Engineering
the Financial Crisis

Engineering
the Financial Crisis

Systemic Risk
and the Failure
of Regulation

Jeffrey Friedman
and
Wladimir Kraus

PENN

UNIVERSITY OF PENNSYLVANIA PRESS

PHILADELPHIA

Published by
University of Pennsylvania Press
Philadelphia, Pennsylvania 19104-4112
www.upenn.edu/pennpress

Printed in the United States of America
on acid-free paper
10 9 8 7 6 5 4 3 2 1

Library of Congress Cataloging-in-Publication Data
Friedman, Jeffrey, 1959–
Engineering the financial crisis : systemic risk and the failure of
regulation / Jeffrey Friedman and Wladimir Kraus. — 1st ed.
   p. cm.
ISBN 978-0-8122-4357-4 (hardcover : alk. paper)
Includes bibliographical references and index.
   1. Basel Accord (1988).   2. Basel II (2004).   3. Global
Financial Crisis, 2008–2009.   4. Bank capital—Law and
legislation.   5. Banks and banking—Risk management.
6. Economics—Political aspects.   7. Financial crises—United
States—History—21st century.   I. Title.   II. Kraus, Wladimir.
HB3717 2008.F75   2011
330.9′0511—pcc   2011024456

CONTENTS

FIGURES AND TABLES

GLOSSARY

ABCP	asset-backed commercial paper (short-term funding issued by OBSEs)
ABS	asset-backed securities (such as an MBS)
ABX	a source of price indices for MBS insurance via CDS
AIG	American International Group
ARM	adjustable-rate mortgage
BCBS	Basel Committee on Banking Supervision
BHC	bank holding company
BIS	Bank for International Settlements (located in Basel, Switzerland)
CCF	credit conversion factor
CDO	collateralized debt obligation (derivative that tranches pools of MBS)
CDS	credit-default swap (insurance against default)
CFTC	Commodities Futures Trading Commission
Fannie Mae	Federal National Mortgage Association
FDIC	Federal Deposit Insurance Corporation
Fed	Federal Reserve Bank
FAS	Financial Accounting Standards
FASB	Financial Accounting Standards Board
Freddie Mac	Federal Home Loan Mortgage Corporation
GDP	gross domestic product
Ginnie Mae	Government National Mortgage Association
GLBA	Gramm-Leach-Bliley Act
GSE	government-sponsored enterprise (e.g., Fannie Mae, Freddie Mac)
HELOC	home-equity lines of credit
HUD	Department of Housing and Urban Development
IFRS	International Financial Reporting Standards
IMF	International Monetary Fund
IRB	internal ratings-based option of Basel II
LIBOR	London Interbank Offered Rate
LTCM	Long-Term Capital Management

LTV	loan-to-value ratio (of a mortgage)
MTM	mark-to-market (or ``fair value'') accounting
MBS	mortgage-backed security
NRSRO	Nationally Recognized Statistical Rating Organization
OBSE	off balance-sheet entity
OCC	Office of the Comptroller of the Currency
OTS	Office of Thrift Supervision
OTTI	other-than-temporarily impaired
PLMBS	private-label MBS
SEC	Securities and Exchange Commission
SIV	Structured Investment Vehicle
S & P	Standard & Poor's
SPE	special-purpose entity
SPV	special-purpose vehicle
TARP	Troubled Asset Relief Program
TBTF	too big to fail

INTRODUCTION

This is not the ordinary book about the financial crisis. The product of a collaboration between an economist (Kraus) and a political theorist (Friedman), it is designed for readers who are interested not only in what caused the financial crisis, but in what those causes indicate about the nature of capitalism and of modern government. Along the way to considering these questions in Chapter 4, we discuss some of the methodological and logical conundrums of contemporary economics and of the modern political culture that shapes contemporary economics (Chapter 1). In Chapters 1, 3, and 4, and Appendix I, we criticize the tendency of both contemporary economics and contemporary politics to overlook *human ignorance*—as a general phenomenon and as a possible cause of the crisis. We hope that these aspects of the book make it interesting to historians, philosophers, legal theorists, political scientists, and sociologists as well as to economists and educated laypeople.

In brief, we argue that:

1. There is no evidence that the crisis—as opposed to the housing bubble—was caused by the lending practices of Fannie Mae and Freddie Mac (Chapter 1).
2. There is no evidence that the crisis was caused by banks' conviction that they were "too big to fail," and thus that they would be bailed out by the government if they made wild bets on mortgage-backed securities (Chapter 1).
3. There is no evidence that the crisis was caused by banks' compensation practices, which tended to reward profit making but not to penalize loss making (Chapter 1).
4. There is no evidence that the crisis was caused by anyone's "irrational exuberance" (Chapter 1).

5. There *is* evidence, of a kind, that deregulation caused the crisis. What
   we mean is that regulations can be envisioned that, in retrospect,
   would have prevented the crisis. But in Chapter 1, we criticize the
   conflation of ex post facto policy prescriptions with causal explanations. This confusion of what did happen with what "should" have
   happened is a deformity of scholarship that we attribute to the "policy mindset" encouraged by modern politics.

6. There *is* evidence that the crisis was caused by capital-adequacy regulations, which influence the leverage ratios of banks around the
   world and, more important, the types of assets banks hold. Basel I
   (1988), the first international agreement on capital-adequacy regulation, required banks to use twice as much capital for business and
   consumer loans as for *mortgages*. Basel II (2005) required banks to
   use five times as much capital for business and consumer loans as
   for *mortgage-backed securities* (MBS) that were rated AAA. During
   the consultative process that eventually culminated in Basel II, U.S.
   financial regulators enacted a capital-adequacy regulation that was
   applicable only to American banks, the Recourse Rule (2001), which
   also required five times as much capital for business and consumer
   loans as for triple-A MBS. The Recourse Rule, in particular, appears
   to have encouraged U.S. banks to accumulate nearly a half-trillion
   dollars of triple-A MBS. This, we contend, was the proximate cause
   of the financial (i.e., banking) crisis (Chapter 2).

7. The financial crisis was transmitted into the nonfinancial or "real"
   economy through a lending contraction that began in mid-2007, as
   banks were required to "mark to market" their holdings of mortgage-backed securities in line with market fears (which culminated
   in the panic of September 2008) about the value of these securities,
   due to rising rates of subprime mortgage delinquencies. Our evidence concerning the lending contraction is presented in Chapter 1,
   in the section entitled "How the Great Recession Began"; our evidence about the role of accounting rules is presented in Chapter 3.

8. The triple-A ratings on MBS were conferred by three bond-rating
   corporations—Moody's, Standard and Poor's (S&P), and Fitch—
   that had been protected from competition by a Securities and
   Exchange Commission regulation dating back to 1975. Not only
   bankers but investors of all kinds were either unaware that these
   three corporations were protected, or they were unaware of the

implications of this protection for the accuracy of their ratings. This lack of awareness was apparently shared by the banking regulators, who had incorporated the three companies' ratings into the Recourse Rule and Basel II (Chapter 3).

Chapter 1 assesses (and chiefly debunks) various elements of the conventional wisdom about what caused the financial crisis. Readers who are interested solely in our own explanation for the crisis, however, should not pass up Chapter 1 entirely, because it contains a key element of the story: the mechanics of mortgage-backed securities. These are explained, as accessibly as possible for a general readership, in the section of Chapter 1 entitled "How Private Mortgage Bonds Worked."

As for the broader questions raised by the crisis, we do not offer unequivocal answers, but the answers we offer are, at least, unusual ones.

From what we can tell, the crisis was caused by ignorance on all sides. The bankers who bought mortgage-backed bonds were ignorant of the vulnerability of these securities to a downturn in housing, or (more likely) they were ignorant of the likelihood of such a downturn; the regulators who encouraged banks to accumulate mortgage-backed bonds were similarly ignorant. Clearly the regulators had no idea that their actions might eventually have such disastrous consequences, but in retrospect the chair of the Federal Deposit Insurance Corporation (FDIC) has now admitted that the Recourse Rule was a terrible mistake that is explained by the regulators' ignorance of the potential consequences (Chapter 4).

John Maynard Keynes once wrote, about the unpredictability of the future: "We simply do not know!" A casual observer of the financial crisis might think this to be obvious—after all, why else would bankers take actions that could well have destroyed their banks, or regulators actions that could well have destroyed the banking system?—but the academic discipline of economics is, we contend, so preoccupied with "incentives" that economists tend to think that whatever happens in our complex world is *deliberately* brought about by agents who have a self-interested stake in the outcome, no matter how disastrous that outcome. Genuine mistakes caused by our ignorance of a complicated reality have little place in mainstream economists' theoretical models.[1] Caricaturing only slightly, economists tend to think that everything that happens must have been envisioned by economic "agents" who had a perfect understanding of the world, and thus an infallible grasp of the results to which their actions would lead.

The world these agents navigate must, by implication, be a very simple one, pellucid and easy to understand. This simplistic perspective has an eerie similarity to the conspiracy theorizing that haunts popular political discourse, so the economists' theory-driven "too-big-to-fail" (TBTF) and corporate compensation stories were perfectly suited to gain wide popularity, and they have. But in this case "the people" are wrong.

More important for present purposes is that economic experts were the ones who created these myths about the financial crisis. We believe that this fact gets to the heart of the wider, systemic issue raised by the crisis, so in writing this book we have not hesitated to name the names of celebrated economists whose pronouncements about the crisis amount to unintentional mythmaking, as we see it. The fallibility of experts strikes us as crucial, not only because so many of them have been mistaken in their retrospective evaluations of what caused the crisis, but because other experts were just as mistaken when they forecast benign results from the capital-adequacy and accounting regulations that, we contend, contributed mightily to the crisis and the recession. Yet none of these experts are blameworthy (we would be the last to contend that they *knowingly* committed their errors); they did their best, given the constraints of human ignorance and fallibility.

This situation produces a genuine dilemma for political as well as economic theory, for if not experts, who else can we turn to when dealing with a complex world? What alternative is there but to place the regulation of capitalism in expert hands? We discuss these questions in Chapter 4.

1

Bonuses, Irrationality, and Too-Bigness: The Conventional Wisdom About the Financial Crisis and Its Theoretical Implications

By the end of 2010, six elements of conventional wisdom about the causes of the financial crisis had taken root:

1. The very low interest rates from 2001 to 2005 fueled a virtually unprecedented nationwide housing bubble in the United States.
2. Fannie Mae and Freddie Mac, the two government-sponsored enterprises (GSEs), helped cause the crisis by loosening their lending standards.
3. Deregulation of finance allowed the "shadow banking sector" to originate subprime loans and securitize them.
4. The compensation systems used by banks, especially the payment of bonuses for revenue-generating transactions, encouraged bankers to bet huge amounts of borrowed money (leverage) on the continuation of the housing boom by buying mortgage-backed bonds. The bankers would be richly rewarded if these bets paid off, but they would not be penalized if the bets went sour.
5. The bankers knew their banks were "too big to fail" (TBTF), and they invested recklessly because they were confident they would be bailed out if disaster struck.
6. Irrational exuberance led investors to buy securities backed by subprime mortgages, oblivious to the fact that when housing prices eventually declined, such mortgages would be likely to default.

In this chapter, we will confront the six items of conventional wisdom with hard evidence and, we hope, sound reasoning in order to clear the ground for our own argument: that, stripped to its essentials, the crisis was a regulatory failure in which the prime culprit was none of the usually targeted factors, but was, instead, the set of regulations governing banks' capital levels known as the Basel rules.

When we began researching the financial crisis in the early months of 2009, we were driven by our dissatisfaction with the analyses then on offer. At the time, there were (understandably) only hypotheses that lacked evidence, and many of them, while equally plausible, contradicted each other. Additionally, there were more hypotheses than the six we have just listed, and partly as a result of the profusion of theories about the crisis there was also a widespread recognition that nobody had yet explained convincingly what had gone wrong. The extant paradigms of economics were found wanting, and fresh thinking was deemed not only possible but mandatory. This made the financial crisis not only an important topic because of the human tragedy to which it led, but an exciting field of research intellectually.

Very soon, however, politicians and political ideologues began to treat the hypotheses that confirmed their predilections as if they were established facts, and these theories eventually formed the conventional wisdom. Thus, conservatives were eager to blame the crisis on the government by means of hypotheses 1, 2, and 5, while liberals were eager to blame the crisis on capitalism by means of hypotheses 3, 4, and 6.

There were also scholarly forms of special pleading. Most of the academic commentary on the crisis has been written by professional economists, and for all practical purposes, the one weapon in professional economists' armory is rational-choice theory. This amounts to saying that the one causal variable that economists are able to identify is the "incentive," known to the rest of us as "the profit motive." If an economic catastrophe occurs, then to most economists it *must have been* due to perverse incentives. Items 4 and 5, the bonus hypothesis and the TBTF hypothesis, fit the economists' template perfectly: each theory posits an incentive for bankers to have engaged in reckless behavior so they could profit from it.

However, there has been a tendency to confuse the mere assertion that these incentives existed with a demonstration that they actually caused the crisis. Nobel laureate economist Joseph E. Stiglitz (2010b, 153), who embraces both the TBTF and the bonus hypotheses, writes without irony that "the disaster that grew from these flawed incentives can be, to us economists, somewhat comforting: our models predicted that there would be excessive risk-taking and short-sighted behavior, and what has happened has confirmed these predictions." Even when Stiglitz wrote those words, however, evidence was already available that, as we shall see, seriously undermines the assumption that the disaster *did* grow from these flawed incentives.

The crisis has also provided grist for the mill of economists who would like to jettison the orthodox academic focus on the incentives faced by *rational* agents. These economists (e.g., Akerlof and Shiller 2009) have popularized the notion of irrational exuberance, hypothesis 6. Our objection to this hypothesis is that its misuse of psychologistic terminology has created the impression that there was something peculiarly *emotional* about the behavior that caused the crisis, even though there is evidence that bankers merely *erred*—not that they "went crazy."

Our criticisms of the conventional wisdom may seem unfair. Journalists first popularized many of the dominant claims about the crisis, and under the pressure of deadlines they often have little choice but to repeat the pronouncements of experts and to draw on the analysis of ideologues. For this reason, journalism is usually seen as, at best, the first draft of history: in the long run, journalistic conclusions are supposed to be corrected and superseded by scholarship. The same process of correction and supersession is also, as Max Weber ([1918] 1946) reminded us long ago, the fate of all scholarly endeavors. As the hasty pronouncements about the financial crisis that have been made by many journalists—and scholars—are challenged over time, specialists may come to repudiate what is today the received view.

However, the received view has immediate and important consequences. The informed public's impressions of the crisis are based in part on journalists' and scholars' hasty pronouncements. These impressions have now hardened into convictions. Political movements of the right and the left are already acting upon dogmas about the crisis that have little or no basis in fact, and policy changes have been made on the basis of these dogmas. Moreover, mass attitudes that have been formed in the crucible of an economic catastrophe cannot be expected to change even if, in the future, careful scholars overturn the assumptions that were the basis for these attitudes. Therefore, we think it is crucial to test the various hypotheses against the available evidence immediately, although we are sure that some or all of our evidence is bound to be superseded, as Weber forecast, and that some of our analysis may be flawed. The basic evidence presented in this chapter is already a matter of public record, however, and the analysis of it is relatively straightforward. Once one confronts the conventional wisdom with this evidence, most elements of the received view crumble, and we are left with the questions that initially made the crisis interesting as well as significant.

The conventional wisdom about the causes of the crisis contains kernels of truth, but most of the rest is demonstrably incorrect. In this chapter, we clear away the underbrush of myth so that we can reclaim the topic for scholarly inquiry. In the process, we will explore some of the tacit assumptions that have commonly led very intelligent and knowledgeable scholars, especially economists, to endorse theories about the crisis that have no apparent basis in reality.

The Limited Role of Low Interest Rates

There *is* empirical evidence for a modified version of the first thesis—that low interest rates fueled the *housing bubble*, as opposed to the financial crisis. Stanford's John B. Taylor (2010) has demonstrated rigorously that not only in the United States, but across the European Union, low interest rates correlated with housing booms during the first half of the decade.

The Federal Reserve Bank (the Fed) and the European Central Bank lowered interest rates from 2001 to 2004, with the Federal Funds Rate falling from 6.5 percent in January 2001 to 1 percent in June 2003, the lowest level in more than four decades (Figure 1.1). It remained at 1 percent for a year before beginning a slow, steady increase to 5.25 percent in 2006. We take no position on whether the central bankers' actions in lowering interest rates merely reflected a "global savings glut" (e.g., Bernanke 2010; Greenspan 2010) or whether instead it reflected monetary expansion designed to forestall deflation (e.g., Taylor 2010).

What is important for our purpose is that, whatever the ultimate cause of the low Federal Funds Rate, mortgage rates followed the rate Fed Funds Rate downward—although, as seen in Figure 1.1, the rates on fixed 30-year prime mortgages stopped going down when they hit the record low of 5.25 percent in 2003. To have gone lower would have caught banks in a trap when the ultralow interest rates at which they were borrowing money (indicated by the Federal Funds Rate) inevitably began to rise. The Federal

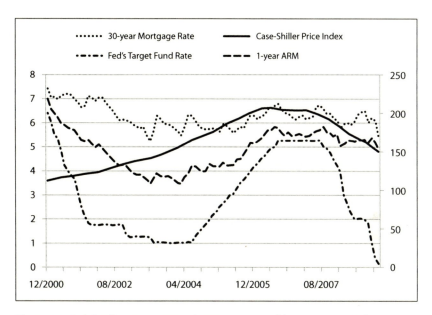

Figure 1.1. Fed funds rate, mortgage interest rates, and house prices. Fed Target Fund Rate: Federal Reserve Statistical Release, Selected Interest Rates; 30-Year Mortgage Rate and 1-Year ARM: Federal Reserve Monetary Policy Report to the Congress, February 24, 2009; Case-Shiller Price Index: S & P/Case-Shiller Home Price Indices.

Funds Rate could not stay at 1 percent forever, and in anticipation of its imminent rise, banks began issuing adjustable-rate mortgages (ARMs) in huge numbers in 2004. The initial ARM rate is shown by the dashed line in Figure 1.1. After the initial period (usually two years), ARMs would reset in accordance with prevailing interest rates. This is generally accepted as a major cause of the trouble experienced by subprime borrowers, strictly defined as those with low credit scores (e.g., Barth 2010).

By 2006, more than 90 percent of all subprime mortgages were ARMs, as were 80 percent of all Alt-A mortgages, meaning mortgages to borrowers who were shy of the income, credit-score, or income-documentation standards required for a prime loan (Zandi 2008 Table 2.1). Beginning in 2006, as the Federal Funds Rate rose, subprime borrowers' inability to pay the higher reset rates triggered the deflation of the housing bubble and a widening concern about the actual value of mortgage-backed bonds. By the third quarter of 2007, "43 percent of foreclosures were on subprime ARMs, 19 percent on prime ARMs, 18 percent on prime fixed-rate mortgages, 12 percent on subprime fixed-rate mortgages, and 9 percent on loans with insurance protection from the Federal Housing Administration" (IMF 2008a, 5n7).

All of this is part of the conventional wisdom, and we do not have reason to challenge it here. But it leaves us with two questions: (1) Why did the new money injected into the U.S. economy, as reflected in low interest rates, cause a bubble in housing, rather than, for example, a bubble in the price of cars, food, airplanes, computers, or clothing? And (2) why did this housing bubble cause a *financial* crisis—which is to say, a banking crisis—when it popped?

In the next section and in Chapter 2, we will first offer an answer to question 1, which the conventional wisdom has largely ignored. Then, for the remainder of this chapter, we will examine the usual answers to question 2, on which the conventional wisdom has justifiably focused.

The Limited Role of Fannie Mae and Freddie Mac

In principle, low interest rates might have caused an upturn in lending across the board, and thus in overall economic activity, instead of an asset bubble in housing. However, as Simon Johnson and James Kwak (2010, 147) note, during the 2000s, "business investment in equipment and software grew more *slowly* than in the 1990s, despite the lower interest rates. The problem was that the cheap money was misallocated to the housing sector, resulting in anemic growth." Why did this happen?

Part of the reason, we believe, was stimulation of the housing market by two government-sponsored enterprises (GSEs): Fannie Mae (the Federal National Mortgage Association) and Freddie Mac (the Federal Home Loan Mortgage Corporation). Even though Fannie Mae and Freddie Mac are private corporations, they were sponsored by the federal government,[1] and this made a substantial difference: they were not taxed by the states, and they were able to borrow money more cheaply than ordinary private corporations. Investors assumed that the GSEs, having been created by the U.S. government, would be bailed out if they got into trouble. Therefore, investors were willing to lend money to the GSEs (by buying their bonds, including their mortgage-backed bonds) on much easier terms than the money they lent to ordinary corporations. "Agency" MBS (issued by the two housing "agencies," Fannie and Freddie), therefore typically paid a 0.45 percent lower interest rate than did privately issued mortgage-backed bonds. The low interest rates that investors required in exchange for lending money to Fannie and Freddie (by buying their MBS) reflected investors' confidence that the GSEs would be bailed out by the federal government if they became insolvent.

Fannie and Freddie's role is central in conservative narratives of the crisis (e.g., Wallison 2011a). But the GSEs' implicit government guarantee became explicit when they were, in fact, bailed out by the federal government on September 7, 2008—a week before the peak phase of the banking panic, which began with the bankruptcy of Lehman Brothers on September 15. We initially assumed that the pre-panic bailout of Fannie and Freddie falsified the conservative view that their reckless mortgage lending caused the financial crisis, for like many observers (e.g., Taylor 2011), we equated the crisis with the nerve-wracking weeks following September 15, when interbank lending around the world froze.

During this period, each bank was afraid that sister banks to which it lent money might own so many "toxic" MBS that they would soon be insolvent and thus unable to pay back any loans. We assumed that this interbank lending crisis, in turn, caused a contraction of bank lending into the "real" economy of businesses and consumers (as opposed to other banks). A contraction in bank lending to businesses and consumers would account for the Great Recession, and this, we assumed, started to occur in September 2008, as each commercial bank, unable to obtain loans from other banks—and perhaps fearful for its own solvency—hoarded cash rather than lending it out.

Since Fannie and Freddie were bailed out a week *before* the interbank panic, it seemed impossible that fears about whether the federal government would honor its implicit guarantee of their debt could have contributed to the panic, and thus to the recession. However, research by Victoria Ivashina and David Scharfstein (2010) changed our minds about the timing of the contraction in bank lending. This research is also essential to our analysis of the recession in Chapter 3.

How the Great Recession Began

Ivashina and Scharfstein showed that bank lending to businesses began to decline sharply in the third quarter of 2007, long before the panic in the

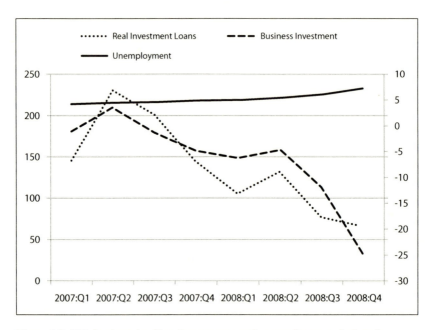

Figure 1.2. U.S. business lending, investment, and unemployment. Left scale: billions of dollars per quarter. Right scale: U.S. unemployment rate/annual change in business investment. Business lending, Ivashina and Scharfstein 2010, Fig. 2; business investment, Federal Reserve, Flow of Funds Accounts, Z.1 Statistical Release.

autumn of 2008—and long before the bailout of Fannie and Freddie. This chronology is consistent with what was happening in the mortgage markets in 2007 and even earlier. Once house prices stopped rising in mid-2006, subprime ARM mortgage default rates began to rise (Jarsulic 2010, 40). A year later, on July 11, 2007, ratings downgrades were issued for 1,043 subprime nonagency, or "private-label" mortgage-backed securities (PLMBS).

Figure 1.2 reproduces some of Ivashina and Scharfstein's data on business lending,[2] with the rates of business investment and unemployment superimposed. These data show that business lending and investment started to decline almost precisely when the ratings downgrades occurred— more than a year before the panic of September 2008. These trends are also consistent with the "official" judgment of the National Bureau of Economic Research, which dates the recession to December 2007. (The decline in new bank loans to businesses was immediately reflected in a decline in business

Table 1.1.   Distribution of Mortgage Bonds (billions)

	Agency (Fannie, Freddie, Ginnie) MBS	AAA tranches of PLMBS	AAA tranches of CDOs	Mezzanine tranches of PLMBS and CDOs*	Total mortgage bond exposure
U.S. commercial banks/thrifts	$ 852	$ 383	$ 90	0	$1,325
GSEs/FHLB**	$ 741	$ 308	0	0	$1,049
investment banks	$ 49	$ 100	$130	$ 24	$ 303
REITs	$ 82	$ 10	0	0	$ 92
hedge funds	$ 50	$ 51	0	$ 24	$125
insurance cos.	$ 856	$ 125	$ 65	$ 24	$1,070
overseas	$ 689	$ 413	$ 45	$ 24	$1,171
financial guarantors	0	0	$100	0	$ 100
Others	$1,044	$ 246	$ 45	$ 24	$1,359
Total	$4,363	$1,636	$475	$120	$6,594

*CDOs are collateralized debt obligations, which tranche tranches of PLMBS.
**FHLB is the Federal Home Loan Bank.
Source: Derived from Lehman Brothers 2008, Figure 4.

investment, but this logically would not translate immediately into unemployment, and Figure 1.2 shows that there was indeed a lag.)

The fact that bank lending began to decline in mid-2007 opens the door to the possibility that bankers contracted lending because they worried that their own insolvency might be brought about by their immense holdings of agency MBS—totaling $852 billion among U.S. commercial banks. The commercial banks held nearly twice as much in agency MBS as in PLMBS, as can be seen in Table 1.1, and the implicit government guarantee of these securities was not made good until September 7, 2008.

An MBS is a pool of thousands of mortgages repurchased from mortgage originators, including "thrifts," or savings and loans; mortgage specialists, such as Countrywide; and commercial banks, such as those controlled by the huge bank holding companies (BHCs): Bank of America, Wells Fargo, Citigroup, and JPMorgan Chase. Commercial banks accept federally insured deposits from the public and they lend them out, along with funds raised by issuing corporate stock and bonds, to businesses, home buyers (through mortgages and home-equity loans), and consumers

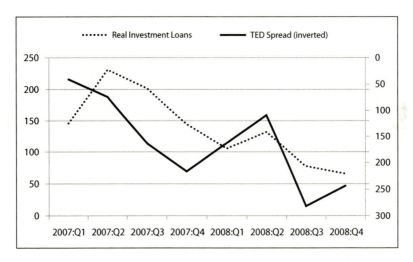

Figure 1.3. Decline in bank lending to businesses. Left scale: billions of dollars per quarter. Right scale: "basis points" (bps). Real investment loans, Ivashina and Sharfstein 2010, Fig. 2; TED spread, Federal Reserve, Selected Interest Rates, H.15, Historical Data.

(primarily through credit cards). By contrast, *investment banks* underwrite the equity and bond offerings of corporations and accept only uninsured deposits, which go into clients' brokerage accounts.

In Figure 1.3, the solid line shows an indicator of banks' perception of each other's riskiness: the "TED spread." This is the difference between the interest rate, or "coupon," paid on Treasury bills (T), and the rate that banks charge each other for overnight loans (the London Interbank Offered Rate, or LIBOR, abbreviated as ED for Eurodollar rate). When banks fear that other banks to which they are lending money overnight may not be able to pay it back, the TED spread goes up. The dotted line shows Ivashina and Scharfstein's data on bank lending to businesses. The TED spread is inverted so it can be compared to business lending.

The TED spread had averaged 25 basis points (bps) since December 2001, but it leapt to 189 bps by August 21, 2007, after two Bear Stearns subprime hedge funds filed for bankruptcy and Countrywide, the largest subprime mortgage specialist, had required an $11 billion emergency loan from a group of banks (Barth et al. 2008, 5; Jarsulic 2010, 66). The TED spread then remained high—an average of 89 bps, or nearly four times the usual rate—until September 2008, when it began skyrocketing to a peak of

364 bps on October 10, 2008. This jitteriness appears to have caused the decline in bank lending to businesses, and thus (we assume) the recession.

During the 2007–2008 period, as the fears about subprime mortgages ebbed and flowed, the yields that the largest banks had to pay in order to get people to buy their corporate bonds rose and fell in tandem. The spread of Citigroup bonds over Treasury bonds stayed at around 200 bps for most of the period, but it skyrocketed to more than 1,000 bps (i.e., 10 percent interest on Citi bonds) when the government's decision not to bail out Lehman Brothers raised the prospect that other big banks might be allowed to fail. Much the same can be said about the yield spreads of JPMorgan Chase and Bank of America corporate debt (Barth 2008, Fig.4.8). However, during the same period, the spread of Fannie and Freddie debt over Treasuries *never* exceeded 160 bps, and that peak was just before Fannie and Freddie were bailed out in September 2008. Until then, the GSEs' spread spiked above 80 bps only twice, and usually was closer to 60 bps (ibid.). Roughly speaking, then, it seems that investors were about three times as concerned about the default risk of the banks as they were about the default risk of Fannie and Freddie. As we discuss toward the end of the chapter (when we consider the "too big to fail" theory as a cause of the crisis), the implicit government guarantee of Fannie and Freddie appears to have been much more widely perceived than any implicit guarantee of the big banks. We infer that the GSEs' implicit government guarantee assured investors, and bankers, that agency MBS, unlike PLMBS, would be bailed out.

Nonetheless, the conservatives' emphasis on Fannie and Freddie is not entirely misplaced. The GSEs inarguably helped to pump up the housing bubble, having funded 45 percent of all mortgages outstanding as of the second quarter of 2008 (Barth 2010, Fig. 5.20). This may provide part of the explanation[3] for why the low interest rates of the 2000s ended up fueling a housing bubble rather than an across-the-board increase in prices.

To be sure, housing had been subsidized like no other industry for decades. The most prominent subsidies had been the income-tax deduction for mortgage interest payments and the repurchasing of mortgages for securitization by Fannie and Freddie. However, until the end of the 1990s, a family that wanted to buy a house with a mortgage that "conformed" to Fannie and Freddie's standards for repurchase—the type of prime mortgage that banks preferred to issue—would have had to put down an initial payment of 20 percent of the cost of the house. In 1995, the Clinton administration set as a goal a 67.5 percent homeownership rate for the U.S.

population, compared to the 65 percent rate at the time (Johnson and Kwak 2010, 112). The Department of Housing and Urban Development (HUD) accordingly mandated that increasing proportions of the mortgages repurchased by Fannie and Freddie be issued to low- and moderate-income borrowers (Johnson and Kwak 2010, 145; Barth 2010, Table 5.6). Thus, in 1997, Fannie Mae began to repurchase mortgages with a mere 3 percent down payment, and by 2001, as part of its commitment to an "ownership society," the Bush administration made the Clinton policy its own. Thereafter, Fannie and Freddie began repurchasing mortgages with no down payment at all (Wallison 2011a).

The reduction in down payments made homeownership more affordable to the poor. Millions of people who could not afford down payments were now able to buy houses because of the GSEs' willingness to assume the risk by repurchasing these loans from the mortgage originators. This had to have had the effect of driving up the price of housing.

Fannie and Freddie also helped to inflate the *subprime* housing bubble by buying $308 billion of PLMBS, but too much can be made of this (e.g., Lane 2010). These purchases consisted largely of PLMBS containing subprime or Alt-A mortgages, (GAO 2009, 27–28), which must have added to the demand for securitized subprime PLMBS issued by investment banks— but, at most, by 29 percent (Table 1.1, row 2, column 2). Even without the GSEs, the subprime portion of the bubble, although smaller, would have been largely sustained by the PLMBS purchases of private investors.

The U.S. home-ownership rate peaked at 69 percent in 2006 (Johnson and Kwak 2010, 112)—an unprecedented 4 percent increase in just ten years. In raw figures (not controlling for population growth), the number of owner-occupied homes increased from 68 million in 1998 to 75 million in 2006. The farther house prices went up (Figure 1.1), the farther they would eventually fall. This would have a devastating effect on subprime borrowers' ability to keep making payments. A family that might once have feared whether it could make mortgage payments on a relatively expensive house might have purchased it anyway during the housing boom, due to the rising general level of house prices and the lower mortgage rates. This is because as long as the price of one's house goes up, it can usually be resold at a profit in case one is unable to make the payments on it. Once house prices start declining, however, it may no longer make sense to keep making mortgage payments. To the extent that the GSEs helped pump up house prices, they bear that amount of responsibility for the severity of the burst housing bubble, and especially for the high delinquency and default rates among subprime borrowers when the price bubble burst—even though the GSEs did not make subprime loans directly.

On the other hand, it is important to keep in mind that the housing bubble is not the same thing as the financial crisis or the recession that followed. The housing bubble was not an evil in itself, and its bursting triggered, but did not cause, the Great Recession—which *was* an evil in itself. The negative effect of the burst housing bubble on the world economy was mediated by its role in generating the financial crisis, which is to say the banking crisis. And as we have seen, it is unlikely that agency MBS played much of a direct role in the banking crisis, because the financial markets remained relatively confident that if necessary, GSE debt would be repaid by means of a government bailout. In contrast, widespread market concern about the value of commercial banks' PLMBS—about which there was much less confidence of a bailout—was the proximate cause of the financial crisis and, thus, of the Great Recession.

An alternative view targets the decline in house construction as the cause of the recession.

> The economy lost 125,000 construction jobs between the peak in early 2006 and late 2007. By December 2007, residential construction activity had fallen by more than a third from its all-time high in March 2006 (from an annual rate of $676 billion to $414 billion). At the same time, retail sales of building materials fell by 13 percent between early 2006 and the end of 2007. (Wesbury 2010, 108)

Over the same period (2006–7), however, real GDP grew at an annual rate of 2.5 percent, and the collapse of house building is estimated to have reduced real GDP growth by only 1.2 percent (from what would otherwise have been 3.7 percent) (Wesbury 2010, 109). Thus, the collapse of the housing market probably would not even have caused a recession on its own, let alone the devastating recession we experienced. Figure 1.2 shows no detectable increase in overall unemployment until *after* the construction and house-building jobs were lost in 2007. The real problem, then, seems to be the lending contraction that began a year after the housing contraction started, and a year before the financial crisis seized the attention of the world.

Financial Deregulation and the "Shadow Banking System"

The liberal counterpart to the role played by GSEs in the conservative narrative is the role played by financial deregulation. Deregulation (and in some cases nonregulation) created what is sometimes called a "shadow banking system," consisting of financial entities other than commercial banks and thrifts. The shadow banking system included mortgage specialists such as Countrywide and IndyMac; off-balance sheet entities (OBSEs), including structured investment vehicles (SIVs) and conduits for asset-backed commercial paper (ABCP); and free-standing investment banks (unaffiliated with commercial banks), such as Bear Stearns, Lehman Brothers, Morgan Stanley, Merrill Lynch, and Goldman Sachs, as well as the investment-bank arms of BHCs such as Citigroup.

Contrary to what is sometimes asserted (e.g., Madrick 2009b, 15), few of these entities were unregulated. The mortgage specialists were savings and loans regulated by the Office of Thrift Supervision (OTS). The investment banks, like commercial banks and most OBSEs, were regulated by the Basel accords, named after the location of the Bank for International Settlements, a central banking secretariat that includes the Basel Committee on Banking Supervision (BCBS). The BCBS negotiates agreements among member nations to adhere to sets of banking regulations that have become known as Basel I (1988), Basel II (2005), and Basel III (2010); these regulations are then adopted by most world governments.

That said, the regulations imposed on the shadow banking system were in various respects lighter than those covering commercial banks. In addition, credit-default swaps (CDS), or "derivatives," are sometimes included under the "shadow banking" rubric, and they were indeed unregulated.

Because of the complexity of the topic and the surprisingly small quantities of mortgage-backed bonds in OBSEs, we confine a discussion of their regulation to Appendix II. We shall treat each of the other aspects of deregulation or nonregulation here, with sections covering subprime mortgage origination, derivatives, and the repeal of those sections of the Glass-Steagall Act that had prevented investment banks from being affiliated with commercial banks. This discussion will raise theoretical questions about how one thinks about historical causality in a political culture that is relentlessly focused on the future—that is, on debating policies that will prevent problems in the future—despite the obvious relevance of the origin of these problems in the past.

How Private Mortgage Bonds Worked

First, however, we need to explain how the pieces of the shadow banking system fit with the commercial banking system in generating the financial crisis (and thus the Great Recession). We will not follow the usual practice of starting at the "bottom" of the pyramid—with subprime mortgage origination by specialists, commercial banks, and savings and loans—before working our way up to mortgage securitization and sale by investment banks, because the relevant question in explaining the financial crisis is why so many PLMBS bonds were ultimately *retained or bought by commercial banks*, leading them to start to contract lending in mid-2007. Our dependent variable is thus Table 1.1 (p. 13), row 1, columns 2 and 3.

Put differently, the relevant question is, to us, a question of demand—why did commercial banks want to buy or keep these bonds?—and not supply. Where there is demand, a capitalist economy will generally supply it, and that was certainly true in this case. The mechanics of the supply side therefore do not strike us as being directly relevant to understanding the cause of the financial crisis.

The question of demand will not be answered fully until Chapter 2, but a logical place to begin is by analyzing the attractions of PLMBS bonds to any investor (not just commercial banks). Agency MBS relied on the GSEs' implicit government backing to gain investors' trust. What did PLMBS put in place of government backing?

The answer is primarily the principal of "subordination." PLMBS were contractually structured into various "tranches." Each tranche had a different rating, from AAA down to B, and each rating corresponded to a different level of risk. The "senior" (AAA) bonds were the safest, with each "mezzanine" tranche (AA +, AA, AA −, A +, A, A −, BBB +, BBB, BBB −, B +, B, and B −)[4] a little riskier. Finally there was an unrated, "equity" tranche.

The differences in risk among the tranches usually did not signify different types of mortgages—for example, prime mortgages in the AAA tranche, subprime in the BB tranche. All the mortgages in a pool could be subprime or Alt-A and yet it would issue a tranche of AAA-rated bonds. This was made possible by the subordination of the mezzanine tranches to the senior tranche, in a "waterfall" payment system. Subordination meant that payments from the mortgages in a PLMBS pool would first flow to the senior tranche; only after all triple-A bondholders had been paid in a given period would holders of AA + bonds receive revenue, followed by the holders of AA bonds, and so on down the line. Each successively lower-rated tranche was subordinate to all the tranches above it. Therefore there was always, by definition, a triple-A or "senior" tranche (and sometimes even a "super-senior" tranche, which received payments before the "junior" triple-A tranche), because some-body—the owners of AAA-rated bonds—had to be the first recipient of the stream of revenue flowing from the pool's mortgage payments.

Looking at it from the bottom of the waterfall, if any of the mortgages in the entire pool defaulted, the sponsoring bank would suffer first by tak-ing losses on the equity tranche, which it generally retained ("equity" meaning "ownership" in financial contexts). The equity tranche provided the other appeal of structured PLMBS bonds: "overcollateralization." None of the bondholders had a claim on income generated by the equity tranche, typically amounting to 1.9 percent of the mortgage pool's revenue (Ashcraft and Schuermann 2008, 30). The number of mortgages that added up to 1.9 percent of the pool was therefore a security cushion of extra collateral for the rated bonds standing above the equity tranche in the subordination waterfall. Only after all income from 1.9 percent of the mortgages in the pool was wiped out by defaults would purchasers of shares in the B or BB tranches suffer any diminution in their stream of income from the mort-gage and interest payments from the pool, followed by holders of shares in the next-highest-rated tranches, and so on. In turn, only if defaults were so great that payments to all the mezzanine tranches—the ones that were subordinate to the senior tranches—had completely stopped would inves-tors in the senior tranches suffer any losses.

The overcollateralization figure appears smaller than it really was, because even if 1.9 percent of the mortgages in a pool defaulted, the houses representing that 1.9 percent could often be resold, and the bondholders would have the rights to revenue from the new mortgages on the houses. "It had been typical to assume that when a subprime mortgage foreclosed, about 65 percent of its outstanding balance could be recovered. Such a 35 to 50 percent loss severity assumption implied that 50 to 65 percent of the mortgages [in an entire PLMBS pool] would have to default before losses would impact the MBS senior tranche" (IMF 2008a, 60), after factoring in the recovery of income from the equity tranche and the number of defaults required to stop all revenue to each of the subordinate tranches.

The logic of subordination and overcollateralization was airtight, and the results were so popular with investors that investment banks began crafting CDOs (collateralized debt obligations) by tranching tranches from various PLMBS and other asset-backed securities, or ABS, such as pools of credit card, student loan, and car-payment debt. This further diversified the collateral of the bonds, and thus reduced the risk of "correlated" defaults—or so it was thought—although by late 2003, CDOs consisted mainly of tranches of *mezzanine* tranches of subprime and Alt-A mortgage pools (Bass 2007), which were, as a rule, more likely to default. (The width assigned to the various tranches attempted to correct for this.) Investment banks also produced "CDOs^2" (which tranched tranches of CDOs) and "synthetic" CDOs, which were essentially two-way bets on the direction in which the CDO market would go; synthetic CDOs were constructed to mimic the movement of CDO prices, but by using derivatives instead of actual mortgages, they did not require the buyers to own any actual housing assets (Lewis 2010).

Apart from the safety that seemed to be offered by the subordination, overcollateralization, and the diversification of assets (in the case of CDOs), the main advantage of all the variants of PLMBS, including CDOs, was that subordination allowed an investor to choose a congenial level of risk. In exchange for the safety assurances that came with the triple-A rating, which were based on the waterfall structure, senior bondholders received a lower coupon (payment) than mezzanine investors did. The higher coupon for mezzanine investors compensated them for the greater risk of being lower in the waterfall. For example, Ashcraft and Schuermann (2008, Table 16) have calculated that a triple-A subprime bond issued in the first quarter of 2007 typically paid a coupon of 9 bps (0.09 percent) higher than Treasury bonds of similar duration, while an AA bond paid a "spread" of 15 bps over Treasuries, an A bond 64 bps, and a BBB bond 224 bps (2.24 percent). (By contrast, subprime bonds issued in the *second* quarter of 2007, when troubling default rates on subprime mortgages started to be recognized, had to pay higher coupons to get investors to buy them: on average, 76 bps for a triple-A tranche, 192 bps for an AA tranche, 369 bps for an A tranche, and 500 bps for a BBB tranche.) Over the course of the housing boom, triple-A CDO bonds typically paid 3.4 percent interest per year, but triple-B CDO bonds paid 4.4 percent a year (Barnett-Hart 2009, Table 1).

Such is always the case with bonds: a higher rating, designating greater safety, produces a lower yield. PLMBS investors could choose between the high coupons paid on low rated, relatively risky bonds, and the lower coupons paid on what were perceived as ultrasafe, high-rated bonds, such as those that were rated AAA. Everyone knows by now, however, that the allegedly safe triple-A bonds proved to be much less safe than advertised. Essentially, the reason for the bonds' lower-than-expected safety was that the rating agencies, like the investors, had underestimated the risk of a nationwide housing bubble (as opposed merely to a housing boom justified by fundamental economic factors, such as population and income growth). The rating agencies had therefore made the triple-A tranches too wide. The logic of tranching was valid, but the proper width of the tranches was an empirical question that just about everyone got wrong.

Ashcraft and Schuermann (2008, Fig. 6) estimate that 79.3 percent of the average subprime PLMBS was allocated to the AAA tranches, 6.6 percent to AA tranches, 5.4 percent to A tranches, 4.3 percent to BBB tranches, and 2.6 percent to BB tranches, along with 1.9 percent to the equity tranches. The precise width of each of the tranches could be fine-tuned by the investment bank or other sponsor, because the rating agencies' models were publicly accessible; therefore the sponsor could vary the width of the tranches to suit investor demand for risk (and thus yield). But the rating agencies' models, while not conservative enough in the end, constituted the ultimate limit on the supply of the tranches that were most in demand—the AAA tranches—because the starting points of the rating models were predictions of the rate of default on the entire pool. Had the rating agencies predicted a 25 percent default rate, for example, then even accounting for the resale value of foreclosed houses, the rating agencies would have had to demand more than the 21 percent subordination (100 percent minus 79 percent) that justified the typical triple-A tranche, which was wide enough to claim 79 percent of the revenue of a mortgage pool. However, by the first quarter of 2009, the default rate on subprime ARMs was indeed approaching 25 percent (Jarsulic 2010, Fig. 1.2).

In Chapter 3, we will examine the role played by the rating agencies in the crisis. What is relevant in considering the role of deregulation is that while these "agencies" were, like the GSE housing "agencies," privately owned, it is misleading to imply that therefore they were unregulated (e.g., Madrick 2009a, 54; Stiglitz 2011, 92). Ever since 1975, SEC regulations had conferred an effective oligopoly on the three rating agencies—Moody's, S&P, and Fitch; and older regulations, at both the state and federal level, compelled two of the three largest classes of institutional investors—pension funds and insurance companies—to buy only highly rated securities. There was no change in the legal status of the rating agencies in the run-up to the crisis, so the effect of deregulation cannot be found by looking to the obvious (and culpable) suspect, the rating agencies.

However, the rating agencies' collaborators in securitization, the investment banks and mortgage originators, *were* in the relevant respects effectively unregulated, and this fact seems to have given rise to the idea that deregulation was responsible for the crisis.

Special regulations have been imposed on *commercial* banks ever since deposit insurance was enacted in 1933, because of regulators' fear of what would now be called "moral hazard": bankers might take advantage of the security blanket offered by deposit insurance to engage in reckless speculative activity. These regulations are the topic of Chapter 2. But since investment banks are not covered by deposit insurance, they have been much more lightly regulated than commercial banks. And it was investment banks that first attracted both investors' and the general public's attention to the crisis.

The two attention-getting events were the March 16, 2008, bailout of Bear Stearns and the September 15, 2008, bankruptcy of Lehman Brothers. These two investment banks were dragged under by the decline in the market value of their holdings of subprime mortgages and PLMBS—held in inventory to be sold to investors (such as commercial banks). The fact that Bear Stearns and Lehman Brothers were investment banks strongly influenced the frenzied search for explanations of the crisis after September 15, so financial deregulation immediately presented itself as a plausible cause; for instance, a September 20, 2008, *New York Times* story (Landler and Stolberg 2008) framed the crisis as having been unquestionably caused by deregulation. The story pointed out that Congress had resisted Republican efforts to rein in Fannie and Freddie by regulatory means. It characterized the Clinton and Bush administrations' efforts to expand home ownership as a "market-based"—and thus, by implication, unregulated—"way to help poor people" (quoting economist Kenneth S. Rogoff). And it cited, as "perhaps the most significant recent deregulation of the banking industry," a "landmark act that allowed commercial banks to expand into other financial activities, like investment banking and insurance." This was a reference to the Gramm-Leach-Bliley Act (GLBA) of 1999.

GLBA repealed the portions of the Glass-Steagall Act of 1933 that had forbidden commercial banks to engage in the trading activities associated with investment banks. Contrary to the *New York Times* story, GLBA maintained this prohibition, but it did allow commercial banks to be affiliated with investment banks under the same BHC (bank holding company). The "repeal of Glass-Steagall," however, immediately became a widely reported cause of the crisis. By September 28, this narrative had become so common that *Times* economics correspondent David Leonhardt (2008) felt compelled to correct the record, with an article in the *Times Magazine* pointing out that criticism of GLBA "is often vague," because in reality "the law didn't really do much to create the current crisis. It is a handy scapegoat, since it's easily the biggest piece of financial regulation in recent years. But . . . the nursemaid of the current crisis isn't so much what Washington did . . . as what it didn't do."

Leonhardt's rebuttal to the GLBA trope was to point out that Bear Stearns and Lehman Brothers were unaffected by the legislation, since they remained stand-alone investment banks, not subsidiaries of BHCs. However, Leonhardt kept the "repeal of Glass-Steagall" story alive by speculating that an investment bank that was part of a BHC could give the commercial bank under the same BHC umbrella "more capital to invest" in subprime housing (which is true, but begs the question of why the commercial bank would want to invest capital in subprime housing—the question of demand).

The main thrust of Leonhardt's story, though, was to shift the "deregulation" narrative toward other targets: first, the failure to regulate the practices of subprime mortgage originators, and second, the failure to regulate "the derivatives market." The trio of deregulatory (GLBA) and nonregulatory actions (nonregulation of subprime lending and of derivatives) fingered by Leonhardt remain, as we write, the three primary meanings of "deregulation" as a cause of the financial crisis. We shall treat them in the next three sections.

Nonexistent Regulation of Subprime Mortgage Lending

It strikes us as relatively uncontroversial to conclude that if the federal government had, in effect, banned subprime lending, the financial crisis would not have occurred. Even setting aside the substantial contribution of subprime loans to the size of the housing bubble, the bursting of the bubble probably would have left the holders of *prime* PLMBS unaffected.[5] Thus, after the subprime part of the bubble started to deflate in 2006 and 2007— driving home prices much farther down than would have otherwise been the case—the rate of foreclosure on traditional prime mortgages barely moved above its traditional rate (less than 1 percent) (Jarsulic 2010, Fig. 1.2). Only the recession itself eventually pushed prime foreclosure rates higher. The main problem lay with subprime ARMs, for which the foreclosure rate approached 25 percent by 2007—far surpassing the 1.9 percent of overcollateralization in a typical subprime bond, and sufficient to wipe out most or all of the mezzanine tranches. Thus, if subprime lending (or ARMs) had been banned, there probably would have been no financial crisis.

It does not follow, however, that we should attribute the crisis to the *deregulation* of subprime lending.

The only deregulatory actions that had been taken in this regard were the enactment of the 1980 Depository Institutions Deregulation and Monetary Control Act, which overrode *state* usury laws that put ceilings on mortgage interest rates; and the 1982 Garn-St. Germain Depository Institutions Act, which "increased the ability of *state chartered banks and thrifts* to make adjustable rate mortgages" (Jarsulic 2010, 159n24, emphasis added). ARMs without ceilings on interest rates could have been prohibited by state usury laws, and this surely would have changed the tendency of subprime mortgages to have adjustable rates. In this respect, too, the 1982 act may have made a difference in facilitating subprime ARMs.

However, if state laws had continued to prohibit ARMs, it is likely that the demand for ARMs would have been met by nationally chartered banks (which originated the lion's share of these mortgages anyway).[6] The demand for ARMs came from a combination of mortgage funders' awareness that ultra-low interest rates could not go on forever, and from borrowers who either were too financially unsophisticated to understand that very fact, or who were *so* sophisticated that they bet on their ability to sell or refinance their house before their ARM reset at a higher interest rate. The first group of borrowers may well have been the victims of predatory lending, and state laws might have prevented their victimization. But the mortgage originators (commercial banks, savings and loans, and mortgage specialists), in meeting the demand for ARMs, were in large part thereby meeting demand from *investors* for mortgages that could be securitized. This demand surely would have been met by *nationally* chartered financial institutions unless there had been a *federal* ban on subprime lending.

Such a ban had been legally possible since the 1994 enactment of the Home Ownership and Equity Protection Act, which, combined with the Truth in Lending Act, authorized the Federal Reserve to prohibit mortgages it deemed unfair (Jarsulic 2010, 110–11). If the Fed had acted on this authority by banning ARMs or subprime lending in general, it surely would have prevented the crisis.

Such counterfactuals, however, present two difficulties. The first is political. Two presidential administrations in a row, with the full backing of Congress, had seized on the idea of increasing homeownership rates as a way to help low-income Americans. The political pressure was so great that GLBA was almost derailed by the eponymous Senator Gramm's desire to exclude from the legislation measures that would have expanded the reach of the Community Reinvestment Act of 1997, which mandated lending to low-income communities. The Clinton administration insisted, however, that "no institution would be allowed to move into any new lines of business without a satisfactory lending record" to low-income borrowers (Labaton 1999), and eventually Gramm succumbed.

The tussle over the Community Reinvestment Act was emblematic of the larger political objective of the Clinton and, later, the Bush administration: expanding the middle class by offering homeownership opportunities to the poor. There was no way to accomplish this objective other than by making subprime loans and securitizing them, since securitization was perceived to reduce the risk inherent in subprime lending. It does not seem realistic to lay blame for the crisis on the absence of a ban on the very practices that would achieve the homeownership objectives of powerful political forces.

The second problem with the counterfactual has to do with the distinction between the housing bubble and the financial crisis. It may well be that a ban on subprime lending, or on ARMs, would have prevented the financial crisis by preventing the subprime housing bubble, or the housing bubble *tout court*. But this fact tells us nothing about the mechanism by which the high default rates on subprime ARMs were, in fact, transmuted into a financial crisis, and then into the Great Recession.

If we are solely interested in an odd (although commonplace) sort of prescriptive theorizing—odd because it is able to prescribe what "should" have been done in the past only because of what we know in the present about how the past turned out—then the counterfactual of a ban on subprime lending suffices. But if we believe that "ought" implies "can," such prescriptions are unsatisfactory. Nobody in 1980 or 1982—including opponents of subprime lending—could have predicted that state laws against usury would prevent a financial crisis of epic proportions, as opposed to preventing mortgage lending to impoverished borrowers. More precisely, nobody in 1980 or 1982 could have predicted that defaults on subprime ARMs would have caused a worldwide banking crisis when, two decades later, (1) subprime ARMs would be securitized into PLMBS, and (2) commercial banks in the United States alone would come to hold approximately $250 billion worth of these securities, with non-U.S. banks holding an additional $167 billion worth (Greenlaw et al. 2008, Exhibit 3.8).[7]

The Tension Between Policy Prescription and Causal Description

Retrospectively prescriptive theories of what "could" have prevented the crisis may be adequate for the usual purposes of modern politics, which of course are not scholarly. Scholars try to understand the past and the present, not predict the future. But in the politics of modern democracies—that is, in the politics of polities that are dedicated to solving and preventing social and economic problems—public debate necessarily centers on policy proposals, and one cannot advocate a given policy without making predictions about its future effects in solving or preventing a given social or economic problem. However, no one can accurately predict what the future effects of present policies will be; the future is inherently unpredictable, especially in a complex modern society. A future-oriented policy debate has the unintended effect of encouraging retrospective "policy analysis" that treats moments in the past as if they, somehow, *could* have been informed by knowledge of the future. We, at time T_3, project onto political decision makers at T_1 our retrospectively acquired knowledge of what happened at T_2—even though a crucial distinction between the past and the future is that only the past is, even in principle, knowable.

Such analysis not only encourages unrealistic policy-making, but it corrals us into thinking about every problem prescriptively (i.e., in terms of what should be done to solve it) rather than descriptively (i.e., in terms of what caused it)—even though an effective prescription is unlikely if we lack an accurate diagnosis of the problem. In effect, then, modern democratic culture diminishes the desire to analyze the *causes* of complex social problems. Such analysis tends to stop as soon as one reaches a cause of a problem that *could have been* prevented by a law or regulation—no matter how unrealistic such a law or regulation would have been at the time, given the political forces then in play; and given the difficulty of predicting the future effects of legal and regulatory remedies under modern conditions. Thus, even as social complexity grows, our understanding of society shrinks, because our interest in the empirics of social and economic problems becomes secondary to thinking up policy solutions for them.

The same policy-oriented mindset can also discourage us from standing back and asking whether a given social or economic problem is actually a symptom of a larger, systemic flaw, regardless of whether any within-the-system policy fixes might be available (or might have been available). Thus, not only our "scholarly," or "descriptive-analytic" thinking, but our *prescriptive* thinking can be inhibited by the policy horizons endemic to modern political debates.

The financial crisis is an opportunity to look beyond these narrow intellectual horizons, and it has been widely recognized as such—in large part, we think, because of its manifest complexity. Even though we might find it politically satisfying to identify, with the luxury of hindsight, policies that would have had the effect of preventing the financial crisis (if only our predecessors knew then what we know now), the multitude of factors that appear to have contributed to the crisis renders policy-oriented thinking about it peculiarly unsatisfying, because such thinking is inherently unable to address systemic issues. The larger questions now legitimately being raised about "the system" due to the crisis cannot possibly be answered even by a somehow omnisciently predictive policy proposal designed to prevent future financial crises, let alone by policies that are only retrospectively "prescribed" so as to have prevented the actual financial crisis.

For instance, the crisis raises the question of whether the status quo should be characterized as "capitalism," despite the authority possessed over the economy by the polity. In short, was capitalism to blame for the crisis? Or was the regulation of capitalism to blame? Or were they both to blame—that is, should they be seen as part of the same system?

It is obvious how one might blame the crisis on capitalism, and we will consider the resulting systemic questions in Chapters 2, 3, and 4; for instance, in Chapter 2 we ask whether there is something about capitalism, or rather capitalist banking, that is inherently unstable. Alternatively, one might blame the crisis on the political system, which we have been calling "modern democracy." Perhaps a better term would be "pragmatic democracy," since the modern public agenda is dominated by the search for policy solutions to social and economic problems. A ban on subprime mortgage lending, or ARMs, or for that matter securitization—or banking itself—were all within the power of democratically legitimated legislators and regulators, but these bans would have been inconsistent with the problem-solving goal of trying to raise homeownership rates among the poor. Thus, the absence of such bans can be considered systemically "normal" products of a modern, pragmatic democracy (at least given its operation within fundamentally capitalist parameters that include home ownership). Finally, in Chapters 3 and 4, we ask whether this means that modern democracies face a deeply ingrained epistemological problem—the problem of predicting the future effects of public policies in a complex world.

Yet if we were to confine ourselves to thinking about how to craft new legislative or regulatory policies that would prevent a crisis of the exact sort that occurred in 2007–8, or to retrospectively imagining policies that would have prevented that crisis, larger questions such as these would not arise. The *systemic* issue of how to ensure that the polity will reliably produce *good* (effective) policy solutions *before* a problem occurs would be displaced by the question of the specific fixes that might have prevented the particular problem we have just experienced—without asking what deeper forces were responsible for it.

Clearly, then, there is a tension between future-oriented "policy debate" and the avoidance of hindsight bias. Yet avoiding this bias is essential to the rigorous investigation of the causes of past and present problems. If we attribute to political actors in the past the knowledge we have gained in hindsight, we are likely to underestimate the possibility of policy mistakes that were caused simply by the decision makers' ignorance of the future.

Economists are particularly prone to hindsight bias for two reasons. First, as we mentioned earlier, economists are prone to "incentives" narratives of strategic interaction among self-interested agents. But incentives cannot operate when even the most highly incentivized agents are ignorant of the actions they should take in order to gain the posited benefit. People who are ignorant of the future may, in hindsight, be seen to have objectively had an incentive to do something that, subjectively, they did not know would lead to a self-interested outcome. The incentives orientation of economists therefore leads to a discipline-wide neglect of simple human error as the reason that, for example, bankers might have bought mortgage-backed securities. Indeed, the entire epistemological dimension of the human condition—not just the fact that we are, all of us, fallible because of our ignorance, but the fact that our *interpretations* of the information we happen to have may differ, driving people with precisely the same incentives and the same information to make radically different decisions—is invisible to modern economists.

The other reason that economists have a special weakness for hindsight bias is that unlike other social scientists, economists are often asked for policy advice. They respond by offering it even when they are *not* asked. This is part of their professional ethos; one is hard-pressed to find a book, journal article, or working paper by an economist that does not conclude with policy recommendations. This orientation often aggravates the "policy-debate" tunnel vision that is natural to any citizen of a modern democracy, in that the research leading up to an economist's policy proposal is usually designed to determine whether a given legal fix would solve—or would have prevented—a given problem. Policy-debate tunnel vision thus encourages hindsight bias because, of course, it is infinitely easier to prescribe a policy to "solve" a problem after the fact—once there are data relating to the problem—than it is beforehand, when one may not even realize that a problem is coming for which one should collect data.

Thus, for example, Stiglitz (2010a), in addition to blaming the crisis on TBTF (a political element), and on the compensation practices of the banks (a capitalist element), also blames the crisis on the same three deregulatory and nonregulatory aspects named by Leonhardt: the nonregulation of subprime housing, the Gramm-Leach-Bliley Act, and the nonregulation of derivatives. His retrospective (and prospective) policy solution is, in every case, more federal regulation or new federal legislation. Yet Glass-Steagall already existed before it was "repealed" *by the federal legislature,* and the possibility of banning or regulating subprime lending was rejected *by the federal regulators.* So how is one to ensure that giving regulators and legislators even more authority, as Stiglitz recommends in every case, would not result in similar errors?

What makes Stiglitz unusual is that he believes that he has a *systematic* argument for his blanket policy recommendation. The argument is a tunnel-vision defense of the *systemic* status quo. Thus, Stiglitz (2010a, 243) points out that when markets are imperfect (as they always are), "there [are] always some government interventions that could make everyone better off." This theoretical truism says nothing, however, about how real-world government decision makers are to know in advance *which* interventions will make everyone better off without causing worse unintended consequences.

Stiglitz's answer to this problem is, we believe, simplistic: elect legislators and hire regulators who would do whatever Stiglitz would do, or would have done in retrospect. Thus, Stiglitz (2011) insists (without providing any evidence) that the legislators who repealed Glass-Steagall were corrupted by the campaign contributions of Wall Street; if only honest Stiglitzian legislators had been elected, they would not have done what they did. As for regulators, the problem was their ideology: they were free-market fundamentalists who did not believe in regulation as a matter of principle. Stiglitz points out that "effective regulation requires regulators who believe in it. They should be chosen from among those who might be hurt by a failure of regulation, not from those who would benefit. Fortunately, there are large numbers of financial experts in unions, nongovernment organizations, and universities" (Stiglitz 2010a, 179). In reality, however, the regulators (and the legislators) *were* drawn from universities, but they had not been trained by Stiglitz.[8] They simply interpreted the information they possessed differently from the way Stiglitz thinks, in hindsight, they should have interpreted it.

In systemic terms, Stiglitz is trying to square modern democracy with the fallibility of the voters and their elected and bureaucratic agents. Essentially, his solution to this problem is consistently to downplay the possibility of human error—that is, to deny that human beings (or at least uncorrupt human beings such as himself) are fallible. In a review essay on Robert Skidelsky's *Keynes: The Return of the Master*, Stiglitz (2010b) takes Skidelsky to task for emphasizing Keynes's sharp distinction[9] between *risk*— "situations in which we have good statistical data so that we can talk meaningfully about the probability that a particular event will happen" (Stiglitz 2010b, 17)—and *uncertainty*, that is, ignorance, which Stiglitz does not even bother to define. "Much of the behavior that led to the crisis," Stiglitz asserts (again without evidence), "did not depend on this distinction. More important, for instance, were the incentives, which encouraged banks to take on too much *risk*" (emphasis added). Stiglitz goes on to say that in addition to "flawed incentives, inadequate regulation and a lack of scruples also help explain the abusive lending practices that played so large a role in the crisis." In other words, bankers *knowingly* took on too much risk (because they had an incentive to do so), and somebody (lenders? borrowers?) "lacked scruples," that is, they *knew* they were doing something wrong. Thus far, Stiglitz has made no allowance for anyone's ignorance, and indeed the point of chastising Skidelsky for emphasizing Keynes's insistence on the role of "uncertainty" is to deny that ignorance played a role in the crisis.

But why was there "inadequate regulation," given that the (federal) regulators had all the powers they needed to have banned subprime lending? Even an ideological regulator, blinded by "market fundamentalism," would have been blinded by this ideology to some *fact* that, if recognized, would have led him or her to do the right thing: that is, the ideologues must have been ignorant of something quite important.

In retrospect, it is easy for us to say that subprime lending or securitization should have been banned, but very few people (not excepting Stiglitz) correctly predicted the effects of these policies. Moreover, political pressure favored both subprime lending and, as a means to that end, ARMs and securitization. One does not even answer the *prospective* "policy questions" raised by the crisis, such as whether there should there be tighter regulation (as Stiglitz demands), if one refuses to explain how the system can be expected to find the cognitive resources to ensure that regulators who *know what to do* will be in charge in the future, unlike in the past. Simply turning over all power to a Nobel laureate economist such as Stiglitz is no answer. There are many Nobel laureate economists, and they quite frequently disagree with one another. Which one of them should be the economist-king who will ensure that regulators do not make even worse mistakes next time?

The Nonregulation of Derivatives

Among the university-trained economists who (in hindsight) may have been ignorant of the consequences of his actions was Lawrence Summers, who was at the time the Nathan Ropes Professor of Political Economy at Harvard University, a past recipient of the John Bates Clark medal of the American Economics Association (awarded to the best economist under age forty), and a future president of Harvard University. Summers, a deputy assistant treasury secretary under President Clinton (and future chief economic advisor to President Obama), was among the key opponents of a proposal by Brooksley Born, of the Commodity Futures Trading Commission (CFTC), to study the possibility of requiring that CDS be traded at a central exchange rather than over the counter (Gjerstad and Smith 2011). Summers resisted Born's proposal on the basis of the consensus of academic economists, who believed that derivatives were important instruments of risk reduction, particularly when they could be tailored to the specific risks of the different parties to a CDS "swap." This custom tailoring cannot be done on an exchange, which requires standardized contracts.

In essence, the derivatives that are now in question were insurance contracts against the possibility that a PLMBS tranche would not pay off the bondholders. This risk (or rather, uncertainty) was swapped by the bondholder to a "counterparty," such as another bank or a branch of the gigantic insurance company, AIG; in exchange for a fee paid by the insured party, the counterparty was obliged to pay a fixed amount if the mortgage bond defaulted (Wallison 2011b). Banks and many other institutional investors used derivatives to hedge the risk that their mortgage bonds (and all sorts of other investments) might turn out to be mistakes. But this did not increase risk levels any more than does a car insurance policy, which transfers risk from the driver to the insurance company.

One might think that derivatives provided false assurances of the safety of PLMBS. But the assurances were not false. Derivative contracts paid off with only one major hitch, which is a story in itself (see Chapter 3): AIG, which had supplied a great deal of PLMBS insurance, did not have the funds to cover these contracts when it was—incorrectly—thought that they had to be paid.[10]

However, the problem at AIG, which resulted in yet another bailout, was just as insignificant as a contributor to the crisis as were the problems at Fannie Mae and Freddie Mac. AIG was bailed out on September 16, 2008, the night after Lehman Brothers failed and a week after the bailout of Fannie and Freddie. Once this happened, the CDS that AIG had sold were a nonissue in the interbank panic that was underway: the bailout had ensured that the CDS would be paid off by the government. Yet the panic sharply escalated anyway. The fear that drove the panic concerned not AIG's CDS insurance,[11] but what the CDS were insuring: subprime mortgage bonds. Nobody would have worried about AIG's ability to pay off these CDS if the value of the bonds themselves had not been called into question by the failure of Lehman Brothers.

None of this is to deny that commercial banks would not have had to worry about their CDS counterparties if the CFTC had required that the contracts be listed on an exchange that would back up the contracts, as Born had proposed studying. If the exchange had built up an immense cash reserve, totaling more than the contracts in question, then there would have

Table 1.2. Securities Exposures of U.S. and Other Banks (rounded, percent)

	U.S. banks	UK banks	Non-British European banks	Asian banks
residential mortgage	42	24	19	5
commercial mortgage	6	5	5	27
corporate	32	27	27	60
consumer	4	6	5	2
other	16	38	43	6
Total	100	100	100	100

Source: IMF 2009a, Table 1.13.

been no panic. One might reasonably conclude, then, that the mandatory placement of CDS on an exchange couldn't have hurt, and might have actually helped, in reducing the severity of the financial crisis.

That might be the end of the matter from a "policy perspective," but if we are interested in the *causes* of the crisis, and their implications for capitalism and modern democracy, the underlying problem remains: Why were so many of the mortgage bonds that were being insured by CDS bought by commercial banks? The CDS per se are irrelevant to this question. The underlying dependent variable remains the *overconcentration* of residential mortgage bonds in the commercial banks, of which Table 1.2 gives a preliminary picture.[12]

Unfortunately, our experience has been that data on non-U.S. banks that are more fine-grained than those shown in this table are difficult to come by. As a result, while in subsequent chapters we will refer to the situation among European banks, our main focus will be limited by the available data to U.S. banks. Since the financial crisis was a global event, or at least a trans-Atlantic one, the full story remains to be told.

The "Repeal" of Glass-Steagall

As we have noted, David Leonhardt pointed out the unlikelihood that the "repeal of the Glass-Steagall Act" played much of a role in the failure of Bear Stearns and then Lehman Brothers—stand-alone investment banks that were unaffected by the GLBA's repeal of the Glass-Steagall sections that separated commercial from investment banking. However, even

Leonhardt's rebuttal to the conventional wisdom about financial deregulation causing the *crisis* does not go far enough, because investment banks do not have the power to cause *recessions*. Unlike commercial banks, investment banks do not lend to businesses in the real economy (as opposed to lending to speculative investors and engaging in speculative investments themselves), except when, as part of the underwriting process for a stock or bond issuance being handled by an investment bank, a bridge loan to the firm issuing the securities is required. Thus, the problems of investment banks could only have been transmitted to the real economy through some process that produced a decline in *commercial* banks' lending.

If the amendment of Glass-Steagall by GLBA were to have had any role in causing the recession, then, it would have had to be by allowing the investment-bank arms of bank holding companies to transmit losses to the commercial banks with which some of them were affiliated through bank holding companies (BHCs). The troubled investment banks, therefore, not only would have had to be BHC affiliates rather than stand-alones, as Leonhardt pointed out; but contrary to his own hypothesis, their losses on PLMBS would have had to have *reduced* the capitalization of the commercial banks with which they were affiliated. However, it is difficult to envision how this might have occurred under the terms of GLBA. Under GLBA, a bank holding company is merely a shareholder in its affiliates; it has no liabilities for their debts, and if either an investment-bank subsidiary of a BHC or the BHC itself fails, the commercial bank subsidiary is unaffected. Moreover, "banking law and regulations prevent the activities of a bank securities affiliate [investment bank] or subsidiary from adversely affecting the condition of a related bank" (Wallison 2009b).[13]

GLBA also allowed commercial banks themselves (as opposed to holding-company parents of commercial banks) to have investment-bank subsidiaries. But similar restrictions apply to them. For instance, the commercial bank's investment in its investment bank is deducted from the commercial bank's net worth when the investment is initially made, so no further losses to the commercial bank are possible due to their affiliation. Only profits are possible, in the form of dividends paid by the investment bank to its parent entity—whether the parent is a commercial bank or a bank holding company.

Even more than Leonhardt realized, then, GLBA was irrelevant. The key problem, we reiterate, lay with the commercial banks, not the investment banks.

Bankers' Bonuses

The corporate-compensation theory of the crisis is, like the theory that legal capital buffers are necessary because of deposit insurance, a story of "moral hazard." In this case, bankers were put into a hazardous moral position, in which they might act contrary to the interests of their employers and society at large, by the incentives created by their performance bonuses. Those who, like Stiglitz and Judge Richard A. Posner (2009), espouse this theory claim that bankers deliberately took excessive risks because their compensation packages encouraged excessive risk taking. Bank executives received performance bonuses for profits; but if profits turned to losses and the executives were fired, they often had "golden parachutes" to protect them from financial damage. Meanwhile, lower-level employees (particularly traders) got annual bonuses for their own profitable actions in the short term, even if their actions cost the bank huge losses in future years (Posner 2009, 93–99).

Note that, as with Stiglitz's earlier criticism of Skidelsky on Keynes, this theory reduces the crisis to a matter of *risk* taking: that is, deliberately taking "known" risks, not inadvertently taking risks of which the executives or subordinates were unaware (due to their ignorance of the future). In short, the corporate-compensation theory is a typical economists' incentive narrative, one that treats economic actors as being, for the purposes at hand, omniscient.[14]

Cash performance incentives are especially likely to encourage short-term risk taking, since they "are typically awarded annually based on single year objectives" (Balachandran, Kogut, and Harnal 2010, 11)—objectives such as profits generated by the entire bank, in the case of executives, or profits generated by the unit in which subordinate employees such as traders work. However, *equity-based* incentives (payment in stock or in stock options), which are the preferred form of incentive compensation for executives, tend to favor a longer time horizon, since there is a vesting period of three to five years before bankers receive these bonuses. This should eliminate any incentive for them to deliberately take excessive risk in order to drive up the price of the stock in which they are paid, at least if the risks thus incurred might have the opposite effect on the stock price within three to five years. Moreover, each year begins a new vesting period for any equities awarded during that year. If executives want to keep working at the bank, the time horizon beyond which they might (theoretically) be willing to let short-term risks turn into long-term disasters will keep resetting three to five years into the future every year, although this counterincentive to risk taking will presumably diminish as the executives accumulate stock over the years. On the other hand, if executives hold onto these equities instead of selling them, their overall incentive will be to strike a balance between aggressive actions that further increase the share price, and conservative actions that guard against losses that would depress the share price of unsold stock and of bonus payments yet to come—let alone actions that are so risky that they would threaten the solvency of the bank.

There are other countervailing factors as well, such as the personal disgrace if an executive runs his or her company into the ground. There is also, conceivably, a sense of responsibility to the company's employees and shareholders. Such factors can also apply to subordinate employees compensated with cash bonuses, who may feel a sense of responsibility to each other, to their employer, or to society at large. Finally, a bank's risk-taking employees are supervised by risk managers paid to control excesses. In short, there are many cross-cutting "incentives" at work in banks, just as there always are when human beings act in an institutional and cultural context—which is to say, always.

It is by no means obvious, then, that performance-based incentives must have caused the crisis. The widespread acceptance of this theory may stem from its appearance in one of the first scholarly books about the crisis, Posner's *A Failure of Capitalism*, published early in 2009 by Harvard University Press. However, Posner provided no evidence that actually linked his hypothesis to the financial crisis (see Kraus 2011), and neither have any of the other scholars who have used the corporate-compensation theory to explain the crisis (e.g., Rajan 2008; Thanassoulis 2009; Stiglitz 2010a, 151–63). The corporate-compensation theory, like any logically valid theory, *might* be a sound explanation for a given real-world event; but if we are going to differentiate between logical possibilities and empirical realities, we need evidence showing that the forces posited in the theory were present in the case at hand and that they were not counteracted by other factors (Mill 1836 [1967]; Friedman 1996).

To date (November 2010), however, scholars have produced just three empirical studies touching on whether corporate compensation contributed to the financial crisis,[15] none of which support the theory as an explanation of the crisis. In Appendix I, we subject two of these papers to detailed analysis. Here, we shall summarize by saying that only the third paper (Cheng, Hong, and Scheinkman 2009) came up with *any* evidence that corporate compensation played a role in the crisis—and a role not for performance bonuses, but for the *amount* paid to executives. The paper found that banks and bank holding companies that paid relatively *more* to their executives (regardless whether this was in the form of performance incentives) tended to hold 1 percent more PLMBS than average (2009, Table 6). The remaining 99 percent is unexplained by any evidence yet adduced.

Of course, absence of evidence is not evidence of absence. The fact that nobody has yet discovered that corporate compensation practices contributed to the crisis does not mean that nobody will ever find such evidence, or that even if nothing is found, the corporate-compensation thesis is false. (It may well be true even if we remain ignorant of the evidence for its truth.) However, there is extremely powerful evidence *against* the thesis, and it is central to the alternative theory of the crisis that we defend in Chapter 2.

Before producing this evidence, it is important to keep in mind the role played in the corporate-compensation thesis by the deeply rooted economists' assumption that economic "agents" know everything they need to know if they are to make "rational" economic decisions (Simon 1985; Colander et al. 2011).[16] This assumption appears to have two roots. First, the political demand for policy advice from economists could not be satisfied if economic models fully incorporated agents' *ignorance* of key information, since an ignorant yet fully rational[17] agent might, at least in the limit case, exhibit any behavior at all in pursuit of his or her self-interest.[18] Second, an economic agent must be *aware* of an incentive and *know* how to achieve the objective addressed by the incentive if it is to affect his or her behavior predictably. Since microeconomics is almost completely reducible to game-theoretic incentive stories, economists are heavily dependent on the working assumption that agents are subjectively aware of the existence of an objectively posited incentive and that they know how to take advantage of it.

The bias toward hyperknowledgeable agents manifests itself in the corporate-compensation theory. In blaming performance incentives for bankers' "reckless" actions, one is saying more than that bankers had an incentive to make money in the short term. One is saying that because they had an incentive to make money in the short term, they deliberately took extra or "reckless" risks—risks that they knew could be justified by the positive effect they would have on their personal wealth—but that they also knew those risks would jeopardize the medium- or long-term viability of their banks.

Consider what happens if we remove the deliberateness assumption and replace it with the assumption that bankers were *inadvertently* "reckless" (i.e., that they were mistaken). According to this assumption, the bankers' actions were reckless only in retrospect, but were not perceived by the bankers as being reckless at the time; therefore, their recklessness could not have been influenced by incentives that might otherwise encourage recklessness, since these could operate only after having been perceived (the banker would have to realize that if he or she took "reckless risk" X, payoff Y might follow). Thus, the ex post facto "riskiness" of a banker's actions would better be attributed to her ignorance of the risk than to her incentive to be reckless.

Thus, granting for the sake of discussion that the effect of short-term performance bonuses is, in the absence of countervailing incentives, to encourage reckless behavior, a banker ignorant of the extra riskiness of her behavior *cannot* have been prompted by performance incentives to take the actions that turned out to be extra risky. If she took those actions, it must have been because she was unaware that she was being reckless. A corporate-compensation argument that does not empirically demonstrate *deliberate* recklessness therefore amounts merely to saying that, after the fact, we have decided to impute to bankers who made what turned out to be imprudent investments in triple-A mortgage-backed bonds the *knowledge* that they were "gambling" with the bank's money because of their incentive to do so (Dewatripont, Rochet, and Tirole 2010, 45).

A priori, there is no reason to prefer the deliberateness assumption to the inadvertence assumption. Merely establishing the existence of corporate-compensation structures that *could* have encouraged risk taking therefore proves nothing about whether they actually *did* encourage risk taking—except by assumption. Thus, the corporate-compensation theory is well put by Marc Jarsulic (2010, xix): "Because short-term returns on these assets were high, and the returns to traders and managers were outlandish, executives were happy to put the long term existence of their firms in harm's way," where "happy" indicates the assumption they *knew* that they were putting the long-term existence of their firms in harm's way.

Setting aside attempts to make assumptions substitute for research, we find two reasons to think that in the aggregate, deliberate risk taking was not a significant factor in causing the crisis. First, if the bankers responsible for acquiring the mortgage bonds that proved toxic were, as the corporate-compensation thesis holds, reckless gamblers, oblivious to risk, then they should have attempted to place their bets with *the maximum leverage (borrowed money) allowed by law.* This would have magnified their potential gains.

In the case of American commercial banks, the relevant laws were the Basel I accords of 1988, which were implemented in the United States in 1991 by the FDIC, the Federal Reserve, the Office of the Comptroller of the Currency, and the Office of Thrift Supervision. These regulations required that in order to maintain the legal privileges granted to "well-capitalized" U.S. banks,[19] a bank would have to fund at least 10 percent of its investments and loans with its own (unborrowed) capital. Under the Basel accords, then, the total amount of borrowed funds allowed to well-capitalized commercial banks was capped at 90 percent of the value of the bank's assets.

Banks run by reckless gamblers should have been very close to this limit—but most banks were not. In 2007, the twenty largest U.S. commercial banks' regulatory capital levels averaged 11.7 percent, nearly 20 percent above the legal minimum (Kuritzkes and Scott 2009). When one includes smaller commercial banks, the regulatory capital level as of mid-2007 was 12.79 percent (Pittman et al. 2008), nearly 30 percent higher than legal minimum for well-capitalized banks, and 60 percent higher than the "adequately capitalized" 8 percent level that was the absolute legal minimum for all banks.

These figures, moreover, underestimate U.S. commercial banks' aggregate conservatism before the crisis. Leverage is usually calculated by dividing total assets by what Basel I defined as "Tier 1" capital—funds received from sales of common equity shares and from retained earnings. Since these funds represent capital in the strictest and most secure sense, as explained in Chapter 2, Tier 1 capital is considered a truly reliable cushion against the unknowable future. The maximum legal Tier 1 leverage ratio for well-capitalized U.S. banks is 20:1 (a 5 percent Tier 1 capital minimum), but the Tier 1 leverage ratio of all U.S. commercial banks on the eve of the crisis was slightly lower than 10:1 (Barth 2010, Fig. 5.13). In short, banks were about half as leveraged, using this measure, as allowed by law.

Moreover, the regulatory capital ratios of different banks varied considerably, even though they all had the same "incentive," according to the corporate-compensation theory, to maximize their leverage. For instance, using Tier 1 leverage ratios, Citigroup was leveraged at 19:1, JPMorgan

Chase at 13:1, and Bank of America at 12:1 (Barth 2010, Fig. 5.14).[20] As Jean-Charles Rochet (2010, 97) has recently put it, "It is not at all rare for those managing banks to adopt prudent policies on their own initiative, maintaining some capital as a precaution in addition to the regulatory minimum." The persistence of such prudence up to the eve of the financial crisis disproves the notion that bank executives, at least (as opposed to traders), were deliberately taking excessive risks so as to boost earnings. Indeed, even the commercial banks that actually became insolvent had significantly higher regulatory capital levels than required by law (Kuritzkes and Scott 2009). This suggests that the chief cause of their insolvency was not (as a rule) deliberate risk taking but *inadvertent* risk taking—or, to be precise (because all investments and loans are risky in the colloquial sense), risk taking in which the bankers were ignorant of the true level of risk.

The second reason to doubt that bankers were deliberately taking excessive risks in pursuit of revenue, at least in the aggregate, is that they bought the least-lucrative MBS available—either agency bonds, issued by the GSEs and thus implicitly guaranteed by the U.S. government; or triple-A rated PLMBS or CDO tranches (Table 1.1). Not only were agency and triple-A MBS rated as "less risky" than lower-rated PLMBS bonds; as a result of these ratings, triple-A-rated bonds paid lower coupons than did lower-rated bonds. A banker trying to maximize his or her revenue, heedless of risk, so as to maximize his or her performance compensation, *never* would have purchased agency bonds or triple-A bonds instead of bonds with higher coupons due to lower ratings. Yet that is what commercial bankers did.[21]

A more detailed look at the MBS portfolios of the commercial banks allows us to put a finer point on the bankers' risk aversion. Even though all of the commercial banks' CDOs were rated triple-A, they tended to be *objectively* more dangerous than triple-A PLMBS tranches or agency bonds, because CDOs often tranched the mezzanine tranches of PLMBS. The stated rationale of CDOs was that they were even safer than PLMBS, because of the greater diversity of assets included in them. But when they tranched higher-paying mezzanine bonds, triple-A CDO bonds were more lucrative than triple-A PLMBS, just as triple-A PLMBS were more lucrative than agency bonds. Since the rule of thumb in bond investing is that higher returns connote greater risks, it is possible that commercial-bank traders who acquired CDOs did recognize their greater risk, despite their AAA ratings.

Table 1.3 displays the distribution of commercial banks' assets among these three types of "safe" investment, with the safest and least lucrative

Table 1.3.   Bankers' Preference for Safety (percent)

	Agency MBS	AAA PLMBS	AAA CDOs	AAA PLMBS plus agency MBS
proportion of U.S. commercial bank and S&L mortgage bonds, by type	64.3	28.9	6.8	93.2

Proportion of U.S. commercial banks' mortgage securities invested in government-guaranteed or triple-A PLMBS and CDO tranches. AAA-rated CDOs consisted largely of mezzanine tranches of PLMBS, and thus were objectively riskier than senior (AAA-rated) PLMBS bonds.

Source: Derived from Lehman Brothers 2008, Figure 4.

bonds in the first column, the objectively riskier bonds in the middle, and the riskiest but most lucrative third. The final column adds the two safest categories of mortgage bonds for comparison to the riskiest ones. The table demonstrates that risk taking in pursuit of higher revenue was not a significant factor in commercial banks' bond purchases, in the aggregate. The bankers consistently tended to choose the least-lucrative available MBS (agencies) and the least-lucrative PLMBS (those rated AAA)—instead of CDOs.

We acknowledge that these data are less conclusive against the corporate-compensation theory than are the leverage ratios, because while we know the leverage ratios of individual banks such as Citigroup, we do not have individual-level data on asset composition that is as fine grained as the aggregate figures presented in Table 1.3. Presumably the banks that got into worse trouble tended to have higher proportions of riskier bonds.

However, one should also keep in mind what is missing from the table: *any* bonds (PLMBS or CDO) rated lower than triple A. These would have been the most lucrative choices of all. The universal avoidance of double-A, single-A, and lower-rated mortgage bonds by commercial banks suggests that, at worst, bonus-hungry traders were getting around their risk managers by sneaking triple-A CDOs past them: the risk managers' "screen" may well have been the ratings, not the details of the collateral. In that case, however, we would want to know why anyone believed the ratings produced by a ratings cartel; we explore this question in Chapter 4.

"Too Big to Fail"

The same two considerations hold against the TBTF theory of the crisis, which, like the corporate-compensation theory, is an economistic, moral-hazard story that presupposes that managers of the largest banks were well informed about the objective (ex post) level of risk they were taking (e.g., Volcker 2010, 12). As Stiglitz (2010a, 164, his emphasis) puts it (again without providing evidence), banks *"knew* they were too big to fail, and consequently they undertook risk just as economic theory predicted they would."

In other words, the reason the bankers knowingly took risky bets is that they also "knew" they would be bailed out if the bets went sour. Had this been the case, however, the bankers would have levered their bets to the legal maximum; and they would have bought disproportionate quantities of bonds from the high-yielding mezzanine tranches of PLMBS and CDOs, not from comparatively low-yielding triple-A PLMBS and CDO tranches and even lower-yielding agency bonds.

The TBTF theory also suffers from defects of logic and evidence that do not apply to the corporate-compensation theory. First, the evidence *for* the TBTF theory consists mainly of two historical episodes, the bailouts of Continental Illinois Bank in 1985 and of a hedge fund, Long-Term Capital Management (LTCM), in 1998. These episodes are supposed to have assured executives at the largest commercial banks that they, too, would be bailed out. However, when Continental Illinois failed, its managers were fired and its shareholders were wiped out, and when LTCM was bailed out, its principals were essentially wiped out, too. It would not be logical for any self-interested bank executive to run a bank into the ground because of his or her belief that *it* would then be bailed out if *she* would then be fired (and, if compensated with equities, wiped out). Not only does public obloquy follow from destroying a major bank, but "the reputational impact of insolvency is likely to include the loss of opportunities to manage another banking firm or to be appointed to the board of other banking firms" (Mehran and Rosenberg 2009, 8–9). In addition, "a higher standard of accountability according to law and well-defined regulatory expectations for bank CEOs (and bank directors) can facilitate their prosecution relative to non-bank CEOs." It is therefore not at all obvious that the incentives created by the Continental Illinois and LTCM bailouts were *in favor* of risk taking at other TBTF banks. If anything, the leverage ratios and asset composition of the banks suggest that bankers might have taken quite the opposite lesson from those bailouts.

There is a subtler theory of TBTF, however, according to which the earlier bailouts created incentives for recklessness not among bank executives but among certain bank *creditors*—that is, the buyers of corporate bonds issued by TBTF banks—because the creditors of Continental Illinois (although not the creditors of LTCM) were bailed out.

As we noted before, the higher the (perceived) "risk" of a bond, the higher the coupon its issuer must offer to investors, lest they refuse to take the risk. According to this version of TBTF, then, the Continental Illinois bailout in 1985 led creditors to be satisfied with lower coupons on the corporate debt of TBTF banks in the 2000s than would have been acceptable if they thought these banks would be allowed to fail if they engaged in risky activity. Thus, without the implicit TBTF guarantee, creditors of the large banks would have been vigilant about recklessness on the part of the banks, raising the coupons paid by banks that engaged in excessively risky behavior, thereby costing those banks money paid out in higher interest on their debt; this would have discouraged bank managers from allowing risky behavior. With the implicit TBTF guarantee, however, bond buyers' vigilance flagged, because they no longer had the incentive to watch for risky behavior: a big bank that took too many risks would be bailed out, so the bank's creditors need not be concerned.

The theory is implausible on its face, not only because the most recent bailout, of LTCM (in 1998), did *not* make creditors whole; but because the theory assumes that vigilant creditors somehow would have been more aware than bank executives, whose careers and stock holdings were at stake, that buying triple-A mortgage-backed securities was "risky" behavior. In short, the theory credits creditors with the same omniscience that the corporate-compensation theory attributes to bankers.

Moreover, this version of the TBTF theory can be tested empirically, and it fails the test. Dean Baker and Travis McArthur (2009; cf. Hart and Zingales 2010) test the theory by comparing the coupons paid on the corporate debt of large banks (defined as those with more than $100 billion of assets) to the coupons paid by small ones. They discover that large banks had to pay an average of 0.29 percent less interest on their bonds than did small banks—amounting to a 29 bps "risk premium" for small banks. This is supposed to confirm the TBTF theory, but there are many non-TBTF reasons that small banks might be considered riskier than large ones. For instance, the national and international depositor and investment bases of large banks reduce their probability of default in case of regional or national economic downturns, to which smaller banks have always been more vulnerable.

More logical than comparing the borrowing costs of large versus small banks would be to compare the borrowing costs of supposedly TBTF banks against the borrowing costs of Fannie Mae and Freddie Mac. If the TBTF theory is true, then the corporate bonds of TBTF banks must have been considered by creditors to be similar to the corporate bonds issued by Fannie and Freddie: that is, TBTF banks' bonds should have been seen as implicitly guaranteed by the government, just like Fannie and Freddie's bonds. However, the comparison falsifies the theory. During the years 2004–7, for example, when most of the mortgage debt was added to commercial banks' balance sheets, the average spread above "riskless" Treasury bonds for Fannie and Freddie bonds was roughly 20 bps (Barth 2010, Fig. 6.19), while the average spreads for the corporate bonds issued by the three biggest U.S. banks—Citigroup, JPMorgan Chase, and Bank of America— were, respectively, 53, 75, and 55 bps.[22]

In addition to the much higher spreads on all three of the biggest banks' corporate bonds relative to those of Fannie and Freddie, the 22 bps spread between JPMorgan Chase and Citigroup demands special attention. It is nearly as large as the 29 bps spread between banks that were definitely too small to be bailed out and the large, supposedly "TBTF" banks. Yet nobody could have thought that JPMorgan Chase, the second-biggest bank in America, was too small to be bailed out—at least not anyone who thought that the biggest banks were indeed too big *not* to be bailed out. Instead, JPMorgan Chase's lower profitability during these years (Tett 2009a, chap. 8) is a plausible explanation for its greater risk premium, even though it turned out to be the safest of the big banks once the crisis erupted. If anything, creditors, who were, in the aggregate, demanding a much higher risk premium for Morgan bonds, should have (according to the TBTF theory) reacted to whatever fears prompted this demand by vigilantly inspecting Morgan's actual holdings, and then—effectively omniscient about the good news these holdings conveyed about the future—they should have driven Morgan's risk premium much *lower* than the risk premia of Citigroup and Bank of America.

It is possible, however, that all three of the biggest banks had much higher risk premia than did Fannie Mae and Freddie Mac because bank-bond investors who were convinced that big banks *probably* would be bailed out in a crisis might still have thought that Fannie and Freddie were even *more* likely to be bailed out. Or perhaps *some* of the large banks' creditors were skeptical about the TBTF notion, driving up these banks' risk premia, while a *smaller* proportion of Fannie and Freddie's creditors were bailout skeptics.

Both scenarios are undoubtedly true, to some extent: millions of diverse people invested in these bonds, and surely they must have had differing perceptions of risk. However, one could say something very similar about banks' performance-compensation plans: tens of thousands of executives and subordinate traders at the commercial banks might have had an objective incentive to take on excessive risk, and some fraction of them might subjectively have realized that this incentive could be taken advantage of by getting around risk-management supervisors and any ethical qualms they might have had. In other words, both the TBTF theory and the corporate-compensation theory provide logical explanations for *some quantity* of the behavior that produced the crisis. The question, however, is, *How much*? This is the question that economists have all but ignored, for the moral-hazard theories are, as Stiglitz admits, so comforting to economists' a priori assumptions about the primacy of "incentives" that it does not seem to occur to economists that other factors may have been at work.

We are not demanding an impossible degree of precision when we ask how important these incentives actually were; we simply want to know whether either of the two moral hazard theories (corporate compensation and TBTF) describes "relatively little" actual behavior or "a great deal" of it. The data in Table 1.3, for instance, suggest that bankers who were heedless of risk because of the short-term incentive for risk-taking offered by bonuses did not affect banks' mortgage-backed securities portfolios *very much*—especially considering that none of the PLMBS or CDOs bought by the commercial banks paid the higher returns offered by double-A-and lower-rated bonds. Similarly, the data on banks' risk premia suggest that in fact, the prospect of a bailout for banks that were allegedly TBTF was not the primary determinant of their access to relatively inexpensive credit; sheer size, national and international scale, and profitability seem to have served as most investors' heuristics for the risk of banks' default.

Of course, in light of the subsequent bailouts, TBTF can be expected to be a very real factor in the future, but there is no evidence that it was a major factor in causing the financial crisis.

"Irrationality" and Interpretation

Once housing prices leveled off in 2006 and began falling in 2007, a negative synergy can be expected to have hit nonprime borrowers. This can be seen by examining the behavior of loan-to-value ratios (LTVs) when house prices rise and when they fall.

The initial LTV of a mortgage is 100 minus the percentage of the house price that constitutes the down payment. A conventional 20 percent down mortgage has an initial LTV of 80, while a mortgage with no down payment has an initial LTV of 100. The average LTV of a subprime loan issued in 2006 was 95 (i.e., a 5 percent down payment), and the average Alt-A LTV was 89 (Zandi 2008, 33).

Mortgages with low LTVs are considered less likely to default, because a borrower who can put 20 percent down is likelier to be in better financial shape than one who cannot, and is likelier to be committed to staying in the house, and thus to making the required payments—unlike house flippers, who buy a house solely as a speculative investment and put as little money into it as possible. However, a high LTV may decline during a housing boom merely because the price of the house is going up. A 25 percent increase in the price of a house would reduce the initial 100 LTV of a 0 percent down mortgage to a respectable 80. If the price of the house is rising, a financially stretched subprime borrower has an incentive to keep making difficult-to-afford payments because if the payments become unaffordable, he or she can try to sell the house for a profit.

Therefore, private lenders, not just GSEs, appear to have welcomed the opportunity to provide high LTV loans as the housing boom continued. Low- and no-down payment mortgages proliferated, as did second mortgages: home-equity loans, home-equity lines of credit (HELOCs), and "cash-out refinancings,"[23] all of which effectively raise the LTV by increasing the size of the mortgage. This effect is counteracted as the price of a house rises, making first and second mortgages more affordable for subprime and Alt-A borrowers. Thus, Figure 1.4 shows that as time passed, an increasing proportion of mortgage bonds' collateral consisted of Alt-A or "subprime" mortgages (strictly defined by the low credit rating of the borrower). Many agency bonds were also "subprime" in the looser sense of pooling mortgages to borrowers with high credit scores but also high LTVs.

As the price of a house *falls,* the LTV goes up, and the incentive to keep paying the mortgage declines. Even before a mortgage goes "underwater"

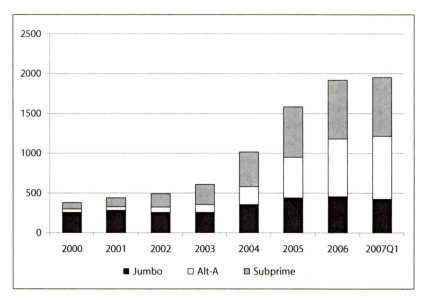

Figure 1.4. Growth of the subprime bond bubble. Privately issued MBS outstanding
(billions of dollars). Shaded: subprime; white: Alt-A (between prime and
subprime); black: jumbo (loan amount above conventional limits). Jablecki
and Machaj 2011, Fig. 8.12

(meaning that it has an LTV above 100), a borrower may decide that payments on a house with a plummeting resale value are not worth making, and
may simply "walk away" from the mortgage if he or she cannot sell the
house, given that he or she has no ethical scruples. This is possible in most
states because of laws that give banks "no recourse" in case of default (Wallison 2011a). And it is likeliest to happen with subprime and nonprime borrowers, who can least afford to make payments in the first place. Thus, the
International Monetary Fund (IMF) reported in April 2008 that "delinquency rates on subprime mortgage loans originated in 2005–6 have continued to rise, exceeding the highest rates recorded on any prior vintage" (IMF
2008a, 5). The "vintage" is the year in which a mortgage was originated;
delinquencies are late mortgage payments, which are often preludes to a
default. The IMF data show graphically that delinquent payments on subprime mortgages that were originated in 2000—before the housing boom—

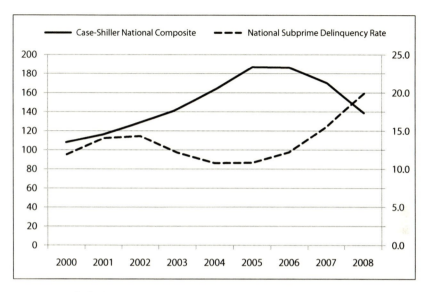

Figure 1.5. The bubble bursts: house prices and subprime delinquency rates. Left scale: house prices (Case-Shiller). Right scale: subprime delinquencies.S & P, U.S. Census Bureau.

peaked four years later, with an average of 25 percent of the loan balance unpaid (IMF 2008a, 6). By contrast, 2006-vintage subprimes had reached 25 percent delinquency values a mere one year after they were issued.

In hindsight, all of this can be seen with perfect clarity, and one might think that by the same token, any sensible person, let alone sophisticated investors and bankers, should have been able to predict the effects of a deflating housing bubble beforehand. The fact that they acted as if they did *not* predict this has led to the popularity of "irrational exuberance" as an explanation of the financial crisis.

The initial problem with this explanation is the same as the problem with the corporate-compensation and TBTF explanations: commercial bankers who were irrationally exuberant about the endless rise of house prices would have levered up more than they did; and they would have purchased the riskier, more lucrative mezzanine tranches of PLMBS and CDO mortgage bonds, not low-paying agency bonds and senior tranches of PLMBS.

However, there are also conceptual problems with the notion of "irrationality" as used in this explanation of the crisis. These problems indicate that the economics of "irrationality" is built on the same assumption of omniscience as the orthodox economics of "rationality."

At least in its vulgar usage, "irrationality" does not actually explain anything. In this usage, "irrational" is a synonym for *inexplicable*: when we say that people are behaving irrationally, we really mean that we don't understand why they are doing what they are doing. Clearly this represents an abdication of the goal of social science, which is to explain behavior; calling people crazy merely explains their behavior away.

Specifically, the vulgar usage of "irrationality" treats people's *errors* as inexplicable. Since the correct interpretation of what was going on—in this case, that the housing *boom* that was driving up prices was actually a doomed housing *bubble*—seems obvious to us ex post, we assume that it must have been obvious to any calm, *rational* person ex ante, such that only emotion or irrationality can explain behavior that did not take account of our retrospectively self-evident interpretation of the housing boom. Another way to put the point is that the vulgar usage does not recognize that reality is complex and can produce many different interpretations, each of them plausible to sane, rational people.

Thus, the vulgar notion of irrationality treats *accurate and representative* "information" about objective reality as if it were there to be had, *sans* interpretation, by any rational agent, such that behavior that does not take our retrospective interpretation of this information into account must have been due to a lack of rationality—rather than to an absence of accurate, representative information, or the presence of an incorrect interpretation of such information.

One way of summarizing our point is to say that the vulgar "irrationality" hypothesis is more normative ("they *should* have known it was a bubble") than it is scientific (explanatory). Another way of summarizing it is to say that the attribution of the financial crisis to irrationality is an exercise in hindsight bias:

> In hindsight, people consistently exaggerate what could have been anticipated in foresight. They not only tend to view what has happened as having been inevitable but also to view it as having appeared "relatively inevitable" before it happened. People believe

that others should have been able to anticipate events much better than was actually the case. They even misremember their own predictions so as to exaggerate in hindsight what they knew in foresight. (Fischhoff 1982, 341)

All these marks of hindsight bias can be seen in even the scholarly (as opposed to the vulgar) wing of the "irrationality" school. For instance, the leader of this wing, Robert J. Shiller, argues in retrospect (Shiller 2008, 39) that a certain Figure 2.1 in the 2005 edition of his book, *Irrational Exuberance*, demonstrated, at the time, that the increase in house prices since the late 1990s could not have been due to fundamental, "secular" factors, such as rising construction costs, population growth, or rising interest rates, all of which, the figure showed, grew more slowly than house prices. Thus, post-2005 investment in housing was "irrational." However, Shiller left out another secular factor that might have influenced many people to interpret the "boom" as being fundamentally sound, instead of being a "bubble": the rise in disposable income after World War II, a period during which house prices barely moved up at all until the 2000s.

As Ben Bernanke put the conventional wisdom in 2005,

House prices have risen nearly 25 percent over the past two years. Although speculative activity has increased in some areas, at a national level these price increases largely reflect strong economic fundamentals, including robust growth in jobs and income, low mortgage rates, steady rates of household formation, and factors that limit the expansion of housing supply in some areas. (Bernanke 2005, 7)

Indeed, despite his 2008 interpretation of his own Figure 2.1, in 2005 Shiller himself did not recognize that there was a nationwide housing bubble, as opposed to bubbles in a few "big glamour cities" (Shiller 2005, 18)—local bubbles that were widely recognized as such at the time, which Shiller devoted a large part of the book to explaining with great insight. By 2008, however, the ex ante "predictability" of the nationwide housing bubble had become so obvious to Shiller ex post that he derided former Fed Chairman Alan Greenspan's 2007 book, *The Age of Turbulence*, for containing a passage in which Greenspan recounts that he used to " 'tell audiences that we were facing not a bubble but a froth—lots of small local bubbles that never grew to a scale that could threaten the health of the overall economy'" (Greenspan 2007, 231, quoted in Shiller 2008, xii). In hindsight, this sounds so ludicrous to Shiller that he attributes it to willful blindness and religious zeal (i.e., irrationality). Whatever the cause of the housing boom had been, Shiller writes, "it was not seen by national leaders, especially . . . in the United States, where pride in the superiority of our capitalist system some-times seems to approach religious fervor."

However, Shiller does not notice that in the next paragraph of Green-span's book, Greenspan had suggested that by 2005—when Shiller's Figure 2.1 appeared—he *was* aware of widespread reports of house flipping, and that by then, as a result, it was clear to him that "the party was over." Moreover, in the previous paragraph, Greenspan (2007, 230) makes it evi-dent that it had been in 2002 or 2003 that he used to tell audiences that there were merely local housing bubbles. Similarly, 2003 was the year in which Shiller said that "he'd only predict a nationwide housing slump if a worldwide economic slump 'kills' consumer confidence. Only some 'high-flying' cities like San Francisco, Denver and Boston are at risk of price depreciations, and the chances of declines in those regions are less than a third."[24] Although Shiller predicted in 2003 that housing prices would rise "everywhere," he *denied* that this would constitute a bubble. "'It would be quite daring to predict' a nationwide housing bubble, he said"—at the time.

We invoke this episode not to call out a prominent economist or to dismiss the substance of his arguments about the origins of bubbles, with which we have no quarrel. However, Shiller *interprets* this substance as "psychological" or "emotional"; he calls it "*social contagion*" (Shiller 2008, 41, emphasis original), and concludes that it produces "irrational" behav-ior—even though this behavior turns out, on closer examination, to be *error* that is not caused by any real psychological process, and certainly not by the emotional processes suggested by such terms as "irrationality" and "exuberance."[25] Rather, Shiller is describing purely *epistemological* lapses with *cultural*, not psychological, roots.

Shiller's "irrationality" is actually *market participants' ignorance of important information,* or *market participants' misinterpretation of informa-tion.* The "social contagion" of which he writes is actually a "contagion of ideas" (Shiller 2008, 41). Without the pseudo-medical terminology, a social "contagion" of ideas simply means a widespread acceptance of incorrect beliefs. Yet when people relate to each other, or hear from the media, *sound* beliefs, we assume that Shiller would not call it a "social contagion," since the very point of the medical terminology is to suggest "irrationality."

We agree with Shiller that people get their beliefs socially, meaning from other people (although we prefer the term *culturally*, since the beliefs must be mediated by symbols). But there is nothing irrational about this. Where else would people get their ideas if not from other people—either personal acquaintances, or journalists, or other symbolic mediators of various interpretations of reality? Socially transmitted ideas are not inherently erroneous, let alone "diseased." Moreover, when a socially transmitted idea is unsound, it bespeaks ignorance of some aspect of reality or logic on the part of the transmitter or the recipient of the idea, not *irrationality* on the part of anyone. (To make an error in logic, let alone to be unaware of a fact, is not the same thing as to be irrational.)

Thus, for example, Shiller and George Akerlof write in *Animal Spirits* that these "spirits" arise from "our peculiar relationship with ambiguity or uncertainty" (Akerlof and Shiller 2009, 4). In Akerlof and Shiller's view, ambiguity and uncertainty produce asset bubbles and thus economic crises by way of the "changing thought patterns" to which ambiguity and uncertainty lead—specifically "changing stories about the nature of the economy" (Akerlof and Shiller 2009, 4). Indeed, "stories" are one of the five types of "animal spirits" in their account, along with "confidence," "fairness," "bad faith," and the "money illusion." Yet *animals* do not tell stories, notice ambiguity, or believe in fairness, faith, or wealth. All of these supposed animal spirits, or emotions, actually function in Akerlof and Shiller's book as *ideas*, including the all-important "confidence": *overconfidence*, which simply means "a misperception that one is correct," is supposed to be the upshot of irrational exuberance, such that the emotion causes the misperception rather than the other way around.

In reality, we suggest, the causal arrow often (or always?) runs in the opposite direction. If one believes that one is investing in a *safe* bond because it is tranched, overcollateralized, and rated triple A, and because it represents exposure to a housing *boom* in a country that has never experienced a significant nationwide housing *bubble*, then one may be *overconfident* that the investment will turn out well, and as a result, one may feel *exuberant* if one can buy a lot of these bonds. But the feeling is not irrational, even if it is based on erroneous ideas. Moreover, if the feeling turns out to be unwarranted, this says nothing about the *source* of the feelings in emotions or animal spirits rather than in what those who shared the feelings thought were good reasons, such as the growing wealth of the United States.

As Benjamin Friedman (2009, 44) puts it,

> Akerlof and Shiller's substantive arguments fall victim to . . . circularity. The element of animal spirits on which they place the most emphasis in their account of the current crisis is confidence. It is, they say, "the first and most crucial of our animal spirits." Is it rational or not for me to put money in a bank in which I have confidence? Or to buy a stock if I have confidence in the company's business prospects? According to Akerlof and Shiller, this kind of behavior is, by definition, irrational since "confidence" for them is a kind of faith, not a matter of rational analysis: "The very term *confidence* [they write] implies behavior that goes beyond a rational approach to decision making."

In other words, Akerlof and Shiller define away the very possibility that emotions can be based on reasons (whether they turn out to be good or bad reasons). This definition is the only "evidence" they present that actions were taken in the runup to the crisis that we would need psychological diagnosis or animal-behavior studies to understand.

Like Friedman (no relation), we are objecting only to Shiller's (and Akerlof's) vocabulary. Shiller's use of his Figure 2.1 exemplifies the conceptual damage that this vocabulary can cause. Shiller treats the Figure as if it has a single "rational" interpretation, even though, as we have seen, there are other rational (if erroneous) ways of interpreting it—including Shiller's own interpretation at the time (i.e., that it did *not* signify a nationwide housing bubble). We can conclude either that Shiller was "irrational" at the time, or that he, like most human beings, was ignorant of what the future would hold. In the latter view, Shiller—just like Greenspan, the rating agencies, and the investors in mortgage-backed securities, including the bankers—was ignorant of the looming nationwide housing bubble, either because he misinterpreted information that he possessed or because he failed to possess what turned out to be accurate, representative information.

Even though it might seem clear that predicting the future is a task that generally surpasses human capacities, we have already seen that economists are poorly equipped to acknowledge either our ignorance of the future, resulting in the many incorrect predictions that we make and transmit to each other culturally; or the complexity of the "data" that we are interpreting, which leads to the misinterpretations on which those faulty predictions are based. Economists such as Shiller and Akerlof, who *do* reject the assumption that economic agents are omniscient, have unfortunately equated this with the assumption that economic agents are "rational," such that their unwitting attempt to create an economics of ignorant agents is transformed, verbally, into an economics of economic agents' irrational "animal spirits." Yet one's use of *reason* has nothing to do with how well informed or perspicacious one is. Only if we conflate rationality with the possession of perfect information, and then conflate the possession of perfect information with perfect reasoning abilities, does a rejection of the perfect-information assumption appear to entail "irrationality" as the alternative.

Rationality, as economists use the term (Max Weber's *Zweckrationalität*, or instrumental rationality), is not an unemotional state. It is the disposition to treat one's own actions as means to other ends, rather than as ends in themselves. Weber ([1968] 1978, vol. 1, 25–26) distinguished the opposite disposition from this economistic—or, better, this consequentialist—rationality by using the term "value-rationality" (*Wertrationalität*). Value rationality is epitomized by Kant's injunction never to tell a lie, *regardless* of the consequences. Neither value rationality nor instrumental rationality prevent those who in a given situation display either disposition from making *mistakes* because of ignorance or poor reasoning abilities. Rationality and irrationality have nothing to do with ignorance or ineptitude.

We are left, then, with some of the elements of the conventional wisdom intact, at least pending further investigation: low interest rates and Fannie and Freddie contributed to the housing bubble. And predatory lending (as well as mistaken beliefs) encouraged people to accept subprime, Alt-A, and adjustable-rate mortgages that, ex post, many people turned out not to be able to afford.

However, if the housing bubble had burst before those mortgages had been converted into private-label mortgage-backed securities, and if commercial banks had not acquired nearly $500 billion of these securities, there probably would not have been a financial crisis and recession. Low interest rates, GSEs, deregulation, banks' compensation systems, the notion that large banks were too big to be allowed to fail, and irrational exuberance do not explain why nonprime mortgages were privately securitized or, more importantly, why such a substantial sum of these assets found their way into the investment portfolios of commercial banks. Our interpretation of why this happened, and how it caused the Great Recession, will be given in the next two chapters respectively.

We begin with the Basel rules on bank capital, which governed not only the level but the type of assets that commercial banks acquired during the years preceding the crisis.

2

Capital Adequacy Regulations and the Financial Crisis: Bankers' and Regulators' Errors

A bank's "capital" is the security blanket it needs because of the fragile nature of banking. Any corporation's capital boils down to its net worth, or *"the residual after subtracting liabilities from assets"* (Gilliam 2005, 293, emphasis added). "The greater a bank's capital, the more it can absorb net losses before liabilities exceed assets": capital serves as a buffer against bankruptcy, which occurs when a corporation's assets dip below its liabilities. Capital is thus rightly seen as a "cushion" for any corporation, but it is especially important for banks. This is because of the unique nature of a (commercial) bank's assets, from which its liabilities are subtracted to determine its net worth.

A manufacturing corporation's assets, for example, will probably consist largely of cash and items that could be sold in case of bankruptcy to meet its liabilities, such as its factories and equipment, inventory of unsold goods, real estate, and so on. In the case of a bank, however, most of its assets are not plant or equipment; they are loans—mortgages, business loans, and credit-card accounts, for instance. A sufficient "capital" buffer, in the accounting sense of the term with which we are concerned here, is important to banks because of the general unpredictability of these assets.

A factory may unexpectedly burn down, but such possibilities are actually "risks" in Keynes's sense, and therefore they can be insured against.

The insurance company calculates the odds of a fire based on its interpretation of relevant historical factors: the neighborhood in which the factory is located, the type of manufacturing performed in the factory, and so on. It makes predictions of future probabilities based on these factors, although, since interpretation is involved, the predictions may be wrong. Meanwhile, however, the insured corporation is guaranteed payment in the case of fire—as long as the insurance company itself remains solvent.

The idea behind using CDS to insure mortgage bonds was that the risk of mortgage holders' defaults could also be calculated based on historical data. These calculations were performed by the rating agencies, the interpretations of which were apparently erroneous. We discuss that further in the next chapter, but here, we deal with the question of why so many commercial banks ended up, in effect, building factories (income-producing assets) in neighborhoods that were extra vulnerable to fires.

On the other side of the ledger from assets are a corporation's *liabilities*. These are funds legally owed to a corporation's employees, vendors, and anyone else from whom the corporation has borrowed money or entered into legal obligations to deliver payments, goods, or services. In addition, corporations will often incur liabilities in the form of loans, lines of credit, and corporate bonds. All of these liabilities must be paid off before any profits are distributed to investors in the form of dividends. With commercial banks, however, there is an additional type of liability: customers' bank-account balances.

The defining feature of a commercial bank is that it gets some of its funds from customers' accounts. But with the exception of certificates of deposit and other bond-like (time) deposits, which need only be paid off at specified dates, banks must stand ready at any time to pay a given customer the full amount she has lent to the bank by depositing funds in her checking or savings account. Like other corporations, banks borrow funds from other banks and from bond purchasers; unlike other corporations, they also borrow funds from depositors. The special fragility of banking stems from the fact that banks then *lend* much of the money they have borrowed to mortgagors, credit-card account holders, and businesses: banks are both borrowers and lenders of the same money. The borrowed money constitutes part of the bank's liabilities, yet when it is lent out, it also constitutes part of the bank's assets.

To be sure, those who borrow money from a bank are legally obliged to pay back these loans; but they might prove unable to do so. If they default on their obligations, the bank is left holding the bag; it is still obligated to its creditors (depositors, bond holders, and so on). This makes a capital cushion especially important for a bank to cover unexpected declines in the value of its principal assets, i.e., loans.

The "cushion" metaphor can be misleading, since a bank's capital is not kept in a vault as cash reserves. Instead, it too is lent out at interest to credit-card holders, mortgagors, and businesses; or is invested in, for example, corporate debt, equities, government debt, or asset-backed securities, such as subprime mortgage bonds. However, most of the money that commercial banks lend out (or otherwise invest) is *not* capital; it is debt borrowed from depositors and purchasers of a bank's bonds. Hence the widespread concern about commercial banks' leverage ratios—the proportion of borrowed funds to capital. This proportion was legally limited at 10:1 for "well-capitalized" commercial banks and 12.5:1 for "adequately capitalized" banks under the version of Basel I that was imposed in the United States. That is, Basel I set an 8 percent minimum capital cushion, which U.S. financial regulators raised to 10 percent for banks considered "well capitalized" under U.S. law. If *all* the money that a bank lent out or invested in assets were borrowed, with no remainder (the capital cushion), then assets and liabilities would precisely match each other, and a bank would teeter on the edge of insolvency. But if, say, 8 percent of the bank's mortgages and other assets are funded not by debt (a liability) but by capital, then 8 percent of the bank's loans can default before the bank reaches the breaking point.

The special qualification needed by capital to serve as a "cushion," then, is that it has not been borrowed, hence is not owed, to anyone. Profits—"retained earnings"—are one source of capital. Issuing shares of stock (instead of bonds) is the other chief means by which a bank can obtain capital. The shareholders obtain ownership (equity) rights in the bank, meaning the right to a portion of the accumulated capital, including profits, if the bank liquidates itself or is bought by another company. In exchange for this right, buyers of common shares in an initial public offering of a bank's stock, or buyers of common shares in future offerings, hand over cash to the bank free and clear.[1] Unlike borrowed funds, such as funds raised by selling bonds, cash raised from the sale of equity shares is not owed back (let alone with interest) to the purchasers of these shares, so it provides part of the needed cushion against future vicissitudes.

Capital Becomes a Requirement: The Dilemma
of Capital Adequacy Standards

The most dramatic illustration of the difficult spot in which bankers inherently find themselves is the bank run. If a bank's depositors suddenly try to withdraw all their money, the bank will become insolvent long before the last depositor is paid off, because most of the depositors' funds have been lent out or have been devoted to other investments. The Great Depression prompted an unprecedented wave of bank runs in the United States, to which one response was a provision of the Banking Act of 1933 that instituted deposit insurance for commercial banks and savings and loans. This would prevent future bank runs by reassuring depositors that they would be bailed out if their bank became insolvent.

Because of deposit insurance, commercial banks and savings and loans were immediately subjected to legal capital minima by the federal government. What are now called "capital adequacy requirements" were designed to ensure against the "moral hazard" that, because of deposit insurance, bankers would gamble depositors' money on reckless loans or investments. The idea was that the threat of a bank run had impeded bankers from operating their banks as casinos, since depositors might take flight if they found out about risky practices. When deposit insurance effectively eliminated the threat of a bank run, bankers were free to be (deliberately) reckless. Therefore, a mandatory capital cushion was necessary, just in case. As several economists put it,

> Given the existence of deposit insurance, when a bank defaults on its obligations, losses are incurred that are not borne by either the bank's shareholders or any of its other financial claimholders. Thus bank management has no reason to internalize its losses. This observation yields a simple and powerful rationale for capital regulation: a bank should be made to hold a sufficient capital buffer such that, given realistic lags in supervisory intervention, etc., expected losses to the government insurer are minimized. (Kashyap et al. 2008, 16–17)

In addition to removing the fear of a bank run from the hearts of bank managers, deposit insurance is held to have "reduced depositors' incentive to monitor banks" (Dewatripont et al. 2010, 5). Thus, the theory that we saw standing behind economists' a priori dedication to the TBTF theory (as well as the corporate-compensation theory) stood, and stands, behind capital requirements, too.

It is thought that in the absence of deposit insurance prior to the Depression, bankers and depositors monitored banks' capital cushions, which (in the aggregate) ranged from 11 to 15 percent in the years immediately preceding the Depression. After the Banking Act of 1933, the newly established FDIC, which administered deposit insurance, also set capital minima for all banks that it insured, to prevent reckless behavior that would require it to close down a bank and repay depositors' funds. Initially, the FDIC required that insured banks maintain capital amounting to 10 percent of their deposits (FDIC 1984, 115). In addition to technical questions such as how to define capital and whether to calculate it against deposits (debt), on the one hand, or against the total assets funded by both debt and equity, on the other, the main question with which regulators and academic researchers grappled once capital controls were established was whether to require a fixed capital level, such as 10 percent (e.g., New York State Bankers Association 1952; Freeman 1952; Norton 1995) or to impose a less rigid form of regulation (e.g., Cotter 1966; Ryon 1969).

The dilemma was created by the fact that any fixed capital minimum will be a percentage of another number (such as total assets) that will illogically lump together "safe" loans and investments with those that are likelier to default or to pay off at less-than-expected rates. Since the purpose of a capital cushion is to buffer against losses, it makes all the difference in the world if it is buffering against, for example, possible defaults on loans to huge corporations that are unlikely to go out of business or, instead, possible defaults on loans to impoverished families to buy houses.

The intuitive solution to this problem is to allow federal bank examiners the discretion to be flexible—say, by making exceptions for banks primarily invested in what the supervisor considers to be ultrasafe loans or securities, or by excluding from the asset number "assets classified as worthless or of doubtful value" (FDIC 1984, 116). However, the discretion required to make exceptions or to determine which assets are indeed worthless or of doubtful value amounts to the power to supersede the bank's own judgments about the riskiness of various assets. If federal regulators are thought to have better judgment about risk than the bankers themselves (due to the bankers' presumed moral-hazard problems), then there is really no reason to allow private banking to continue.

The only ostensible purpose of private banking (or any other private economic activity) is the possibility that, at least overall, private parties will somehow have better judgment than government employees. Just beneath the surface of arcane banking regulations, then, lie questions about the nature of capitalism and modern government as profound as those we encountered in Chapter 1; however, we postpone consideration of these questions until Chapter 4.

International Capital Regulation: Basel I

In the years after the Depression, each country reached different solutions to the quandaries of capital regulation, which was seen as being required by deposit insurance (although Canada did not adopt deposit insurance until 1967). However, in 1974, following a German bank failure, the Group of Ten established the Basel Committee on Banking Supervision (BCBS) at the Bank for International Settlements (BIS), the international organization of central bankers located in Basel, Switzerland. In 1988, the BCBS agreed to the regulatory framework for bank capital that came to be known as Basel I. By the early 1990s, Basel I was effectively implemented in most countries, including the United States. At the time of the financial crisis, it was still in effect (as later amended) for commercial banks and savings and loans in the United States, although the rest of the world began adopting Basel II (see below) as early as 2005. At this writing (November 2010), Basel III is being formulated by the BCBS and, after modifications by the G20, will be imposed over a period of several years.

The main effect of Basel I was to internationalize and standardize the efforts of several countries to address the main defect of *flat* capital minima, such as 8 percent: the undifferentiated treatment of all bank assets as if they were equally risky, and thus required the same capital cushion.[2] Under Basel I, a bank's regulatory capital level was determined by the ratio of capital divided by the *risk-adjusted* value of a bank's assets; the result had to be 8 percent or higher (a leverage ratio of 12.5:1). The "risk-adjusted" value of the assets, in turn, was determined by grouping different types of assets into four "risk buckets" and then multiplying the value of each bucket by a percentage, called a "risk weight." Assets in the bucket that the BCBS deemed ultrasafe (gold, cash, and government bonds) received a 0 percent risk weight; obligations issued by "public-sector entities," such as the GSEs, were considered slightly riskier and therefore went into the 20 percent risk bucket; "whole" (unsecuritized) mortgages were risk weighted at 50 percent; and all other assets—everything from corporate bonds and equities to business loans, loans to individuals, and a bank's physical plant and real estate—went into the 100 percent risk bucket, which required the full 8 percent capital, or $8 for every $100 in, say, business loans. In contrast, whole mortgages required just $4 for every $100 in assets ($100 x 8 percent x .50), and $100 in GSE bonds required just $1.60 in capital ($100 x 8 percent x .20). Assets in the zero risk bucket required no capital at all.

There was a clear logic to these categories—the 0 percent and 20 percent categories relied on the relatively riskless nature of "sovereign debt" and semisovereign debt (BCBS 1988, para. 38), at least at that time. As for the 50 percent bucket, "loans fully secured by mortgage on occupied residential property have a very low record of loss in most countries" (ibid., para. 41).[3] Yet obviously the round numbers—0 percent, 20 percent, 50 percent, 100 percent—continued the practice of lumping together disparate risks, both generically and individually.

Generically, British, Greek, Portuguese, Irish, Spanish, and U.S. government bonds, for example, were treated as equally riskless. In other words, even though the riskiness of three general categories—sovereign debt, GSE debt, and mortgage debt—had been distinguished, many subcategories with different risk profiles were still being combined within these categories, and especially within the catch-all 100 percent risk bucket. Individually, the buckets could not possibly distinguish among the variegated risks of different assets, such as a loan to a growing business that a bank judged as having an established market versus a shrinking business with untrustworthy management. These contradictions, however, were inevitable in any regulatory system that did not completely substitute individual bank examiners' judgments for those of individual bankers, loan by loan and investment by investment.

The Basel Committee was clearly trying to make sound risk generalizations from past experience. While these generalizations certainly can be questioned—especially in retrospect—the attempt to distinguish among risk categories can be seen as a logical step away from the even greater anomalies inherent in flat capital minima. To be sure, the various risk weights, and the 8 percent starting point itself, were not based on a "scientific" calculation of asset-default probabilities, since that would be impossible. Default "rates" agglomerate a variety of heterogeneous loans and

investments whose past rates of default will never be precisely duplicated
in the future. Their lack of rigor, then, is not a reason to criticize the Basel
regulators: it was the best they could do, given the fundamental tension
between refusing to make any distinctions among risks, or else making
distinctions so fine that only successful bankers could make them.

Bankers' judgments about risk, like all human judgments, are themselves
subjective and somewhat arbitrary. By substituting its own judgment for that
of bankers, the BCBS was inevitably going to be subjective and somewhat
arbitrary, too. However, even a fixed capital minimum that does not distinguish among types of assets will supersede a given banker's judgment about
the overall riskiness of the bank's asset portfolio; and since no bank's assets
are homogeneous, there is no logical stopping point once one tries to make
allowances for the heterogeneity of risk. Given the premise that bankers' risk
judgments could not be trusted once deposit insurance was in place, Basel I
was a logical step in the evolution of capital regulations, as would be any
further step toward finer-grained distinctions among types of assets or,
indeed, among individual assets. Moreover, this step was consistent with the
initial rationale for capital-adequacy regulations of all kinds: the notion that
bankers could not be trusted because of the morally hazardous situation into
which deposit insurance had thrust them. With a flat leverage ceiling/capital
cushion, bankers could use their leverage to acquire the riskiest assets they
could find, with the potentially highest payoffs. A capital-adequacy regime
that, like Basel I, calibrated capital requirements according to risk weights
would penalize bankers who did this by imposing higher capital charges on
them.

The Costs and Benefits of Bank Leverage

The establishment of different risk buckets, however, allowed bankers to
engage in what economists call "regulatory arbitrage" in order to reduce
the amount of scarce capital that they needed. For instance, a bank could
(in principle) originate a $100,000 mortgage risk weighted at 50 percent,
which it would need to fund with $4,000 in capital ($100,000 x .08 x .50);
or it could sell the mortgage to Fannie Mae or Freddie Mac for securitization and then buy it back as part of an agency bond risk weighted at 20
percent, reducing the amount of capital required to $1,600 ($100,000 x .08
x .20). Since $1,600 is 40 percent of $4,000, such transactions would free

up 60 percent of the capital that had been used for the mortgages. This capital could then be used as the basis for making 60 percent more loans or investments than before, generating (*ceteris paribus*) 60 percent more revenues and thus profits.

Regulatory arbitrage achieves such results by increasing a bank's leverage. To understand why this might be desirable from a banker's point of view, consider a well-capitalized U.S. commercial bank,[4] which adheres to the U.S. financial regulators' 10 percent capital minimum instead of the standard Basel I 8 percent minimum. The vast majority of American banks are "well capitalized," and since 10 percent makes for easier arithmetic, the following thought experiment will assume a well-capitalized bank.

Suppose that this bank had $100 in regulatory capital in 1992, when Basel I had taken effect in the United States. The bank's managers might have used this $100 as the basis for $1,000 in business loans—given that they could attract $900 in checking and savings deposits and in income from bond sales. ($1,000 in business loans, multiplied by the 10 percent capital minimum, multiplied by the risk weight of 1.00 for business loans, requires $100 in capital.) This bank, fully invested in business loans and levered to the maximum extent allowed by law, would thus have assets of $1,000, liabilities of $900, and a leverage ratio (equity against total assets) of 10:1. To keep things simple, assume that the bank is able to make the same rate of return—let us stipulate 5 percent—on all its loan and investment options (the various assets it can buy), and let us assume that it can pay all its depositors and bond holders a single interest rate, 2 percent, producing a 3 percent spread. At these rates, the bank would garner $50 in revenue on its $1,000 in business loans (.05 x $1,000), less $18 in interest (.02 x $900), leaving a $32 profit.

However, since the Basel I risk weight for mortgages is 50 percent, the bank could have doubled its balance sheet to $2,000 by putting all $100 of its capital into mortgage loans. This would have required raising $1,900 in debt, increasing the bank's leverage to 20:1. With $2,000 in assets, the bank would make twice as much revenue at 5 percent interest—$100 instead of $50—assuming, however, that none of the mortgages defaulted. Paying the depositors and bondholders 2 percent on the $1,900 they had lent the bank would cost $38 in interest payments, leaving a profit of $62.

A third option would have been use its $100 in capital to buy $5,000 of agency MBS from Fannie or Freddie, carrying a 20 percent risk weight: $5,000 x .20 x .10 = $100. The same $100 of capital, now leveraged at 50:1, would yield $250 if the MBS carried a 5 percent coupon, less $98 in interest payments on the bank's debt, for a profit of $152.[5]

One lesson of this exercise is that as the regulators intended, the Basel rules created incentives for bankers to engage in certain types of lending rather than others. The rules encouraged mortgage lending by requiring twice as much capital for business and consumer loans as for home loans, and they encouraged mortgage securitization by requiring five times as much capital for business and consumer loans as for agency bond purchases. The "encouragement" of mortgage lending and GSE securitization can also be seen as a penalty for other types of lending. A bank that insisted on lending to businesses or consumers, as in the first scenario, would be penalized by a loss of $122 in profits compared to a bank that devoted all its capital to securitized mortgages, as in the third scenario. The first bank is only 21 percent as profitable as the third bank because of this penalty.

A second lesson, then, is that leverage can be very lucrative. Obviously, the rub is that with leverage comes not only the hope of large gains, but the risk of great losses. Every penny that a bank's creditors have lent the bank must be paid back eventually, so if a portion of the business loans, mortgages, or mortgage-backed bonds largely funded with this debt should default, the bank could be rendered insolvent—depending on the rate of default. A default rate of 10 percent on the business loans made in the first scenario, or 5 percent on the mortgages in the second scenario, or 2 percent on the agency bonds in the third scenario would bring the bank to the edge of insolvency. The shrinkage of the bank's capital cushion in proportion to the increase in its leverage leaves half as much room for error in judging risk in the second scenario as compared to the first, and a fifth of the room for error in the third scenario compared to the first. Therefore, the decision to lever up is not always the obvious choice. If a bank expects that the assets it might acquire with higher leverage are excessively risky, it might well pass up the opportunity to make higher returns, since that opportunity is premised on everything turning out well. Moreover, if a bank becomes concerned that the assets it already owns have become riskier than expected, it might well *deleverage*, preferring a lower level of profit on a less risky portfolio to the possibility of bankruptcy.

This assumes, of course, that moral-hazard theory as applied to deposit insurance is wrong, and that real-world bankers do not, in general, deliberately court bankruptcy merely because they don't have to worry about a run on the bank. As we pointed out in discussing the moral-hazard theories of the financial crisis—the corporate-compensation and TBTF hypotheses—real-world banks generally were not even close to being leveraged to the maximum extent allowed by law at the start of the crisis. In the aggregate, the regulatory (risk weighted) capital level of U.S. commercial banks as of mid-2007 was 12.85 percent (Jablecki and Machaj 2011, Fig. 8.3), nearly 30 percent higher than the 10 percent level mandated for well-capitalized banks, and 60 percent higher than the 8 percent level mandated for "adequately capitalized" banks. These levels are comparable to the level of U.S. banks *prior to* 1933, when deposit insurance was created. We therefore see no more reason to accept the moral-hazard story about deposit insurance than to accept the stories about corporate compensation and "TBTF."

Still, in light of bankers' ignorance of the future, one might think that the best course is for a bank not to incur any debt at all: a bank could obtain a 100 percent margin of error by maintaining a 100 percent capital cushion (zero leverage).

This would achieve the aim of prudence but at the cost of putting an end to banking, which is essential in any advanced economy. Even a non-capitalist economy would require banks to "intermediate" between people who have earned money (or created goods) that they do not currently need—the bank's creditors—and people who need money (or goods) now that they have not yet earned: a family buying a house or a business seeking to expand. Mortgage-backed securities, for example, are pools of hundreds of loans made to such families, enabling them to live in houses now by borrowing against their future income. Since that future is uncertain, the borrowers' and the bank's expectations that the loan will be paid off may turn out to be overly optimistic. For this reason, a capital cushion of some size is needed. But a capital cushion of 100 percent would cut off the largest source of funds for potential mortgagors and businesses: current savings, lent to the bank in the form of deposits and bond purchases. All actions are risky—in the colloquial sense—in the face of our ignorance; capital cushions of less than 100 percent are one way to try to strike a balance between risk and benefit.

However, as the Basel Committee recognized when it tied leverage levels to the predicted riskiness of mere asset classes, capital cushions are more art than science, since accurate predictions are unlikely and are therefore matters on which reasonable people will disagree. Thus, some bankers will, depending on their confidence in general economic conditions and the particular assets in their portfolio, seek a lower capital cushion (more leverage);

more pessimistic bankers will seek a higher cushion. However, by virtue of the perceived need to impose leverage maxima on bankers (in the form of capital minima), the regulators were put into the position of determining in advance, and from afar, the riskiness of business loans, mortgage loans, securitized mortgages, and sovereign debt—without having any idea of how risky (or "uncertain") a particular bank's loans and investments in these categories might really be. The mechanism through which this was accomplished was to impose heavier "capital charges" on assets in the risk buckets that were deemed riskiest by regulators than on assets in risk buckets they deemed safest. Thus, to the extent that a banker in a particular place and time was optimistic enough about general economic conditions to want to increase leverage, Basel ensured that the most economical way to do so would be to reduce business and individual loans relative to mortgages, agency MBS, and sovereign debt. The Basel Accord was criticized on precisely these grounds. "In particular, Basel I was accused of prompting a contraction of credit extended to individuals and firms" (Rochet 2010, 80), causing a "credit crunch" for businesses and individuals.

The Recourse Rule and the Financial Crisis

In response to criticisms about the depressive effect of the undifferentiated 100 percent risk bucket on lending to businesses and individuals, the BCBS "determined on a thorough revision, a process that in 2004 culminated in the second Basel Accords, Basel II" (Rochet 2010, 80), which appeared in its final form in 2005. For many years before the June 2004 conclusion of this process, it was clear that the BCBS[6] was determined to use "external credit ratings" (i.e., from Moody's, S&P, and Fitch) to refine the risk-sensitivity of its capital-adequacy standards.

For instance, in "A New Capital Adequacy Framework," the first consultative paper issued as part of the process of formulating Basel II, the BCBS in 1999 proposed using credit ratings to sort assets into the various risk buckets. The BCBS also proposed expanding the number of risk buckets to accommodate very low-rated assets. For example, instead of all sovereign debt going into the zero-risk-weight bucket, government bonds would now receive risk weights of 0, 20, 50, 100, or 150 percent depending on whether they were rated, respectively, AAA or AA (and their subcategories, such as AA+ and AA-), A (and its subcategories), BBB (and its subcategories), BB or B (and

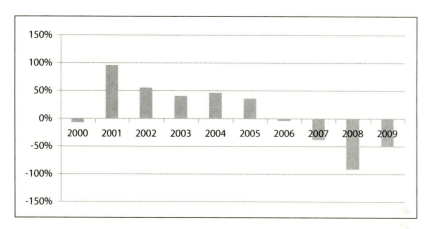

Figure 2.1. Rise of PLMBS (annual change). Derived from IMF Global Financial Stability Report, October 2009b, Fig. 2.7.

their subcategories), or below B- (BCBS 1999, Table 1). The proposed reliance on ratings would eventually be included in Basel II.

Because of the financial crisis, Basel II was never implemented in the United States. But the process leading to Basel II had an important effect on the United States at the very moment that the housing bubble, the subprime bubble, and the growth in PLMBS issuance all began: 2001.

In Figure 2.1, we display the annual rates of growth in PLMBS issuance. We believe that the timing of the growth spurt in 2001 and subsequent years may be due, in part, to the so-called Recourse Rule,[7] a regulation governing capital requirements for asset securitization and sale by U.S. banks that was first proposed in 1994,[8] refined in 1997 and 2000,[9] and finalized on November 29, 2001. The Recourse Rule, issued by the FDIC, the Federal Reserve, the Office of Thrift Supervision, and the Office of the Comptroller of the Currency, applied the developing Basel II ratings-based approach to privately issued securitized assets to U.S. commercial banks and "thrifts," or savings and loans.

"Recourse" as used in the Recourse Rule means, to oversimplify, the credit risk that a bank incurs in providing credit enhancements to investors in a securitization of its assets.[10] The Recourse Rule sought to encourage securitization, which, the regulators wrote, "provides an efficient mechanism for banking organizations to buy and sell loan assets or credit exposures and thereby to increase the organization's liquidity."[11] But it also sought to discourage risk. The riskiest form of credit enhancement for the originating bank is overcollateralization, i.e., the retention of an equity tranche to absorb the first losses from (for example) delinquent mortgage payments or defaulting mortgages. Under Basel I the assets in equity tranches fell indiscriminately, like the rest of an asset-backed security, into the 100 percent risk bucket, requiring an 8 percent capital cushion (10 percent for well-capitalized U.S. banks). The Recourse Rule, like Basel II, increased this to a dollar-for dollar capital requirement—$100 of capital for a $100 equity tranche, as opposed to $8 (or $10). This was equivalent to a 1000 percent risk weight for a well-capitalized bank, or 1250 percent for an adequately capitalized bank.

On the other hand, tranches higher up in the waterfall structure required less capital, as they were less risky. The specific capital requirements were to be based on the external (ratings-agency generated) ratings of the bonds issued against the various tranches. The Rule put asset-backed securities, including PLMBS, into a new 200 percent risk bucket if the bonds were rated lower than B; it left them in the 100 percent bucket if they were rated BB or BBB; it put them into the 50 percent risk bucket, along with whole mortgages, if they were rated A; and into the 20 percent risk bucket, along with agency bonds, if they were rated AA or AAA. These risk weights were exactly the ones that had been proposed in the 1999 BCBS consultative paper for Basel II, except that the BCBS document had proposed dollar-for-dollar capital reductions, instead of a 200 percent risk weight, for B-rated tranches.

The net effect was to dramatically raise the capital requirement for the riskiest parts of a securitization, the equity tranche and the B tranche, but to reduce the capital requirement by 80 percent for the top-rated tranches. By the same token, the Recourse Rule penalized banks that did not invest in top-rated ABS by requiring them to devote 400 percent more capital to business or commercial loans than to double- or triple-A ABS, and 150 percent more capital to whole mortgages than to such ABS. We believe that this may be the primary explanation for the overconcentration of securitized mortgage risk in the commercial banks.[12]

As we explain in Chapter 3, the Recourse Rule had been under development since 1994, going through several public iterations before the "Final Rule" was adopted in 2001. Investment banks had plenty of time to get ready for this event, and Figure 2.1 suggests that in 2001 they were prepared to take advantage of it by issuing PLMBS that would, as we know from

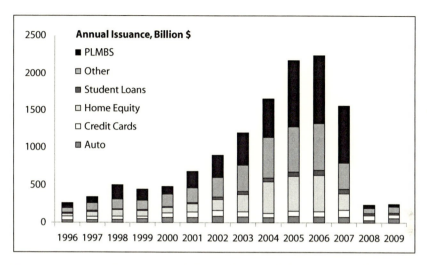

Figure 2.2. Rise of ABS. Acharya and Richardson 2009b, Fig. 1, reprinted with the authors' permission.

their very wide triple-A tranches, meet the Recourse Rule's prerequisite for 80-percent capital relief for U.S. commercial banks and savings and loans. Figure 2.2 tends to confirm this interpretation of Figure 2.1, inasmuch as *all* ABS rated AA or AAA, not just PLMBS, received the same 20 percent risk weight under the Recourse Rule.[13] (Note that this Figure displays the gross dollar value of ABS rather than the percent change in issuance, so the dramatic change in 2001, shown in Figure 2.1, is not as apparent in comparison to the larger gross amounts securitized in later years.)

Figure 2.3 displays a similar pattern. It shows the issuance over time of asset-backed commercial paper (ABCP). Appendix II explains how ABCP was used to fund the creation of PLMBS, as the details are too complicated to go into here. We can see from the figure, however, that at the same time that PLMBS and ABS issuance spiked and then began their long ascents in 2001, so did ABCP issuance in the United States.

One of the most interesting aspects of the figure is that it shows a second spike in the creation of ABCP, primarily but not exclusively among European issuers, beginning in 2005, when the final version of Basel II was introduced. While Basel II never went into effect in the United States, it was implemented in other countries at varying points during the years 2005 to 2008. Before turning to Basel II, however, it is important to note that

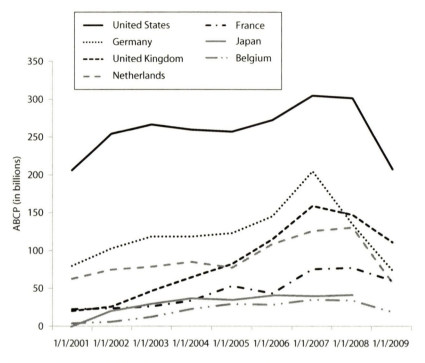

Figure 2.3. Rise (and fall) of asset-backed commercial paper (issuance by country). Acharya and Schnabl 2010, Fig. 4, reprinted with the authors' permission.

during the years before its implementation in countries outside the United States, and during all the years leading up to the crisis in the United States itself, Basel I's 50 percent risk weight for unsecuritized mortgages remained in effect. This in itself may help to explain why low interest rates were steered into mortgage lending. It may also help to explain why, of all the ABS that banks could have acquired, MBS were more popular than student-loan, car-loan, and other securitized-loan ABS. Student loans and car loans would be risk weighted at 100 percent when first extended by a bank (that is, before they were sold to an off-balance-sheet asset pool funded by ABCP; see Appendix II). Mortgages, however, received only half the balance-sheet capital charge applied to student loans, car loans, and all other loans. Of course, mortgages are most people's major expenditures, and any given person has a relatively fixed demand for more student loans and car loans, while one rarely finds people who would be averse to living in a bigger, newer, nicer house. Still, without proving the point, we suggest that the 50 percent risk weight applied across most of the world by Basel I may contribute to the explanation of both the housing booms that occurred in many countries and the boom in the mortgage variety of ABS. Basel II made matters worse: it reduced the risk weight for mortgages from 50 to 35 percent.

Basel II

Just as the Recourse Rule essentially duplicated the 1999 BCBS ratings-based proposal for Basel II's treatment of ABS, so did both the "standard-ized" and "internal ratings-based" (IRB) options that were to be made available to the largest banks under Basel II. Both options based their capital charges on "external ratings," and the standardized approach assigned the same risk weights to the various ratings as had the Recourse Rule, with the exception of B-rated bonds.

Table 2.1 provides (some of) the details of Basel II in comparison to the Recourse Rule and Basel I. (It is important to note that while the Recourse Rule "amended" Basel I in the sense that it put double- and triple-A-rated ABS into the same 20 percent risk bucket into which Basel I had put agency bonds, the Recourse Rule left alone the rest of U.S. regulatory law that had implemented Basel I; the figures shown in the first two rows of column 2 are simply carried over from that law.)

Figures 2.1, 2.2, and 2.3 suggest that the Recourse Rule encouraged U.S. banks to shift toward holding AA- or AAA-rated PLMBS in anticipation of its implementation at the end of 2001. And Figures 2.2 and 2.3 may suggest that Basel II had a similar effect elsewhere in 2005. But these graphically visible spikes in PLMBS, ABS, and ABCP issuance just before the effective dates of the Recourse Rule and Basel II, while suggestive, are not conclusive.

For instance, interest rates were also plummeting in 2001, and might account for the sudden availability of mortgages to be securitized. More-over, while the second Basel Accords were agreed upon in 2004, Basel II was not issued in final form until December 12, 2005, and was not officially implemented in various countries around the world, each of which had the power to make alterations in it, until (variously) 2006, 2007, and 2008. (It was scheduled for U.S. implementation in 2008, but the financial crisis intervened.) This may not have left time for it to have affected non-U.S. banks' decision making prior to the crisis in a substantial way.

Table 2.1. Risk Weights Under the Three Basel Regimes (percent)

	Basel I	Recourse Rule**	Basel II (standardized)
business loans, corporate equities, bonds, private-label ABS, and all other	100	100	varies according to external rating
whole (individual) residential mortgages	50	50	35
agency bonds	20	20	20
AA/AAA-rated ABS	100	20	20
A-rated ABS	100	50	50
BBB/BB-rated ABS	100	100	100
lower-rated ABS	100	200	dollar-for-dollar capital expenditure
equity ABS	100	dollar-for-dollar capital expenditure	dollar-for-dollar capital expenditure
AA/AAA-rated sovereign debt (government bonds)	0*	0	0
A-rated sovereign debt	0*	0	20
BBB-rated sovereign debt	0*	0	50
BB/B-rated sovereign debt	0*	0	100
lower-rated sovereign debt	0*	0	150

    * Risk weights for sovereign debt under Basel I were 0% for OECD governments, 100% for other governments.

    ** Applied only in the United States. The Recourse Rule changed the risk weights for private-label ABS; the other risk weights in the Recourse Rule column are carried over from Basel I, implemented in the United States in 1991.

    Sources: BCBS 1988 and 2006; 66 Fed. Reg. 59614 (November 29, 2001).

On the other hand, as Adrian Blundell-Wignall and Paul Atkinson (2008) have pointed out, in some countries, including Germany and Britain, banks were extended Basel II capital treatment by their countries' financial regulators in advance of the country's official implementation date, and in other countries banks may have begun to shift their portfolio composition in anticipation of Basel II once they knew their countries' regulators' intentions as to the final form the Accord would take in law.[14] Therefore, the effects of Basel II might have been felt, in a given country, as early as 2004.

Our approach will be to follow Blundell-Wignall and Atkinson in allowing that the implementation and anticipation of Basel II *may* have helped to lay the groundwork for the financial crisis outside the United States, but to use the demonstrable U.S. effects of the Recourse Rule, whose risk weights for ABS were essentially the same as those of Basel II, as a template for what might have been happening in other countries in 2004–7 because of Basel II. Future research will have to determine whether this template is appropriate.

Capital Regulation as a Primary Cause of the Financial Crisis

Given the limitations of currently available data, which are particularly unilluminating about non-U.S. banks and off-balance-sheet assets (see Appendix II), we must confine ourselves to analyzing the effect of capital regulation on the mortgage-securitization exposure of U.S. banks. In this regard, however, if we are to go beyond observing the temporal spikes in the issuance of securitized assets and asset-backed commercial paper in 2001 and 2005, we need to infer the net possible effect of the Recourse Rule from the aggregate data shown in Table 1.1.

An indirect approach to demonstrating this effect is to infer from aggregate data the overall priorities of U.S. commercial bankers. We have already seen that in the aggregate, U.S. commercial banks chose the "safest," lowest-yielding MBS—agency bonds—twice as often as AAA-rated private-label MBS, which paid higher yields; and nearly ten times as often as even higher-yielding AAA CDOs (Table 1.3). This appears to establish that, contrary to some economists' favorite theories of the crisis, U.S. bankers were not, on the whole, sacrificing safety for revenue. Where, however, did the quest for capital relief fit into bankers' aggregate priorities?

The Recourse Rule established virtually laboratory conditions to find out whether banks were choosing either capital relief plus safety in preference to yield, or capital relief plus yield in preference to safety. The Rule did this by allotting the same 20 percent risk weight, hence the same 80 percent capital relief, to lower-yielding AAA bonds and higher-yielding AA bonds. Recall from Chapter 1 that a bond against a triple-A PLMBS tranche issued in the first quarter of 2007 typically paid a spread of 9 basis points (0.09 percent) over Treasuries, while a double-A bond paid nearly twice as much, 15 bps (Ashcraft and Scheurmann 2008, Table 16). Similarly, in July 2006, triple-A CDO bonds paid a spread of 10–15 bps over Treasuries, while double-A CDO bonds paid a spread of nearly three times as much: 30–40 bps over Treasuries (McDonald 2009, 110n). Bankers who preferred capital relief to yield, and yield to safety, would have bought AA-rated bonds instead of triple-A bonds whenever they could. Bankers who were heedless of risk and indifferent to capital relief would have bought BBB- or BB-rated PLMBS, which received no capital relief under the Recourse Rule but paid 224 bps at the beginning of 2007; or, better yet, BBB- or BB-rated CDO bonds, which presumably paid even higher spreads. Yet all of the PLMBS and CDO bonds held by U.S. banks appear to have been rated AAA (Table 1.1).

Thus, we can rule out the possibility that bankers preferred yield to safety, or yield to capital relief. Their preference for triple-A bonds suggests that U.S. bankers' aggregate preference was for either safety or capital relief first and yield last.[15] In turn, their preference for implicitly guaranteed agency bonds suggests that the order of priority was safety first, then capital relief, then yield. In the first quarter of 2007, the spread for agency bonds was 0.4 percent, less than half of the spread for triple-A PLMBS, even while PLMBS offered the same capital relief as did agencies.

As we indicated in Chapter 1, the preference for safety before yield undermines the leading theories of the cause of the crisis: the corporate-compensation thesis, the TBTF thesis, and the irrational-exuberance thesis. But if we are to defend the alternative thesis that the Recourse Rule was the chief culprit in the United States, we need to see whether the objective "incentive" that the Rule created for investing in highly rated PLMBS and CDOs actually had much of an effect on commercial bankers' behavior.

Perhaps the best way to find out would be to ask the bankers (in strict confidence)—particularly those who made the asset-allocation decisions at

Table 2.2.   U.S. Commercial Bankers' Search for Capital Relief (percent)

	Agency bonds as proportion of total assets	AAA PLMBS as proportion of total assets	AAA CDOs as proportion of total assets	All 20%- risk- weighted MBS as proportion of total assets
Commercial banks and thrifts	7.7	3.5	0.8	12
Non-bank U.S. investors (except GSEs, monolines, and investment banks)	4.7	1.0	0.3	6

Sources: Bank holdings: Lehman Brothers 2008, Figure 4. Bank assets and total assets: IMF 2009a, 177. GSE, monoline, and investment-bank assets: U.S. Census Bureau, Flow of Funds Accounts—Financial Assets of Financial and Nonfinancial Institutions by Holder Sector, Table 1129.

the biggest commercial banks. One of us intends to do this and to report the results in a future work. In the meantime, however, we can compare the proportion of commercial banks' total assets that were invested in mortgage bonds, and particularly in PLMBS and CDO bonds, to the proportion of *other* investors' total assets that were invested in these instruments. This should reveal by inference whether capital-adequacy regulations were responsible for the banks' particular vulnerability to a downturn in the housing market, since the Recourse Rule did not apply to any category of investor other than commercial banks.

In Table 2.2, we contrast the proportions of U.S. commercial banks' portfolios that were devoted to agency MBS, triple-A PLMBS, and triple-A CDO bonds against the proportion of all other U.S. investors' portfolios that was invested in these instruments—excepting the portfolios of the GSEs, investment banks, and monoline insurers, because the latter two were part of the mortgage-bond production line, while the GSEs acquired PLMBS to help meet their HUD targets for affordable housing (see Chapter 1). The results appear to indicate that Basel I (in the case of agency bonds) and the Recourse Rule (in the case of PLMBS and CDOs rated AAA) had a dramatic effect on the composition of banks' assets.

The 2:1 ratio between the proportion of mortgage bonds held by commercial banks and the proportion held by other investors (column 4) represents our independent variable—the influence on banks' balance sheets exerted by capital-adequacy regulations, both Basel I (in the case of agency bonds) and the Recourse Rule (in the case of triple-A PLMBS and CDOs). Our dependent variable is the overconcentration of PLMBS and CDOs in commercial banks' portfolios in comparison to the portfolios of other investors, since these, rather than agency bonds, are the mortgage bonds that made commercial banks particularly vulnerable to the deflation of the housing bubble in 2007 and 2008. The overconcentration of PLMBS and CDOs in the commercial banks is displayed in Table 2.3.

The 3:1 ratio of PLMBS/CDO investments made by U.S. commercial banks to those made by investors who were not governed by Basel I and the Recourse Rule (column 4) speaks, as we see it, to the counterfactual that we need to consider if we are to address the question raised in Chapter 1: Was capitalism responsible for the crisis? To answer this question, we need to infer whether the crisis would have occurred had it not been for capital-adequacy regulations, which, despite the forms of deregulation and nonregulation discussed in Chapter 1, still strictly governed the practices of U.S. (and, in the form of Basel I and Basel II, most other) commercial banks. In the absence of capital-adequacy regulations in general (i.e., in this context, Basel I), U.S. commercial banks would have been free to invest in whatever assets they chose, whether mortgages, business loans, corporate bonds, asset-backed bonds, or corporate equities. And in the absence of the Recourse Rule, U.S. commercial banks would have had no particular reason to favor PLMBS more than other investors did. Thus, it seems to us that Table 2.3 strongly suggests the following: Without the favorable treatment of highly rated PLMBS by the Recourse Rule, U.S. commercial banks might have acquired only a third of the exposure to PLMBS that they did, in fact, acquire. Thus, causal responsibility for the crisis should be attributed not so much to capitalism—which is to say, to the errors made by capitalist investors, including bankers—as to capital-adequacy regulations—which is to say, the errors made by the regulators of capitalism.

To be sure, capital-adequacy regulations did not operate alone. Low interest rates needed to be present, sparking an asset bubble of some kind. Other factors, such as the GSEs' promotion of housing, may have been needed to steer the flow of cheap credit into housing. And as we noted in

Table 2.3.   Overconcentration of Private-Label MBS in Commercial Banks (percent)

	AAA PLMBS as proportion of total assets	AAA CDOs as proportion of total assets	Mezz. bonds as proportion of total assets	All private MBS as proportion of total assets
Commercial banks and thrifts	3.5	0.8	0	4.3
Non-bank U.S. investors (save GSEs, monolines, and investment banks)	1.0	0.2	0.2	1.4

Sources: Bank holdings: Lehman Brothers 2008, Figure 4. Bank assets, total assets: IMF 2009a, 177. GSE, monoline, and investment bank assets: U.S. Census Bureau, Flow of Funds Accounts—Financial Assets of Financial and Nonfinancial Institutions by Holder Sector, Table 1129.

Chapter 1, many possible regulations can be contemplated that, in retrospect, could have prevented the crisis.

Finally, the bankers were not compelled to take advantage of the low risk weights of highly rated ABS tranches, nor to prefer mortgage bonds to other highly rated ABS. Had they known they were buying into a mortgage bubble, they could have absorbed the penalties established by the Recourse Rule for investing in commercial loans or corporate securities rather than highly rated ABS: those penalties would have been less severe than the penalties exacted by the financial crisis. But as we saw in Chapter 1, the evidence suggests that they did not know. The failure to anticipate the mortgage bubble was shared by banker and regulator alike. Nonetheless, it does seem that the unintended effect of the Recourse Rule was to push commercial banks to load up on highly rated mortgage bonds, and thus to have caused the financial crisis when the bubble burst.

However, Table 2.3 leaves us with a puzzle. Given that the Recourse Rule steered U.S. banks toward the senior tranches of PLMBS and CDOs (just as Basel II would have done, where it was being enforced), the net effect of tripling commercial banks' exposure to these securities was to concentrate a mere 4.3 percent of their assets in what turned out to be dangerous instruments. How did this 4.3 percent cause such a huge banking crisis? This is a question we shall seek to answer in Chapter 3.

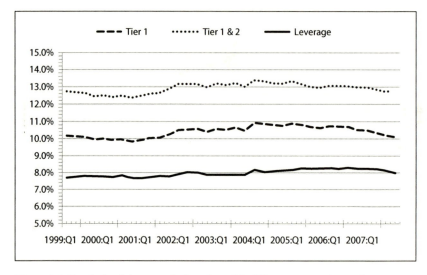

Figure 2.4. Steady bank leverage before the crisis. The top curve shows the regulatory capital of U.S. commercial banks divided by their risk-weighted assets. The middle curve shows Tier 1 capital (equity and retained earnings) divided by risk-weighted assets. The bottom curve shows Tier 1 capital divided by assets unweighted by risk. The higher the capital level as shown in these curves, the lower the banks' leverage; rising leverage would result in downward-sloping curves. FDIC Quarterly Banking Profile.

Why Weren't Banks Leveraged Even More Than They Were?

We conclude our primary argument by considering an objection to it.

In common with every observer of whom we are aware, we have been assuming that capital-adequacy regulations offer "favorable" treatment to low-risk-weighted assets only inasmuch as a bank wants to increase its leverage. For such banks, low-risk-weighted assets offer capital relief, meaning that they enable a bank investing in such assets to borrow more money on a slender base of capital than they would have been able to borrow by investing in high-risk-weighted assets. By the same token, high-risk-weighted assets penalize only banks wanting to increase their leverage, because these assets require the investment of more capital. Yet as we noted in Chapter 1, banks did *not*, in the aggregate, increase their leverage during the run-up to the financial crisis, as can be seen in Figure 2.4, which shows three measures of U.S. commercial bank leverage. None of these curves display any overall trend except a slight increase in bank capital, i.e., a slight *reduction* in bank leverage, in the first and second curves. Admittedly, if leverage were increasing, the top two curves might not reveal it, since the new assets might be "hidden" by their low risk weights, which are factored into these two curves. However, the bottom curve should slope downward if bank assets grew in proportion to bank capital—that is, if leverage was increasing—because this curve compares bank capital to total bank assets without artificially reducing the size of those assets if they were in low-risk-weight buckets. Yet the bottom curve does not slope downward, revealing that there was no tendency toward higher leverage among U.S. commercial banks as a whole.

Why, then, would banks have invested in the senior tranches of PLMBS?

The top two curves of the Figure suggest that in 2001, the year before the Recourse Rule took effect, this was indeed starting to happen. Bank capital divided by risk-weighted assets rose noticeably—which is to say that (in the aggregate) U.S. banks were deleveraging, from a regulatory-capital perspective: risk-weighted assets were shrinking in proportion to bank capital. Yet the bottom curve shows that in the same year, assets unweighted by risk weight were staying roughly proportional to capital levels: capital levels rose slightly, but not as much as in the top two curves. This confirms the hypothesis that banks were shifting their portfolios into low-risk-weight assets, with the logical suspects being mortgages risk weighted at 50 percent and agency bonds or AAA PLMBS, both risk weighted at 20 percent. Yet the aim of capital arbitrage is supposed to be to increase *real* leverage (unweighted by risk) by purchasing *more* low-risk-weighted assets with the *same* quantity of capital—say, twice as many mortgages or five times as many mortgage bonds. The bottom curve shows that this was not happening. Banks shifted into low-risk-weighted assets but did not increase the dollar value of those assets, unweighted, as compared to their capital levels.

Figure 2.5 confirms that what was happening, at least at the world's ten largest banks, was a shift into assets with a low risk weight. Thus, even while these banks' real assets doubled between 2001 and 2007, their assets multiplied by their risk weights barely increased at all. The only possible explanation is that these banks, like the U.S. banks covered by Figure 2.4, were raising enough capital to keep pace with the increase in the size of their balance sheets. In short, just as in the United States, large international

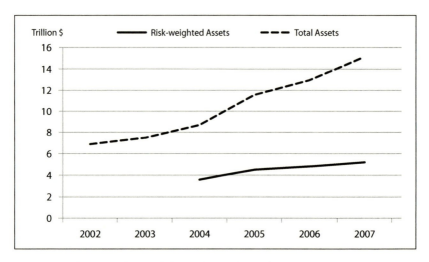

Figure 2.5. The largest banks shift into low-risk-weighted assets. Acharya and Richardson 2011, Fig. 7.3.

banks' real leverage remained constant; even while, as in the United States, the largest world banks were doing as the regulators wished: shifting into the asset types that the regulators considered least risky. Regulatory arbitrage was occurring, but the aim must have been different than to increase leverage, since leverage did not increase.

We believe that the explanation for this seeming paradox is twofold.

First, the aggregate figures hide considerable diversity among different banks. We noted in Chapter 1 that various banks had widely varying levels of capital on the eve of the crisis; by the same token, some banks were levering up (in real terms, unadjusted for risk weight) in the preceding years while other banks were deleveraging. For example, Citigroup levered up from 13:1 in 2000 to 19:1 in 2007, while Bank of America deleveraged from 13:1 to 12:1 and JPMorgan Chase deleveraged from 17:1 to 13:1 (Barth 2010, Fig. 5.14). In Chapter 4, we consider the political-economy implications of heterogeneous behavior such as this.

Second, however, the aggregate patterns suggest that the prevailing understanding of the reason for capital arbitrage is simplistic. To see why, we need to keep in mind that there is a significant difference between a regulatory capital cushion and a *usable* capital cushion. In fact, a regulatory capital minimum is not a "cushion" at all: if it is breached, negative legal consequences follow for the bank. It is therefore more akin to a hard floor than to a pillow that can absorb unexpected losses.

As Martin Hellwig (2010, 20) puts it, there has been little "consideration of the paradox that the buffer function of regulatory capital is limited because this capital is needed to satisfy the regulator." Thus, a bank with an 8 or 10 percent capital buffer on the eve of the crisis could not use this capital to absorb losses, or else it would fall below the regulators' legal minima. By contrast, if there were no legal capital requirements, a bank with a 10 percent buffer would be able to let it fall to 9, 7, 5, or 1 percent to absorb losses in times of trouble. When the financial crisis struck, however, this was not possible for U.S. banks wanting to retain the legal privileges associated with being a "well-capitalized" bank, capitalized at 10 percent; or for banks not wanting to be seized by the FDIC ninety days after they fell below the 8 percent "adequately capitalized" level.[16]

The distinction between regulatory capital "cushions" and usable capital cushions may resolve a quandary in the banking literature: the question of why banks consistently maintain capital levels well in excess of the legal minima (e.g., Tarullo 2008, 141–50; Hanson et al. 2010). Prior to the crisis, as we noted earlier, the typical well-capitalized bank had 12.85 percent of risk-based capital (Tier 1 plus Tier 2 capital divided by risk-weighted assets—the top curve in Figure 2.4). The "extra" 2.85 percent was the banks' usable capital cushion—their margin for error before they hit the 10 percent capital legal minimum. Much more serious legal consequences follow, however, from going beneath the 8 percent level, so we might say that the banks' usable capital cushion was 4.85 percent. There is little reason for such expenditures of capital if not to serve as a buffer between the bank's assets and the legal penalties that follow from piercing the legal capital minima.

This analysis may explain why commercial banks would have collectively acquired capital at a pace that almost exactly matched the growth of their real, non-risk-weighted assets during the 2000s (the bottom curve of Figure 2.4), even while they shifted the composition of their balance sheets toward low-risk-weighted assets. In conjunction, these two actions suggest that in the aggregate, U.S. bankers were using the Recourse Rule not to lever up, but to increase their usable capital cushions by (1) maintaining their absolute ratio of capital to assets even while (2) they *lowered the hard regulatory-capital floor.*

Consider a well-capitalized commercial bank that on January 1, 2001, had risk-adjusted capital amounting to 14 percent of its $100 in assets, all of which were business loans risk weighted at 100 percent. This bank's usable capital cushion was $4, while its regulatory capital cushion was $10. If in 2001 it exchanged $50 of its business loans for $50 of AAA mortgage bonds, then when the Recourse Rule went into effect, the bank would have lowered its regulatory capital floor by 8 percent of the value of the bonds, or $4, raising its usable cushion by the same amount, 80 percent of the 10-percent regulatory capital cushion is saved by shifting assets from the 100 percent to the 20 percent risk bucket. Regulatory arbitrage need not increase leverage levels and thus risk; it may instead increase usable capital levels at the expense of regulatory capital levels, *reducing* risk (other things equal). The same effect could be achieved by adding (instead of trading for) AAA mortgage bonds while the balance sheet was expanding, as long as the bank also added enough capital to keep pace. This, we believe, accounts for banks' use of capital arbitrage during the years leading up to the crisis, even while their leverage levels remained essentially unchanged.

On the eve of the crisis, the net effect of the banks' acquisitions of AAA-rated PLMBS and CDOs, even while they added enough capital to keep up with the overall growth in their assets, would have been to expand their usable capital cushions, and shrink their regulatory capital cushions, by 0.34 percentage points—that is, 8 percent of the 4.3 percent of their assets that was invested in these instruments (Table 2.3), assuming, for the sake of simplicity, that this 4.3 percent otherwise would have been risk weighted at 100 percent. Using the same assumption for the sake of exposition, the net effect of banks' purchases of *all* MBS, including agency bonds, would have been to reduce their legal capital minimum by 8 percent of the 12 percent of their assets thereby placed into the 20-percent risk bucket (Table 2.2), increasing their usable capital cushion by 0.96 percentage points.

In reality, of course, banks might have been acquiring MBS risk weighted at 20 percent in exchange for whole mortgages risk weighted at 50 percent, not business loans risk weighted at 100 percent. But even if they were thus "exchanging" *no* 100-percent-risk-weighted assets for agency bonds or triple-A PLMBS, the effect of devoting 12 percent of their assets to these 20-percent risk-weighted MBS instead of to whole mortgages would have been to increase their real, usable capital cushion by 0.48 percentage points.

The problem leading to the crisis, then, was not that banks were over-leveraged, except inasmuch as one can always say, in retrospect, that a bank that runs through its usable capital cushion "should" have had a bigger usable cushion. The problem was that, to minimize pointless expenditures on regulatory capital *minima*, which cannot serve the loss-absorbing function of usable capital *cushions*, banks had shifted into assets assigned a low risk weight by the BCBS and by the U.S. financial regulators. Among these were, unfortunately, the senior tranches of PLMBS.

3

The Interaction of Regulations and
the Great Recession: Fetishizing Market Prices

It is doubtful that the U.S. and international financial regulators who, in all three versions of the Basel regime (including the Recourse Rule), assigned a low risk weight to mortgages, anticipated the effect this might have on banks and on the world economy if a housing bubble were to occur—or that they anticipated that this action might have contributed to such a bubble. The same goes for the even lower risk weight that they assigned to securities issued by "public-sector entities" such as, in the United States, Fannie Mae and Freddie Mac; or the equally low risk weight that they assigned, in the Recourse Rule and in Basel II, to highly rated, privately issued asset-backed securities.

The regulators were not irrational; they were simply unaware of some of the consequences of their actions under unanticipated circumstances. But perhaps the worst of the unintended consequences of the Basel rules occurred through their interaction with other regulations. In this chapter we focus on two disastrous instances of this type of unintended consequence: the interaction of the Basel rules with accounting regulations that mandated mark-to-market accounting, and the interaction of the Basel rules with securities regulations that had effectively turned Moody's, S&P, and Fitch into a legally protected ratings oligopoly.

These two interactions allow us to lay out in brief form what we think can be known at this point about why, when the financial crisis occurred, it was transformed into the worst economic calamity since the Great Depression.

Mark-to-Market Accounting and the Problem of Human Ignorance

Mark-to-market or "fair value" accounting was imposed on U.S. corporations, including banks, by the Securities and Exchange Commission (SEC) in 1993, in the form of Financial Accounting Standards Board (FASB) rule 115.[1] European corporations are also covered by mark-to-market accounting under the International Financial Reporting Standards (IFRS). In essence, mark-to-market accounting (MTM) requires that assets be "marked" on the balance sheet of a bank or other corporation in conformity with the current market price of the asset.

The purpose of MTM is to provide investors in a corporation with transparency, that is, a clear understanding of the corporation's "value," by allowing investors to see the value of the corporation's assets if they were to be sold immediately. This requires marking the assets to their current market prices. Otherwise corporations could hide losses from shareholders by marking their assets at unrealistically high prices. Edwin T. Burton (2009, 130) writes,

> The guiding principle of U.S. securities regulation is the concept of "full disclosure," which translates into a demand for "transparency" by shareholder advocates. Transparency means, among other things, that accounting values should reflect current market values to the extent possible.

Or, as Stiglitz (2010a, 156, our emphasis) puts it,

> No one can ever have all they information they [sic] would like before they make a decision. The job of financial markets is to ferret out *the relevant information*, and, on the basis of that limited information, make judgments about the risks and returns. But markets on their own seem not able to provide the proper amount of transparency, which is why government has to step in and require the disclosure of information.

On those grounds, Stiglitz (156) defends MTM, although he concedes that "no accounting system is perfect." This concession is as meaningless, however, as his concession that all decision makers rely on "limited information," since in the same sentence he contends that markets should be judged against the standard of ferreting out "the relevant information." No decision maker needs *irrelevant* information; the problem facing any decision maker is determining which information is relevant *without* knowing all possible information, or, in other words, making sure that the limited information she has *is* the relevant information. But a synoptic perspective on all information, which would allow one to sort the relevant from the irrelevant, is not an option: it would amount to knowing all the information, that is, to omniscience. Therefore, the standard of making merely "the relevant information" transparent is impossible to meet. While verbally conceding our ignorance, Stiglitz is actually trivializing it by contending that as a practical matter, "the relevant information" *can be* in our grasp— given the right accounting regulations.

Our contention is that market participants may be ignorant of the relevant information, or ignorant of which information is relevant, simply because they are human. But Stiglitz (2010a, 332) insists that the source of market participants' (shareholders') ignorance was that "the banks' managers' incentives . . . [we]re not well aligned with shareholders' interests." The quoted passage is from an endnote in which Stiglitz (2010a, 156, emphasis in original) explains why "government has to step in and *require* the disclosure of information." Government can do this by forcing corporations to mark their assets to market; when the corporations are banks, government demands the disclosure of the current market prices of banks' assets. However, as Stiglitz seems not to realize, MTM regulations not only demand the disclosure of this information; they require that the information be used to compute whether a corporation is legally solvent or not, by subtracting declines in the current market prices of a corporation's assets from its earnings and thus its profits. This confers on current market prices the force of law, in that it bars "the market" from investing in a corporation that has been declared bankrupt because the current prices of its assets have gone down—even if some potential investors think that these current prices are merely temporary, or are wrong.

Prices as Opinions

Current market prices reflect the current intersection of "supply" and "demand." But current supply and demand information may be not only irrelevant, but positively misleading, in determining the "true" (i.e., future) value of a corporation's assets, which is all that shareholders would want to know.

To take the simplest case, the "demand" for a *consumer* good is an aggregation of predictions made by various consumers about whether they will value that good in the future, in the sense of needing or being satisfied with the product after they buy it. These predictions are reflected in consumers' willingness to buy the product at a given price; so in the aggregate, these predictions help to determine the current market value of a given product. However, like the predictions made by any fallible human being, consumers' predictions may turn out to be wrong. The product may turn out to be unsatisfactory, and dissatisfied consumers may not repeat their purchases, driving down the price of that product, so the *current* market price of a consumer good cannot be used to predict future prices with any reliability. Moreover, the unpredictable introduction of other products, or changes in their prices, may divert consumers from repeat purchases of a given product even if they *are* satisfied with it.

Similarly, someone who produces a "supply" of consumer good decides what to produce, how much to produce, and the price at which to sell it by *interpreting* what past sales of similar products may indicate about future demand for this specific product.[2] Producers' predictions of consumer demand are even more liable to be incorrect than consumers' own predictions of their need for or satisfaction with a product, because producers do not have direct access to the experiences of consumers.

If the product is not a consumer good but, say, a mortgage-backed security, an additional complication enters in: the bond's purchasers not only have to predict their own future financial needs (perhaps their future needs for putatively riskier, higher-paying bonds; or for putatively safer, lower-paying bonds; or for more liquid securities, such as Treasuries), and to predict the opportunities for satisfying these needs that might or might not be available to them in the future (e.g., if even riskier or even safer securities should appear on the market, or if the liquidity of one's mortgage-backed bond evaporates in a panic about a given type of security). They must also predict the future performance of the mortgages underlying the bond.

As we saw in Chapter 1, such predictions entail corollary predictions about, for instance, the future level of house prices and, in turn, the effect of that level on the idiosyncratic responses of millions of mortgagors to finding themselves "underwater" (with an LTV over 100). How many of these mortgagors will continue to pay their mortgages if the price of their house drops to level x, y, or z? If a mortgagor defaults, how much money will the legal trust that has issued the mortgage bond on behalf of an investment bank be able to raise by reselling the house? The answers to these questions, entailing predictions about the future, cannot be known with any reliability by a non-omniscient being because of the vast array of unique circumstances that will confront each mortgagor in this situation—not only at a personal level, which might be compensated for statistically, but at a societal (e.g., macroeconomic) level, which economists have, as a rule, had little success in predicting (Colander et al. 2010; Caballero 2011; Kling 2011). Indeed, it is this very fact—the unpredictability of the future—that justifies capital cushions.

It is a conceptual error of the first order, then, to tie capital cushions, let alone hard capital floors, to the fluctuating *current* prices of assets. Yet that is what MTM accounting did when it was imposed on all U.S. corporations, a subset of which were commercial banks covered by capital-adequacy regulations.

The reason given by the FASB was that MTM "portrays the market's estimate of the present value of the net future cash flows of [the] securities, discounted to reflect both the current interest rate and the market's estimate of the risk that the cash flows will not occur."[3] The reasonableness of MTM (in the words of one of its critics) "follows from the idea that if markets are efficient, that is, if prices aggregate the information and beliefs of market participants, then this is the best estimate of 'value'" (Gorton 2008, 64). The key word is *beliefs*: FASB's view of market prices effectively equates market participants' beliefs (i.e., predictions) with *knowledge*. This is akin to assuming that all "information" possessed by market participants is accurate, representative, and germane to producing *correct* beliefs (cf. Colander et al. 2010, 269)—or, as Stiglitz might put it, "relevant."

FASB 115 extended this utopian view of the accuracy of market prices, based on the implicit omniscience of market participants (as a group), to financial assets. This view entails understanding the current price of a given financial asset as something much more profound than a fluctuating barometer of how many people are taking the bullish or the bearish side of the argument about such assets' *future value* (Frydman and Goldberg 2009). That is, the regulation treated the current market prices of financial assets as something other than the aggregated, fallible predictions of the buyers and sellers of those assets. Instead, it treated current asset prices as *correct* predictors of the actual future value of the asset—its "fair value"—based on the tacit assumption that the buyers and sellers of financial assets know the relevant information.

The actual future value of an asset is either the price when the asset actually gets sold, or the income it will actually end up producing if it is held to maturity. Neither of these can be predicted reliably based on current prices. If they *could* be predicted reliably, there would not *be* prices for these assets: the existence of a buyer and a seller indicates that the buyer and the seller fundamentally *disagree* about its future value.[4] Far from being omniscient, either the buyer or the seller, or both, must, of necessity, be wrong.

How could defenders of MTM overlook the possible ignorance of the people setting the market prices? One way to make sense of this is to see MTM as a species of *democratic fundamentalism*, in the sense in which some rationales for democracy, like some rationales for capitalism, rest upon the alleged "wisdom of crowds." MTM forces banks to treat "the crowd's" prevailing sentiment about the future value of, say, mortgage-backed bonds as if it were an accurate prediction about the size of the payment stream to be expected from the underlying mortgages. But it is not an accurate prediction, or at least not necessarily; it is an aggregation of various people's divergent opinions about the future, just as an election is an aggregation of people's predictions about which candidate or party will best serve the polity during the term of office.

The Foolishness of Crowds Enacted into Law

Under one set of FAS 115 provisions, assets intended for sale had to be marked to market. Bonds that were to be held to maturity, though, were not to be marked to market. And assets that might or might not be available for sale, depending on contingent circumstances, were marked to market, but not in a manner that reduced *earnings* if the market price of an asset declined.

As we have seen, retained earnings are a crucial component of a bank's Tier 1 regulatory capital. At this juncture the possibility of regulatory interaction arises. If a bank's assets—say, its mortgage-backed securities—are currently the object of the crowd's worries, their price will fall, and if these assets were marked to market, the bank's regulatory capital will fall, too, not because of any actual losses experienced by the bank, but because of the crowd's expectation of losses. If a bank's regulatory capital thus threatens to fall beneath the legal minimum, the bank will have to do something, such as reducing lending, to bring the value of its assets in line with its level of capital.

FAS 115 might have curtailed this effect somewhat, however, because it confined the consequences of asset-price markdowns based on bearish market sentiment to markdowns on assets that were intended for sale, not those being held to maturity or those that may or may not be held to maturity. However, FAS 115[5] also carried forward from FAS 107[6] (1991) and FAS 114[7] (1993) the concept of *permanent* "value" impairment based on the *current* market prices of assets that were *not* intended for sale, and of assets that might or might not be sold before maturity. Thus, if a bank's accountants[8] determined that any of the bank's assets were "other-than-temporarily impaired" (OTTI), then the assets had to be marked down to their current market price, and this markdown *would* reduce earnings—and thus, in the case of banks, regulatory capital—dollar for dollar.

The Office of the Comptroller of the Currency summarized the results of these markdowns as follows:

> A security is considered impaired when its fair [market] value is less than its carrying value. If a bank determines that the impairment is other-than-temporary, the individual security is deemed OTTI and its carrying value on the balance sheet is written down to its fair value, with the amount of the write-down reducing current earnings. . . . Because OTTI reflects a more permanent decrease in the value of the security, the OTTI write-down is reflected in regulatory capital. (OCC 2009, 13)

In reality, of course, OTTI markdowns do *not* necessarily reflect a permanent decrease in the value of the security. They reflect nothing but a current predominance of bearish predictions in the market for that security. The current low price may result from the crowd's overreaction either to *microeconomic* "information" (e.g., regarding subprime defaults) or to *macroeconomic* implications that market participants interpret such information to convey, such as the likelihood of a recession that would reduce the future value of mortgage-backed bonds by diminishing the ability of mortgagors to pay their debts. Thus, in February 2010, John Geanakoplos (2010, 13) noted that in 2008, the market index of JPMorgan Chase *prime* mortgage bonds fell rapidly, plummeting from 100 to 60 by early 2009, even while "the cumulative losses on these prime loans even today are still in the single digits; it is hard to imagine them ever reaching 40 percent," as implied by the 40 percent decline in their market prices. Similarly, William M. Isaac (2009, 2), a former chairman of the FDIC, testified at a March 2009 congressional hearing about MTM that at the end of 2008, a bank that he portrayed as typical had been required to write down $913 million of a $3.65 billion PLMBS consisting of *prime* loans that the bank itself had originated, despite losses to date of only $1.8 million and projected losses over the lifetime of the PLMBS of $100 million.

As the IMF put it, "fair value" or mark-to-market prices reflect

a single, point-in-time exit value for the sum of all the risks the market assigns to the asset, including credit and liquidity risks. If the market overreacts in its assessment of any risk component, then fair value will reflect this. Hence, the heavy discounting during the [financial] crisis of any asset containing securitized instruments produced fair values much lower than their underlying expected future cash flows would imply, even allowing for possible impairment of subprime elements. (IMF 2008a, 65)

Yet the legal enforcement of the crowd's opinion through MTM may turn these otherwise-inaccurate market assessments into self-fulfilling prophecies, through the mechanism described in the Office of the Comptroller of the Currency's summary. For instance, at the end of 2008, Bank of New York Mellon had to write down $1.241 billion on its mortgage bond portfolio, despite having experienced no diminution in revenue from the bonds and despite projecting a loss of $208 million over the bonds' lifetime. The write-downs reduced the bank's earnings by about one third, thereby subtracting the $1.241 billion from its Tier 1 capital (WRCM 2009).

When MTM accounting is combined with legal capital minima, banks may have to reduce lending into the real economy to preserve their capital cushions—inducing or exacerbating a recession, in line with the crowd's macroeconomic prediction. Daniel K. Tarullo (2008, 78) points out that

since raising additional capital is likely to be most difficult and expensive when a bank is already suffering capital losses that bring it closer to the regulatory minimum, reductions in total assets (and, perhaps, corresponding reductions in deposits) will be the more probable response. If, as is likely to be the case, those reductions are substantially achieved through forbearance from new lending, then companies or other borrowers dependent on the bank for their financing needs may be adversely affected. Classes of borrowers, such as small businesses, that lack practical recourse to other sources of financing [such as bond issuance] may be unable to obtain credit, even though they remain creditworthy. If this phenomenon is sufficiently widespread, the inability of economic actors to obtain financing could have a notable effect on economic activity, thereby deepening or prolonging the recession. Thus, regulatory capital requirements may themselves be procyclical.

However, in the case of the financial crisis this procyclicality must have been further aggravated by the *combination* of regulatory capital minima with MTM. Otherwise lending would have been reduced only to the extent that banks suffered *actual* losses, not actual losses plus those that were anticipated by the market crowd. MTM and capital-adequacy regulations interact when MTM write-downs impinge, or threaten to impinge, on a bank's regulatory capital "cushion." Otherwise a bank could simply accept the MTM deductions from earnings without doing anything about it, confident that the current wave of bearish market opinion will pass. However, since MTM reductions in earnings reduce Tier 1 capital levels and thus threaten legal consequences, banks cannot afford to wait. They must take corrective action—at the expense of the real economy.

When the market prices for assets decline and a bank's accountants make the determination that this decline is an "other-than-temporary impairment" in value, banks may, as Tarullo points out, employ a variety of strategies to avoid falling below their regulatory capital minima. Reduced lending into the real economy is not a bank's only option; another option is to sell assets to raise cash. This, too, however, may enact self-fulfilling prophecies about the low "value" of the specific assets (such as MBS) about which there is a market panic:

> When bank A adjusts by liquidating assets—e.g., it may sell off some of its mortgage-backed securities—it imposes a cost on another bank B who [sic] holds the same assets: the mark-to-market price of B's assets will be pushed down, putting pressure on B's capital

position and in turn forcing it to liquidate some of its positions. Thus selling by one bank begets selling by others, and so on, creating a vicious circle. (Kashyap et al. 2008, 13)

Again, however, this effect is magnified by the combination of MTM with regulatory capital minima. If the market prices of MBS have dropped significantly, or if the market in MBS has ceased to be "liquid" (almost nobody will buy the securities), banks may need to sell other assets that have nothing to do with mortgages if they are to make up for the capital reductions caused by MTM markdowns to their MBS. In turn, a "fire sale" of any assets that happen to be on hand will drive down the value of *other* banks' assets, mortgage-backed and otherwise, requiring them, in turn, either to sell assets or reduce lending to compensate.

In a major liquidity crisis of the type experienced in 2007–2009, all securities become highly correlated as all investors and funded institutions are forced to sell high quality assets in order to generate liquidity. This is . . . a feature of any market-based financial system where financial institutions' balance sheets are tied together with mark-to-market leverage constraints. (Poszar et al. 2010, 3)

Thus, "the application of fair value [MTM] rules during periods of market weakness or turmoil can contribute to a downward spiral in asset prices and exacerbate financial instability" (IMF 2008a, 76).

Making matters worse, in September 2006, the FASB promulgated FAS 157,[9] which took effect on November 16, 2007. FAS 157 required marking an asset down to "the price that would be received to sell an asset or transfer a liability in an orderly transaction between market participants at the measurement date."[10] If there were no prices available for an identical asset because nobody was willing to buy it on that date, however, then banks would have to mark down the asset to "observable" prices for similar assets. Thus, the observable prices for CDS insurance on PLMBS were used to mark down the type of asset that they insured. Eighty-two percent of assets marked down by banks in an SEC study of MTM (SEC 2008, 62) were valued in this fashion, with only 11 percent marked against actual prices.[11]

To picture the effect that this provision of FAS 157 can have, consider write-downs that would have had to be taken in the summer of 2008, when the financial crisis had not yet peaked, but when the growing worries about

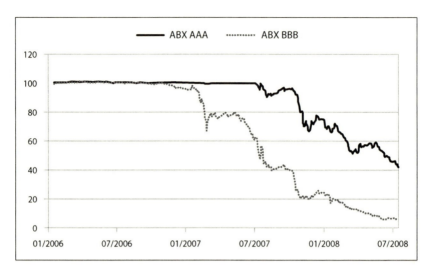

Figure 3.1. The falling "price" of mortgage bonds. IMF 2008b, Fig. 1.9.

mortgage bonds had long since halted trading in actual PLMBS and CDOs. Once trading stopped, CDS insurance prices for indices of mortgage bonds created by ABX (a private indexing firm) were accepted as proxies for actual prices. The aggregate ABX prices for triple-A and triple-B bonds of all vintages are shown in Figure 3.1, with 100 representing the face value of the bonds, and increases in the price of CDS insurance displayed as declining prices of the various tranches being insured.

For triple-A tranches, the price inferred from the cost of CDS protection had fallen by 60 percent in the summer of 2008. Consistent with this decline in market sentiment, the IMF (2008a, Fig. 1.13) reports that from the second quarter of 2007 through March 2008, U.S. banks had to write down about $250 billion on their $472 billion worth of mortgage-backed securities, representing an MTM decline in value of 53 percent.[12] This reduced the paper value of banks' total assets by about 2.2 percent, given the 4.3 percent of banks' assets that was invested in mortgage bonds (Table 2.5 above). In principle, this 2.2 percent write-down could have interacted with the 10 percent capital minimum for well-capitalized banks to reduce U.S. banks' lending capacity by *22 percent of total U.S. commercial bank assets, amounting to $2.5 trillion* (Federal Reserve 2008, Table 1).

The Mark-to-Market Meltdown

Moreover, worried investors, uncertain of precisely what had gone wrong with MBS, were indiscriminately selling all ABS, not just those backed by mortgages. U.S. commercial banks (and savings and loans) held approximately $84 billion of AA/AAA nonmortgage ABS—also risk weighted at 20 percent under the Recourse Rule—as of the end of 2007 (He et al. 2009, Table 10), the prices of which now began to decline. In addition, as we explain in Appendix II, a provision of Basel I had offered complete capital relief to asset-backed commercial paper (ABCP), i.e., very short-term bonds that funded assets held off of banks' balance sheets. These bonds were not backed by tranched, overcollateralized pools of assets, but instead by unstructured pools of assets that included mortgages, credit-card bills, and other bills (all of which are assets because they are claims on debtors to make payments). Banks provided "liquidity commitments" to ABCP bonds—that is, commitments to buy them in the rare event that the market for them dried up.

The market for ABCP did dry up when investors abandoned all asset-backed bonds, and starting in the third quarter of 2007, U.S. banks had to fulfill their liquidity commitments by bringing $245 billion or less in ABCP assets onto their balance sheets (Acharya and Schnabl 2009, 91). Since mortgages, risk weighted at 50 percent, may, using the most generous estimates, have comprised as much as $228 billion of these assets (Acharya and Schnabl 2010, 12), their risk-weighted value would have been $114 billion; added to the other assets, risk weighted at 100 percent, this would have constituted a $131 billion expansion of banks' balance sheets, requiring $13.1 billion of new capital and—in its absence—reducing banks' lending capacity by $131 billion, on top of the $2.5 trillion that, in the previous section, we estimated as an upper bound on the loss produced by MTM write-downs on mortgage-backed bonds.

The bigger problem, however, was that the loss of ABCP funding meant, in itself, a significant decline in the ability of banks to finance consumer and business lending without incurring the risk weight of 100 percent. Basel I and later U.S. regulations of off-balance-sheet commitments (Appendix II) reduced the effective risk weight to zero for assets that could be pooled in ABCP conduits, but this made banks vulnerable to the temporary sentiments that might at any moment cause investors to become unwilling to buy ABCP. Banks took this dangerous route because otherwise, this type of lending would have been subjected to relatively high capital charges on their balance sheets. Once the ABCP market dried up, this type of lending had to stop, especially since the interaction of MTM with capital-adequacy regulations for on-balance-sheet assets had put banks in no position to extend new loans.

Fortunately, several countervailing forces prevented the situation from getting as bad as it could have gotten, even with the shrinkage in banks' lending capacity of (as we have just seen) 22 percent. On September 19, 2008, the Federal Reserve announced plans to loan banks funds to buy ABCP. By then, too, banks had begun to raise substantial amounts of capital to compensate for their paper losses; as of December 2008, when U.S. bank write-downs had doubled to $510 billion, banks had raised $391 billion—including capital injected by the U.S. government—leaving them with MTM losses of $119 billion (IMF 2009a, Table 1.4). That might still have translated into a reduction in lending capacity of up to $1.19 trillion, or 11 percent of total bank assets. Yet as we pointed out in Chapter 2, U.S. commercial banks had, in the aggregate, amassed a usable capital cushion of about 3 percent above the regulatory minimum, and they had shifted into low-risk-weight assets, expanding the usable capital cushion by lowering its legally mandated floor.

Thus, from September 2007 to August 2008, bank lending fell not by 22 percent, nor by 11 percent, but only by 7 percent. This was nonetheless "the fastest pace of credit contraction in 40 years" (Lachman 2008). We cannot attribute the entirety of this contraction to MTM, because banks may simply have been anticipating a recession and reducing lending accordingly. Conversely, however, as Ivashina and Scharfstein show (Chapter 1), new *business* lending during this period fell by 67 percent. Business lending is more important to small businesses than to large ones, since the latter, unlike the former, can borrow money by issuing bonds instead of turning to bank loans. Bank loans to businesses are, of course, risk weighted at 100 percent under Basel I, such that these loans would be among the first things for banks to cut if their regulatory capital cushions were endangered. In that circumstance, it would be better to continue making loans to home buyers or to the federal government rather than to keep lending to small businesses, since mortgages were risk weighted at 50 percent and Treasuries at 0 percent.

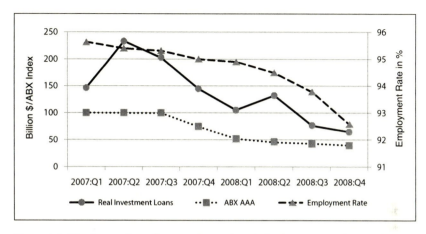

Figure 3.2. The interaction of accounting and capital-adequacy regulations. Loans: Ivashina and Scharfstein 2010, fig. 2; ABX: IMF 2008b, Fig. 1.9; employment: U.S. Census.

Without the ABCP bailout, the bank bailout, the usable capital cushions already in place, and the reduction of the legal capital floor through regulatory arbitrage that had already taken place, regulatory capital minima might well have interacted with MTM accounting to cause a much bigger drop in employment than was experienced, assuming that unemployment would have tracked large lending contractions, particularly business-lending contractions. Nonetheless, the regulatory interaction we have identified appears to have been sufficient to generate the Great Recession in the United States, even though U.S. banks' private mortgage-bond holdings—while three times as great, proportionately, as other investors' holdings, apparently due to the Recourse Rule—remained a small slice of the banks' total asset portfolio.

The situation outside the United States was different. It appears that almost from the beginning, non-U.S. banks were able to raise capital at a pace that matched their MTM losses (IMF 2008b, Box 1.3). Part of the explanation may be that under the International Financial Reporting Standards used outside the United States, there can be "a lag of up to several years" before MTM write-downs must be taken (IMF 2009a, 7n9).

One might, of course, object that no matter how absurd in principle the notion of markets' omniscience—and therefore the requirement that banks mark their assets to market prices—"the crowd" may well have been right in this case. Perhaps the write-downs were justified by the reality of sub-prime delinquencies.

We doubt it. Isaac (2009, 6) testified at the relatively late date of March 2009 that regulators had informed him that they projected *cash-flow* (i.e., "real") losses on subprime mortgage-backed securities at about 20 percent—not 60 percent, as the market price of triple-A CDS suggested at the end of 2008. Recall that about 21 percent of the typical mortgage bond consisted of overcollateralization (an equity tranche that absorbed the first losses) plus subordination (mezzanine tranches that absorbed the next losses). Taking into account the ability of banks to recover some of the value of a defaulted mortgage by reselling the house, default rates of about 28 percent would have been required before triple-A bondholders typically would have suffered any decline in revenue (IMF 2008a, 59). This did not happen. The foreclosure rate for subprime ARMs peaked at less than 7 percent in 2009; the foreclosure rate for fixed-rate subprime mortgages peaked at less than 3 percent (Timiraos 2010).

This is not to say that the interruptions in income flowing to triple-A tranches due to delinquencies plus defaults might not have pierced the 28 percent line and affected triple-A tranches, particularly if a given mortgage pool had a high concentration of mortgages from a particular state or local-ity; and the triple-A CDOs would have been much more vulnerable, given the way they were constructed. But it does appear that "the crowd" pre-dicted absurdly low values for the senior tranches of subprime mortgage bonds—and that these inaccurate predictions sparked an economic calam-ity by reducing banks' regulatory capital levels and thus their ability to lend.

The Case of AIG

Indirect confirmation of our argument can be found in the fate of the CDOs that had bankrupted AIG. AIG had been the CDS counterparty to Merrill Lynch, Goldman Sachs, and Société Générale on CDOs with a face value of $62.1 billion (Sender 2010). In October 2008, the Fed had "decided to take those CDOs onto its own books and pay the banks to extinguish the contracts," even though Goldman Sachs and Société Générale "were willing to tear up the contracts with AIG if they were allowed to keep the underlying CDOs, indicating that both banks thought they could increase in value" (Story and Morgenson 2010). The Federal Reserve, Goldman Sachs, and Société Générale were fighting over the right to keep the CDOs that had, according to the market prices of the CDS written against them, been so worthless that the insurance policies had to be paid off. AIG then had had to take "$25 billion in write-downs [due] to mark-to-market accounting rules, which forced the company to take paper losses that led to debilitating credit downgrades," according to its former CEO (Narayanan et al. 2010). In short, the Fed, Goldman, and Société Générale had reached the conclusion that the market prices of the CDS were wrong, that AIG's MTM write-downs were erroneous, and thus that AIG should have remained solvent.

The Fed pointed out that "there was a 'discrepancy' between 'what [its] advisers [were] saying these CDOs [were] worth and where the firms [had] them marked,'" that is, at $29.6 billion (Sender 2010). The Fed, Goldman, and Société Générale believed that the market prices—or, rather, the "observable" simulacra for market prices, which had been used as the basis for banks' write-downs of their regulatory capital under FAS 157—were too low. This may explain the Fed's controversial decision to pay AIG's counterparties the full value of the CDS contracts when AIG was bailed out, even though "many analysts say they believe the government could have negotiated a price for a fraction of that amount, reducing taxpayer funds used in the rescue" (Story and Morgenson 2010).

In January 2010, a Treasury spokesman told the *New York Times* that "'those investments have turned out to be very sensible, and he added that the fund at the center of the controversy,'" dubbed Maiden Lane III, "may well yield a profit." By then, the value of the CDOs, based on their performance to date, had risen to $45 billion (Sender 2010)—72 percent of their face value.

Explaining the Panic

Why might "the crowd" have been wrong? Was it "irrational"?

Felix Salmon (2007) offers the best explanation we have heard for the gross disjuncture between CDS prices and underlying realities. First, he notes the inconsistency between the fact that in December 2007, the implicit value of mezzanine tranches derived from ABX CDS prices was well above zero, even while senior tranches were priced at a "mere" 34 percent discount to face value. Mezzanine tranches would have to be *completely* wiped out (with a value of zero or close to it) before senior tranches experienced any losses at all, so these prices made no sense.

> Let's say that most AAA-rated bonds are really safe and really will be paid in full, as the residual value in BBB-rated tranches would tend to imply. The problem is that no one knows which AAA-rated bonds are the bad apples which *won't* be paid in full. And because of that uncertainty, the market price of the bonds falls. . . .
>
> The mark-to-market price of AAA-rated subprime bonds, then, does *not* represent the market's best guess as to the present value of those bonds' future cashflows. Rather, it represents an ignorance discount. If you can do your due diligence and work out exactly which AAA-rated bonds are kosher, then you can probably make out very well for yourself. (Salmon 2007)

For example, not all "vintages" of triple-A PLMBS could be expected to suffer similar losses, if any. Delinquent payments on subprime mortgages issued in 2000 and 2001 had peaked at 25 percent by September 2008, while delinquent payments on subprime mortgages issued in 2002 had peaked at 20 percent, and delinquent payments on those issued in 2003 peaked at 15 percent; however, delinquent payments on those issued in 2006 and 2007 had reached 35 percent and 20 percent, respectively, by September 2008, and they showed no signs of having peaked (IMF 2008b, Fig. 1.8). Yet not only were all triple-A mortgage bonds (prime, subprime, and subprime ARM) affected by the panic—so were asset-backed securities that had nothing to do with mortgages, such as those that tranched student-loan debt and those that drew on unstructured pools of business invoices.

The ABX indices did distinguish between separate vintages of PLMBS, but only a handful of PLMBS from each vintage were included in each index. Delinquency statistics by vintage, moreover, lump together hundreds of thousands of individual mortgages from various parts of the country. Moreover, due diligence on CDOs was virtually impossible under the best of circumstances, since they tranched tranches of PLMBS that, in turn, tranched hundreds or thousands of mortgages. Due diligence in the midst of a panic, when quick decision making was needed, was a practical impossibility. These factors—amounting to a classic case of "uncertainty"—created a vicious cycle of falling mortgage-bond prices.

However, market panics of this sort—ignorance cascades, one might say—occur frequently (even in the case of individual stock prices) without causing banking crises, let alone deep recessions (Gjerstad and Smith 2011). The problem was that regulatory capital requirements, which tied legal capital minima to the ratings of asset-backed bonds, combined with MTM accounting regulations, which inadvertently tied bank capital to momentary market prices for such bonds, ensuring that market price fluctuations had devastating economic effects.

The financial regulators and the accounting regulators had accidentally engineered not only a financial crisis but a calamitous recession.

The Regulation of Ratings Firms and the Canonization of Their Opinions

A factor that we have not considered is that the capital regulations not only reduced the capital requirements of banks that purchased or retained highly rated bonds; they also *increased* banks' capital requirements if the rating agencies downgraded these bonds. Once the worries about subprime mortgages began, that is what the rating agencies did. For example, triple-A CDO bonds from the 2007 vintage were, on average, downgraded to CCC+ by 2008 (Barnett-Hart 2009, 23–24), producing a 4,900 percent increase in the capital required for these bonds. In this case, the capital required for $100 worth of bonds rose from $2 to $100 (i.e., a dollar-for-dollar capital expenditure; see Table 2.1), such that the bank would have had to raise $98 in new capital for every $100 in assets.

Fifteen percent of all triple-A PLMBS bonds issued from 2005 through 2007 were eventually downgraded (Barth 2010, Table 5.3). Thus, even while MTM accounting was reducing banks' capital levels based on actual or imputed market prices for similar bonds (and based on the lower prices of other assets being sold in "fire sales"), the rating agencies' downgrades were raising the amount of capital that banks needed if they were to remain well- or even adequately capitalized. The rating agencies had also been responsible, of course, for setting triple-A tranche widths that, at least in the case of CDOs, were too optimistic (i.e., triple-A tranches that were too wide).

Arguably, the errors of the rating agencies were, like the capital-adequacy rules, unintended byproducts of regulations that seemed reasonable when they were adopted. A welter of state and federal regulations going back to 1936 had, by the end of the twentieth century, conferred immense privileges on the three rating "agencies" (Moody's, S&P, and Fitch), which, while being privately owned corporations, had also become unofficial arms of the federal and state governments. Lawrence White (2011) has shown how, over the decades following 1936, a growing number of institutional investors, such as pension funds and insurance companies, had been prohibited from buying bonds that had not been rated "investment grade" (BBB- or higher). Then in 2001 and 2004, the Recourse Rule and Basel II tied regulatory capital requirements to the rating agencies' opinions. In fact, the Recourse Rule and Basel II required that ratings from two of the three rating firms would be necessary for ABS that a bank kept for itself instead of selling to other investors.[13] So income from producing bond ratings was virtually guaranteed to any rating agency, by law.

In 1975, however, the SEC compounded the problem by effectively conferring oligopoly status on the three bond raters then in existence. In this ruling and subsequent actions, the SEC ensured that only these three firms were classified as Nationally Recognized Statistical Rating Organizations (NRSROs)—and that only an NRSRO's ratings would fulfill the numerous regulatory mandates for investment-grade and higher ratings that had proliferated since 1936.[14] The net result was that while the three rating firms could use whatever rating techniques they wished, their financial success did not depend on the ability of these techniques to produce *accurate* ratings. Instead, their profitability depended on government protection. If the rating agencies used inaccurate rating procedures, they would not suffer for it financially—let alone would they go out of business. It is hardly surprising that the rating agencies made mistakes, given that no competitor had been allowed to capitalize on such mistakes since 1975.

The large triple-A tranches that were the norm were premised on these three companies' low estimates of the probability of defaults in the underlying pools of mortgages. Everything rested on these estimates, which, in turn, depended on the companies' mortgage-behavior models, which were based on historical data. However, Moody's had not bothered to update its "basic statistical assumptions about the U.S. mortgage market since 2002" (Jones 2008). This meant that an unprecedented nationwide housing boom had not been factored in. Similarly, Richard Gugliada, who was in charge of S&P CDO ratings until 2005, told a reporter that "the mortgage market had never, ever, had any problems, and nobody thought it ever would" (quoted in Jones 2008). First Pacific Advisors was one skeptic, and sold its investment of $1.85 billion in mortgage-backed bonds in September 2005.

Later, discussing a conference call with Fitch in March 2007, First Pacific CEO Robert L. Rodriguez (2007) described the Fitch representatives as "highly confident regarding their models and their ratings," even though the representatives admitted that the models "would start to break down" if "home price appreciation was flat for an extended period of time" or if it declined.

Why, in contrast to Rodriguez, did the American financial regulators who issued the Recourse Rule, as well as the BCBS in crafting Basel II, place so much reliance on ratings from these three companies? One possibility is that they were ignorant of the companies' legally protected status. This hypothesis is supported by a BIS report issued in 2005, in which a team of staff economists analyzed whether, in light of the rise of "structured finance"—such as tranched, mortgage-backed securities—Basel II should continue on the path toward incorporating NRSRO ratings that had been established by the 1999 BCBS consultative paper discussed in Chapter 2. In advising that this was the proper course, the authors of the report appear to have been unaware of the fact that the rating agencies were shielded from competition by the SEC.

Thus, they reached the naïve conclusion that "the agencies appear to be sensitive to the value of their reputational capital for future business and to market sanctions that would be associated with poor management of conflicts of interest" (BIS 2005, 25–26). Reputational capital was one of the mainstays of contemporary economic theory that were called into question by the crisis (Acemoglu 2011). However, in this case the problem was not with the concept, but with the technocrats' apparent unawareness of the SEC regulation. Reputational capital is of no value to a company if its income is guaranteed *regardless* of its reputation. Since in reality the rating agencies' "future business" was guaranteed by various state and federal regulations, they would have had no reason to worry about future income suffering if their "reputational capital" declined. We infer that the BIS economists were ignorant of at least some of the relevant body of American law.[15]

Similar things can be said of the U.S. financial regulators who enacted the Recourse Rule. The rationale for the use of ratings is discussed in the final version of the Rule, where the rule makers argue that "investors rely on ratings to make investment decisions. This reliance exerts market discipline on the rating agencies and gives their ratings market credibility. The market's reliance on ratings, in turn, gives the agencies confidence that it is appropriate to consider ratings as a major factor in the risk weighting of assets for regulatory capital purposes."[16]

This nearly circular reasoning reveals American economists at their worst. "The market" is attributed with godlike powers of discernment, and in the process the human participants in markets are relieved of their fallibility and ignorance. Similar arguments had been among the rationales for using "external ratings" as the basis for the capital requirements of securitized assets in every official explanation of the Recourse Rule since it was first proposed in 1994.[17] For example, in the second version of the proposal, issued in 1997, the regulators maintained that "the use of credit ratings would provide a way for the agencies to use market determinations of credit quality to identify different loss positions for capital purposes,"[18] and in the third version, in 2000, they defended the idea on the grounds that "ratings have the advantages of being relatively objective, widely used, and relied upon by investors and other participants in the financial markets. Ratings provide a flexible, efficient, market-oriented way to measure credit risk."[19]

We will argue in Chapter 4 that *competitive* markets have certain epistemological advantages, although these certainly do not include omniscience. However, bond-rating corporations did *not* exist in a competitive market. They constituted a legally protected oligopoly of the sort that any economist would identify as lacking the desirable features of competitive markets—if the economist knew that it was a legally protected oligopoly. A reliable sign of a competitive market, for instance, is that some companies fail in the competition. Thus, during the last twenty years of the twentieth century, 202 of the 500 biggest companies in America failed.[20] Yet in the 50 years after the SEC and state governments began to canonize the opinions of the bond-rating "agencies," the number of rating agencies remained constant. Therefore, the only way we can understand the U.S. financial regulators' use of "markets" to justify the use of ratings in the Recourse Rule is to suggest that they, like the BIS economists, were unaware of the legal protection of S&P, Moody's, and Fitch.

Regulatory Interaction in Modern Democracies

In this chapter we have identified two sets of regulations that interacted with the Recourse Rule to contribute to the financial crisis and the Great Recession in the United States: MTM accounting rules established by the FASB, and the regulations that had since 1936 subsidized—and then, in 1975, formally protected—the extant rating "agencies." In the remainder of the chapter we briefly discuss the implications of such regulatory interactions for modern democracy before turning, in the next chapter, to implications of the *reason* for these interactions: the regulators' apparent ignorance of the other regulations with which their rules might interact, which we take to be a particular instance of the regulators' more general ignorance of the future effects of their actions.

The implicit mission of modern democracies is to solve what the *demos* perceives to be important social and economic problems. These solutions necessarily occur on a case-by-case basis, as the mass media bring the problems to public attention. After public concern has been raised, the legislature often creates the authority for specialist bureaucrats to solve the problem, because technical expertise is needed.[21] This case-by-case, problem-solving approach is universal in the West and has, at least in the United States, always been considered the height of pragmatism. Yet if governance is to be truly pragmatic—if it is to solve social and economic problems without creating new, worse ones—then the designer of a new problem-solving law or regulation needs to be able to (1) predict the unintended consequences of the new rule, considered in isolation; and (2) predict its unintended interactions with other rules.

Ideally, of course, the second requirement would mean predicting the new rule's unintended interactions with rules that have yet to be promulgated—rules that will be crafted as solutions to problems that have yet to arise. That being impossible, the most we can realistically hope for in the way of systemically sound regulation is that when a new rule is being designed, possible interactions with previously enacted rules are fully considered. As time passes, however, that gets increasingly difficult, as the number of rules that have been enacted rises.

Currently, a regulator cannot possibly know how a contemplated regulation might interact with previously enacted regulations, since nobody can master the contents of the Code of Federal Regulations, in which all permanent federal regulations are recorded. The Code contains more than 150,000 pages and grows by thousands of pages a year (Crews 2010, 15). Even if they could be read in their entirety, however, regulations are recorded in the Code in isolation from any context. For the context, one needs at least to consult the Federal Register, which gives the rationales of new regulations and examples of how they are intended to operate. But the contents of the Federal Register will soon surpass 3,000,000 pages, of which more than 20,000 per year are devoted to final rules, each one running about 10 pages in length (Crews 2010, Figs. 7–9).

More generally, no human being, or group of human beings, has anything close to a detailed, accurate grasp of the workings of the modern societies that all those regulations are designed to improve. Thus, even if large numbers of researchers and computers were assigned the task of *collating* the hundreds of thousands of regulations that have already been issued, they would not be able, in advance, to *correlate* them with unintended problems that they might cause.

For example, consider the sequence of regulations we have cited as major contributory factors in producing the financial crisis and the Great Recession in the United States.

1. Regulations issued by the SEC and state regulators that had, starting in 1936, mandated minimum ratings for a growing number of institutional investments.
2. The 1975 SEC decision to confer NRSRO status on the three extant rating firms.
3. Basel I (1988), which established favorable risk weights for mortgages and for GSE-issued MBS (Chapter 2).
4. MTM accounting, as established by FAS 115 in 1993, and as refined by FAS 157 in 2006.
5. HUD targets for mortgages to low-income families in the late 1990s, resulting in falling down-payment requirements on the part of the GSEs (Chapter 1).
6. The Recourse Rule, issued in 2001 by the Federal Reserve, the FDIC, the Office of the Comptroller of the Currency, and the Office of Thrift Supervision (Chapter 2).

There is no obvious connection among most of these regulations. Yet without understanding how they intersect, and thus may interact, one cannot—arguably—begin to understand the largest economic disaster since the Great Depression.

The task of researching such interactions illustrates the practical difficulties of minimizing the disasters to which such interactions might lead. The main problem scholars of regulation face—the two of us have noticed it repeatedly—is that there are so many regulations, so many historical circumstances explaining them, so many ways of categorizing them, and thus so many theories about their effects that, inevitably, the scholars will (here as everywhere) be compelled to overspecialize. The predictable cost is that most scholars will overlook interactions between rules in the category in which they specialize with rules studied by specialists in a different subfield, try as they might to see the big, systemic picture. The regulators' task—in this case, to pick what we have categorized as six sets of regulations out of hundreds of thousands or perhaps millions of regulations, so as to *predict* the crisis when it can still be prevented—is logically possible but practically impossible.

The problem of the scholar and the regulator—and of the citizen of a modern democracy—is essentially the same: There is too much information. This is why modern societies seem, and, to less-than-omniscient beings, are, "complex." And it creates the special kind of ignorance with which modern political actors, from citizens to regulators, are plagued: Not the scarcity of information, but its overabundance. This is a curse because, as a practical matter, it becomes impossible to find "the relevant information" among the blooming, buzzing profusion of data about previous political actions and their effects.

The relevant data are the things we would have to learn if we were to arrive at an *interpretation* of the complex world that would steer us away from political decisions that might contribute to a systemic catastrophe. Interpretations depend on categorizations, which in turn (when it comes to regulations) depend on theories about which factors cause which effects, and which effects are important enough to theorize about. The theories, hence the categorizations, hence the interpretations, can always be disputed; disagreement is part of the process by which we attempt to deal with complexity. The most important basis of disagreement would be the prediction of a regulation's specific negative consequence. Yet the very fact that a regulation is proposed and therefore categorized as a solution to, or a preventive of, a specific "type" of social or economic problem suggests the difficulty of envisioning unintended interactions with regulations in an entirely different category.

Thus, in 1936, when the regulations encompassed by item number 1 began to be issued by the SEC (the "securities" regulator), they seemed to be more than reasonable injections of prudence into the "retirement system," for example, as exemplified by pension funds that were now required to invest only in investment-grade bonds. Nobody could have predicted that these "retirement" regulations might, thirty-nine years later, contribute to the perceived need for item 2—a "securities regulation" that, in effect, became a "banking regulation" as of 2001, when item 6 was promulgated.

As a securities or even a retirement regulation, the 1975 decision seemed reasonable—given the proliferation of item-1 regulations that had been issued since 1936. The incorporation of bond ratings into so many laws seemed to demand that "not just anyone" be allowed to rate bonds. As a *banking* regulation, however, item 2 did not necessarily make sense, and if the U.S. "financial" (as opposed to "securities") regulators had known about it, they might not have enacted item 6. Likewise, it seemed perfectly reasonable for "securities regulators" (the SEC) to ensure, through "accounting regulations" issued by the FASB, that corporations were telling their shareholders "the truth" by requiring them to mark their assets to the market price (item 4), and even in the wake of the crisis, we find prominent economists such as Stiglitz defending the reasonableness of this requirement on the basis of economic theory.

At the chronological end of our list—when the Recourse Rule was adopted—it is at least conceivable that someone among the thousands of regulators involved—at the Federal Reserve, the FDIC, the OCC, or the OTS—might have looked backward, selected item 2 out of the vast sea of regulations that had been enacted during the late nineteenth and twentieth centuries, and recognized the danger of directing so much bank capital into securities that had merely won the approval of a legally protected oligopoly—if she had known about item 2. At some point regulators might also have considered the implications of encouraging banks' investment in mortgages and mortgage-backed securities through the low risk weights assigned to them by items 3 and 6, given the encouragement to a housing bubble created by item 5—if the regulators had known about item 5. And in 1993, someone at the FASB might have thought through the implications of requiring bank capital to decline dollar for dollar as market sentiment about bank assets declined—if there was someone at the FASB who knew about and understood item 3.

But as a practical matter, we can hardly fault the regulators for failing to put the pieces together. Nobody else did—not investors, not reporters, not scholars, not bankers, *nobody*, despite the fact that a few claimed that some kind of financial crisis was imminent (on the basis of rising leverage levels, which we have shown were mythical). Thus, despite the accurate claims of some economists to have predicted *a* crisis, no scholars of whom we are aware predicted *this* crisis.[22] Although the housing bubble was noticed by some observers and was a necessary precondition for the crisis, it was not sufficient to cause a banking crisis. That, we maintain, was the product of *interactions* between capital-adequacy regulations and rating-agency regulations; and the Great Recession was caused, at least in part, by the interaction of the banking crisis with MTM accounting. Nobody predicted something so complicated in advance.

Yet one need not agree with our particular analysis of the crisis to see the larger problem in modern governance that the crisis highlights. Suppose one sides with scholars who believe that this was actually a housing crisis caused by irrational exuberance, or that pay incentives were primarily responsible, or that the Federal Reserve was to blame. The problem is that a political system cannot tell reliably *in advance* which scholars' predictions are right, and therefore which theories should inform public policy. One cannot merely rely on disinterested "experts," as Stiglitz (2010a, 179) proposes, since disinterested experts so often disagree. Furthermore, even when they agree, scholarly consensus is, in the social sciences, no proxy for truth, as suggested by the general failure of academic economics to predict anything like the crisis. The problem is not with the *disinterestedness* of the "experts," as if any expert who has the public good at heart therefore magically sees complex realities clearly and can produce the right policy advice. No, the problem is that modern economies are far too complicated to be susceptible to accurate analysis merely by virtue of the analyst's desire— that is, his or her "incentive"—to produce it.

The economists' failure to predict the crisis shows that despite their high reputational and psychological incentives to understand what they are studying, they can be terribly ignorant of how modern economies actually work (Caballero 2010; Colander et al. 2011). Moreover, the economists' failure, after the fact, to transcend the a priori conviction that simple incentive stories explain everything important shows that by virtue of the need to overspecialize, most economists remain ignorant of key institutional features of modern economies: features such as capital-adequacy regulations, securities regulations, and accounting regulations that, to be sure, exercise their control over the economy by rearranging incentives—but regulations that may thereby create new, sometimes catastrophic problems by aligning incentives with economic agents' *ignorance*. This may, in turn, happen because of regulators' own ignorance: their ignorance of the unintended consequences of their own regulations taken alone, and their ignorance of how these regulations will interact with a multitude of other regulations already in force.

4

Capitalism and Regulation: Ignorance, Heterogeneity, and Systemic Risk

"We don't know where the next crisis is going to come from," [Treasury Secretary Timothy] Geithner told me. "We won't be able to foresee it. So we want to build a much bigger cushion into the system against those basic human limitations. I don't want a system that depends on clairvoyance or bravery." He added, "The top three things to get done are capital, capital, capital."

—Leonhardt (2010)

Regulators either did not have sufficient information to understand how concentrated risk was becoming, or if regulators had access to the information, they were unable to understand and identify the risks.

—FDIC Chair Sheila Bair (2010, 28)

We are all prisoners of our preconceptions.

—Paul Samuelson (1973, 11)

The modern democratic method of case-by-case social-problem solving, which Karl Popper (1961, 64–70) called the system of "piecemeal social engineering," rarely rises to the conceptual level at which it can be labeled a "principle," let alone a "system"; and "social engineering" has acquired totalitarian connotations that Popper did not intend. The engineer is not an architect of human behavior or the good society. She simply accomplishes mundane tasks: building a bridge where it is needed, producing a policy fix for reckless banking. Instead of a grand worldview, then, case-by-case "social engineering" is more like a tacit assumption that is absorbed by the citizens of modern countries. It is absorbed from the unarticulated premises of democratic legitimacy conveyed by primary and secondary education and the mass media; and it is absorbed, among the political cognoscenti, from the assumptions implicit in the never-ending "policy debate."

The assumption is simply that government should solve social and economic problems as they arise. As a result of the hegemonic acceptance of this tacit assumption, when social and especially economic problems are recognized, people seek political remedies. This has been the method by which nonsocialist democracies have addressed problems in the development of capitalism ever since the mid-nineteenth century.

There is usually no practicable way to attempt to solve social and economic problems, however, save by authorizing specialist bureaucrats to issue regulations to flesh out a democratically endorsed general direction, since the details are far too complicated for a legislature to handle. The regulators are then, of course, compelled to rely on their understanding— their theory—of the cause of the problem. Thus, every regulation has its own shadow intellectual history, in which legal responses to perceived social and economic problems have their parallel in arguments won or lost in "what is loosely called 'the history of ideas'" (Converse [1964] 2006, 66). If these policymakers' theories are mistaken or simply incomplete, the regulations they issue may unintentionally produce negative consequences: new or worse social or economic problems.

If that happens, then later on (in principle), the original policies may be recognized as mistakes and repealed. But this rarely happens in the real world. Whatever the cultural or cognitive factors that made the theory behind a mistaken regulation seem sensible in the first place, these factors make it likely that its unintended effects will not be attributed to the regulation in the future, given a general continuity in human psychology and in the history of ideas.

Other things held equal, then, subsequent regulators will tend to assume that the problem with which they are grappling is a new excess of capitalism, rather than being an unintended consequence of previous regulators' mistakes in the regulation of capitalism. So it is not unreasonable to suppose that regulators will tend to be ignorant of the role of old regulations in generating the problems they are now trying to address, and instead of repealing the old ones, they will add new ones, creating fresh possibilities for the process to repeat itself—and for new regulatory interactions, such as those discussed in Chapter 3, to occur.

Is Capital Regulation Premised on Historical Ignorance?

Consider Basel I, the Recourse Rule, Basel II—and, now, Basel III—in this light. They are the latest versions of capital minima that were adopted to protect against the "moral hazard" created by mandatory deposit insurance, which in the United States was instituted in 1933. As we pointed out in Chapter 2, the original theory of regulatory capital was that, absent the threat of a run on the bank—a threat that was largely removed by deposit insurance—nothing but mandatory capital minima could protect banks from the consequences of bankers' wild, speculative investments (e.g., Bhattacharya et al. 1998). This is still the leading view. On March 26, 2009, for instance, U.S. Treasury Secretary Timothy Geithner said that "stronger standards on bank leverage are needed 'to protect against the moral hazards presented by [deposit] insurance'" (Graham 2009; cf. Volcker 2010, 12). The original, economistic current in the history of ideas is still running strong.

In turn, the theory behind deposit-insurance legislation was that only it could stop banking panics such as those that had swept the United States at the beginning of the Depression. The legislators implicitly attributed bank runs to the fragility of capitalist methods of finance. We sketched the fragility in Chapter 2, but a fragile object can sometimes be cushioned, and this is what bankers seem to have done, by means of capital cushions, before the advent of deposit insurance. Thus, legal scholar Gary Gorton (2008, 2) tells us that "historically it does not appear that panics are an inherent feature of banking." On the other hand, there was the massive bank panic of 1930–33 in the United States, during which 8,000 banks became insolvent. How can the two facts be reconciled?

Michael D. Bordo (1985, 73) explains that "the United States experienced panics in a period when they were a historical curiosity in other countries" (cf. Selgin 1994). This unfortunate case of American exceptionalism may have been due to a series of state and federal laws, going back at least to the National Bank Acts of 1863, that impeded bank-note issuance, branch banking, and nationwide bank "clearing houses" (Selgin 1988,

12–14; Dowd 1992b; Schuler 1992; Gorton 2009n27; Calomiris 2010, 3).[1] Thus, during the Great Depression, while the United States was undergoing the greatest banking panic in history, Canada experienced no panics or bank failures at all. Like the United States, Canada did not yet have deposit insurance; but Canada also lacked the American laws that inhibited bank-note issuance, branch banking, and clearing houses (Friedman and Schwartz 1963, 353ff.; Carlson and Mitchener 2006).

In this light, deposit insurance, hence capital minima in all their later variations, might have been errors that, at least in the American case, stemmed from the New Deal public's, legislators', and regulators' ignorance of the fact that the recent bank panics were the unintended effects of previous regulations. New Deal legislators, hampered by their understandable focus on solving the current problem, came up with a policy fix—deposit insurance—that *did* prevent bank runs. But the legislators did not have the benefit of scholarship (which did not yet exist) that would have pinpointed earlier state and federal laws as the cause of the wave of bank failures during 1930–33. The earlier laws, moreover, had their own reasonable-sounding rationales, so even if New Deal legislators had been aware of their existence, it probably would not have occurred to them that existing laws—rather than the inherently unstable nature of *unregulated* capitalist banking— could have been responsible for America's proneness to bank runs.

In turn, the new regulatory agency created by the New Deal legislators, the FDIC, had little choice but to institute mandatory capital requirements to guard against the risky behavior in which the regulators—prisoners of their preconceptions—thought that bankers, now protected from bank runs, would be even more likely to engage in the future than they had in the past. Similar preconceptions appear to have guided legislators and regulators around the world (except in Canada, where deposit insurance was not enacted until 1967).

"Policy Tunnel Vision" from Basel I to Basel III

We have argued that the resulting capital-adequacy regulations had an inherent logic that led from flat capital minima to Basel I (1988), which tried to differentiate capital requirements according to asset categories' riskiness. The same logic demanded much finer correlations between the capital required and the riskiness of the assets than was provided by Basel I's risk buckets; and as we showed in Chapter 2, immediately after Basel I was enacted, the Basel Committee on Banking Supervision began formulating such differentiations, based on "external ratings" of riskiness, which, in the form of Basel II, penalized banks that did not invest in highly rated securities of all kinds. While the Basel II process was running its protracted course, the U.S. regulators deployed the same external-ratings approach in formulating the Recourse Rule of 2001.

Chapter 2 establishes what we view as a prima facie case for considering the Recourse Rule to be the most important contributory cause of the financial crisis in the United States. Our evidence is by no means conclusive, but it is uncontradicted by any other evidence of which we are aware. The alternative hypotheses, as we showed in Chapter 1, tend to be unsubstantiated by anything but economists' a priori dogmas, and to be undermined or disproven by the available evidence.

Most economists who pronounce confidently about the causes of the crisis, and particularly those who endorse the theory that deregulation was its cause, appear to be dimly aware, at best, of the existence of contemporary capital regulation; and the consensus view about "policy going forward" among those who *are* aware of it seems to be: the more capital regulation, the better. Stiglitz (2010a, 162) offers a perfect example of how policy tunnel vision leads to this conclusion:

It's easy to curtail excessive risk-taking: restrict it and incentivize banks against it. Not allowing banks to use incentive structures that encourage excessive risk-taking, and forcing more transparency, will go a long way. So too will requiring banks that engage in high-risk activities to put up much more capital.

Yet that is *exactly* what the Basel rules did: they imposed much higher capital requirements on banks that engaged in what the regulators viewed as risky activities. It does not occur to Stiglitz to ask why the capital regulations already in place apparently backfired, perhaps because he does not realize that those regulations followed the model that he recommends.

He writes, for instance, that "the banking system in the United States and many other countries did not focus on lending to small and medium-sized businesses, which are the basis of job creation in any economy, but instead concentrated on promoting securitization, especially in the mortgage market" (2010a, 6). He must be unaware that Basel I penalized lending to small and medium-sized businesses by requiring banks to invest twice as much capital in business loans as in mortgage loans; or that the Recourse Rule required five times as much capital to be invested in business loans as in highly rated mortgage-backed securities—because the Basel and U.S. regulators considered business lending to be much riskier than investments in tranched, over-collateralized, highly rated mortgage bonds.[2] If one knows only of the theoretical rationale for a policy, however, then it seems "easy" to prescribe exactly the right policies, especially if one is unaware that these very policies might, in the past, have caused the problems one is trying to solve.

True to Stiglitz's recommendation, Basel III will, "going forward," require even higher levels of capital than did Basel II. What Basel III will *not* do, it seems, is alter the risk buckets of Basel II, or the entire approach to capital-adequacy regulation—capital requirements calibrated by "risk levels"—that they entail. Therefore, in conjunction with Basel III's higher capital requirements, banks will be under even greater pressure to invest in low-risk-weighted assets, such as mortgages, which Basel II put into a new 35 percent risk bucket (requiring 30 percent less capital than under Basel I); or in double- or triple-A asset-backed securities, risk weighted at 20 percent; or in government bonds, risk weighted by ratings.

Under Basel II, government bonds rated BBB (and its variants) were risk weighted at 50 percent; A-rated government bonds were risk weighted at 20 percent; and double-A and triple-A government bonds were risk weighted at 0 percent (Table 2.1). Basel III will apparently continue this schedule, even though it might already have encouraged banks to overinvest in highly rated government bonds. On April 21, 2010, Moody's downgraded Greek government bonds from A- to BBB +, suddenly requiring banks holding these bonds to raise 150 percent more capital for them and touching off a "minor" European financial crisis that, as we write, has yet to be fully resolved. French and German banks alone held $206 billion in Greek government bonds, as well as $244 billion in Portuguese government bonds and $727 billion in Spanish government bonds, all risk weighted at 0 percent due to their AA ratings (Brereton 2010). These large purchases of sovereign debt must have driven down the cost of funding it (the interest paid by these governments on their bonds), which may have encouraged them to borrow on such a large scale.[3]

We are not suggesting that the next major financial crisis will be caused by banks' overinvestment in government bonds due to Basel II or III. The modern world is too complex to allow even "experts" to make accurate predictions of future events (Tetlock 2005), and we do not consider our-selves to be experts. We are merely highlighting the narrowness of vision that results from what we have been calling, since Chapter 1, the "policy perspective." Our point is that even good policymaking, let alone good scholarship about the causes of past or present social and economic prob-lems, can be compromised by this perspective. If, within two years of two financial crises for which banks' holdings of, respectively, mortgage-backed and government bonds were widely held to be responsible, the Basel regula-tors still have not asked themselves whether the risk weights they adopted in 2004 for these very assets might not have led banks to accumulate them disproportionately, then it seems unlikely that regulators will be even more "backward-looking" than Nobel-laureate economists in seeking out nineteenth-century factors that might have led to contemporary problems through a long-overlooked causal sequence such as the one we described in opening this chapter.

A *Mea Culpa* for the Recourse Rule

There is no *insuperable* barrier to the appointment of regulators who have more historical perspective than the Basel regulators appear to possess. For instance, Sheila C. Bair (2010, 21), the head of the FDIC, testified before the Financial Crisis Inquiry Commission that among the regulatory failures that caused the crisis was that "the regulatory capital requirements for hold-ing . . . rated instruments were far lower than for directly holding these toxic loans" (i.e., for holding unsecuritized subprime mortgages). The relatively low regulatory capital requirements for rated, securitized subprime mort-gages resulted, Bair noted, from the reduction by regulators "in 2001" of "capital requirements for highly rated securities" (29)—that is, they resulted from the Recourse Rule. At least Bair was looking back nine years.

Clearly, Bair (2010, 28) concedes, the regulators who issued the Recourse Rule "were unable to understand and identify the risks." However, Bair does not go on to conclude that we should contemplate the repeal of the National Bank Acts and their successors, thence of deposit insurance—thereby ending the perceived need for regulations such as the Recourse Rule. Her historical perspective does not extend that far, and we are not suggesting that even if it did, she would necessarily agree with the conclusions of the historians we cited at the outset.

Not surprisingly, then, Bair does not draw from the crisis any larger lessons about the fallibility of regulators. Indeed, she blames the crisis on the fact that "the market, abetted by the alchemy of rating-agency assisted securitization, did not prevent the growth of excessively easy access to credit and the resultant massive economic loss." To her, the lesson of the financial crisis is that "markets are not always self-regulating and self-correcting" (2010, 23). This is curious, given Bair's acknowledgement of the role of the Recourse Rule—which, after all, *structured* "the market." Bair seems to be disputing the idea that markets are so "self-regulating and self-correcting" that whatever the regulators do *doesn't matter*, because any erroneous regulation will be corrected for by "the market." But if the market is so perfect that it can correct for erroneous regulations, why must it be regulated at all?

Bair is knocking down a straw man and, in the process, letting the FDIC, the Fed, the OCC, and the OTC off the hook for having issued the Recourse Rule. Or is she? "Well-informed" market participants, who are essential to mainstream models of "the market" (e.g., Samuelson 1973, 48, 69), *would* have known what regulators did not: that the ratings were dubious because the raters were legally protected from competition. Such market participants also would have known that it would be disastrous to invest in MBS during a housing bubble, *regardless* of their ratings; and they would have known that it *was* a housing bubble. Had they known these things, then bankers *would* have absorbed the higher capital charges that Basel I and the Recourse Rule imposed for loans and investments other than government bonds, mortgages, and AA/AAA rated PLMBS. If *Homo economicus* were omniscient, in short, then what *Homo politicus* had done in 1988 and 2001 wouldn't have mattered.

Clearly Bair is right, strictly speaking: markets were not self-correcting in that grandiose sense. Bankers were far from omniscient. So, given Bair's ideal type of "markets" that are so perfect that they cannot be skewed even by regulatory action, the financial crisis counts as a market failure, and future crises must therefore be prevented by more of the same type of regulation—risk-weighted capital adequacy regulation, but with higher capital levels—whose negative effects the regulators did not predict when they imposed a version of it in 2001. Maybe the regulators will get it right the next time. This also seems to be Treasury Secretary Geithner's epigraphic belief, despite his admirable attempt to acknowledge regulators' fallibility and the role of ignorance in human affairs.

Bair (like Geithner, we believe) is in an intellectual trap, but her way out of it follows the same unrealistic path that Stiglitz recommends, as we saw in Chapter 1: somehow get the regulations right; then, of course, they will work well. But while Stiglitz embraces the same "forward-looking" naïveté as do Bair and Geithner, and although he appears to be unaware of the specific regulatory failure (the Recourse Rule) to which Bair is referring, he does provide a better explanation than Bair of recent regulatory failures—including the Recourse Rule.

Stiglitz's broad view is that the regulatory failures were caused by the free-market ideology of regulators—an ideology that, according to Stiglitz (2011, 143–44), deterred them from using regulatory powers that they had or that they easily could have acquired. That is not quite true of capital-adequacy regulation, including the Recourse Rule: the financial regulators did not lack any of the powers they might have asked for, and they used all the powers they had. The problem (in retrospect) is that they used them unwisely.

However, we believe that Stiglitz is right to introduce the notion of *ideological error* as a source of regulatory failure.

The Ideology of the Financial Regulators

Stiglitz's description of the ideology in question as "based on unrealistic assumptions of perfect information, perfect competition, and perfect markets" also has a large kernel of truth to it. Yet in the case of capital-adequacy regulators, clearly there was no ideological belief that "regulation was unnecessary," as Stiglitz (2011, 144) claims. The situation was more complicated than that.

Believers in perfect information, perfect competition, and perfect markets, exemplified by George Stigler of the Chicago school of economics, occupy one pole of a continuum of opinion among mainstream economists that includes at the other pole, most prominently, Stiglitz (Boettke 1997). The difference between Stigler and Stiglitz might be characterized as a matter of political ideology, but all points on the continuum that they represent *share* a non-political ideology that we will call "economism." It was this ideology, not "free-market fundamentalism," that provided the regulators' assumptions.

Economism has two components. First is the view that perfect markets represent a *normative ideal* against which to judge real-world capitalism.

When capitalism displays the characteristics of perfect markets, it should be left alone; when it does not, it should be regulated. The Chicago end of the continuum consists of economists who see real-world capitalism as breathtakingly close to the normative ideal, while at Stiglitz's end of the continuum, market failures appear to be so pervasive that "there [are] always some government interventions that could make everyone better off" (Stiglitz 2010a, 243).

The second component of economism is the assumption that most, if not all, of the deviations of real-world capitalism from the normative ideal are caused by misaligned incentives, e.g., by "moral hazard." One might think that in naming "perfect information" as one of the utopian qualities that real-world capitalism lacks, Stiglitz (2011, 144) is suggesting that human ignorance, not misaligned incentives, constitute a major barrier to market perfection. But his Nobel prize was for his contribution to the theory of asymmetrical information, which essentially reduces ignorance in markets to the deliberate withholding of information by *knowledgeable* parties (such as used-car dealers) because it is in their self-interest to do so (e.g., Grossman and Stiglitz 1980; Stiglitz and Weiss 1981; Akerlof 1970). Knowledge problems are thus transformed into incentives problems (Evans and Friedman 2011).

Bair's post-crisis expression of disillusionment about the heroically "self-correcting" nature of markets may seem to put her, prior to the crisis, at the Chicago end of the spectrum. But if Bair had believed that markets were perfect, she would have called for the abolition of capital-adequacy regulation prior to the crisis. Capital-adequacy regulation is seen by economists as a regulatory solution to a market failure brought about by moral hazard—or, rather, by a succession of moral hazards. First, depositors run on their banks when they suspect bankers of using their deposits for reckless investments that might not pay off, which would leave the depositors holding the bag. However, deposit insurance only aggravates this moral hazard, because once deposit insurance is instituted, bankers are freed from the "discipline" that the fear of bank runs had imposed on their incentive to invest bank funds recklessly. In turn, if this problem is addressed by requiring banks to maintain a flat capital minimum, bankers will still have an incentive to use whatever leverage they are legally permitted to buy the riskiest assets they can find. Calibrating capital requirements according to risk would, in turn, mitigate this problem. Thus, the progression from deposit insurance to capital minima to risk buckets (Basel I) is economistic every step of the way. At each juncture capitalism is regulated because in departing from the normative ideal, markets fail; and the failure is in each case caused by an incentives problem.

However, the Basel I risk buckets were so capacious that they still left enormous scope for moral hazard. For example, a bank could encourage sales of securitized assets by retaining a large equity tranche to absorb first-dollar losses from defaults in the asset pool, putting the bank at high risk for default. This was allowed by Basel I's indiscriminate placement of all securitized assets (indeed, all assets other than government bonds, mortgages, and the debt of semipublic entitities) into the 100 percent risk bucket, despite the very different risk level of an equity tranche, a mezzanine tranche, and a senior tranche.

How, then, should the risk weights for securitized assets be differentiated to better reflect credit risk? This was the question to which the Recourse Rule was the answer. The solution enacted by the Rule was to entrust to the financial markets exactly what Stiglitz (2010a, 156) advises us is their "job": "to ferret out the relevant information, and, on the basis of that limited information, make judgments about the risks and returns." *This* is why the regulators turned to the rating agencies. The regulators believed that the agencies' ratings were endorsed by knowledgeable financial markets. After all, the Recourse Rule points out, "investors rely on ratings to make investment decisions. This reliance exerts market discipline on the rating agencies and gives their ratings market credibility. The market's reliance on ratings, in turn, gives the agencies confidence that it is appropriate to consider ratings as a major factor in the risk weighting of assets for regulatory capital purposes."[4]

This language could not very well have been an expression of free-market ideology, or the regulators who wrote the Rule would not have been engaged in the task of constraining bankers' behavior via capital-adequacy regulations in the first place. Thus, for example, in response to the financial regulators' 1997 recourse proposal, "commentators expressed a number of concerns about the use of ratings from rating agencies to determine capital requirements," arguing that "banking organizations know their assets better than third parties." The regulators responded in 2000 by saying that "ratings have the advantage of being relatively objective, widely used, and relied upon by investors and other participants in the financial markets. Ratings provide a flexible, efficient, market-oriented way to measure credit risk."[5] Read carelessly, this passage, like the repeated invocations of "market discipline" that the financial regulators used to justify their turn to the bond-rating corporations, is an endorsement of free-market ideology. Yet in no case do the regulators contemplate allowing bankers to make their own risk judgments, as a free-market ideologue would insist; "market-oriented" ratings are here being defended *against* the 1997 commenter's suggestion that bankers are the best judges of risk.

The key to understanding the regulators' intentions, then, is not to impute to them a commitment to laissez faire, but to understand their use in 2000 of the term *flexible*. This term refers back to part of the original rationale for using credit ratings, as expressed in the initial 1994 proposal for a recourse rule. There, the financial regulators suggested that the use of credit ratings would "add flexibility to the regulatory capital requirements . . . by taking into account the different degrees of credit risk associated with first dollar loss [equity tranche] and second dollar loss [mezzanine tranche] credit enhancements and senior positions for those asset securitizations where formal credit ratings are provided for the various positions." Moreover, credit ratings could also be "applied to large, well diversified pools of non-homogeneous assets, such as small business loans, because the market would determine the level of credit support necessary to obtain the various credit ratings."[6]

"The flexibility of such a system," the regulators continued,

> would be apparent in transactions that use overcollateralization to provide first dollar loss enhancement because the amount of the excess capital will vary based on factors such as the quality of the underlying assets. One pool of assets may require 5 percent overcollateralization and another may require 20 percent overcollateralization to raise the credit quality of the pools to the investment grade level. . . . The use of credit ratings to determine the amount of first dollar loss protection could provide the [financial regulatory] agencies with an inherently flexible method for identifying when an adequate first dollar loss position has been reached and when the second dollar loss position [the lowest-rated mezzanine tranche] begins.[7]

Just as Basel I had moved away from the inflexibility of flat capital minima by creating the various risk buckets, the U.S. financial regulators wanted to move away from the inflexibility of risk buckets that did not distinguish among the risks of various securitization tranches. The same desire to correct for the possibility of moral hazard was at work in each case. Likewise, BIS economists tasked with investigating whether to go ahead

with Basel II's proposed ratings-based approach to capital-adequacy regulation were concerned primarily with the moral hazard posed by "conflicts
of interest" created by the "issuer pays" system of securitized asset ratings
(BIS 2005, 25–26): that is, the creators of asset-backed securities paid the
rating agencies to rate the tranches, creating an incentive for the agencies
to issue whatever ratings the creators thought could be most profitably
marketed (White 2011). However, this potential misalignment of incentives
was, according to the BIS team, offset by the rating agencies' incentive to
maintain their good reputation, as we saw in Chapter 3. The possibility
that, regardless of the incentives, the rating agencies *might not know how to
rate the tranches accurately* went unremarked, because the BIS economists
appear to have been unaware that the agencies were (1) legally protected
from competition by the SEC, and (2) staffed by fallible human beings.[8]

The Ideology of the Accounting Regulators

We have labored the economistic assumptions of the financial regulators
because we do not want Stiglitz's insight about the importance of ideology
to fall victim to a narrow interpretation of what "ideology" is. Ideology is
not just the province of the politically committed or the dogmatic. Ideology
is one of many heuristics through which fallible, ignorant human beings
try to make sense of the world.

Political ideologies seem to be heuristics that are used much more frequently by relatively well-informed political elites, who are trying to make
sense of more political information than people with other concerns (Converse [1964] 2006). However, given the role of ideologies as heuristics that
allow us to navigate a complex world, Stiglitz is right to point out that
regulators, too (and, we would add, scholars),[9] can fall into ideological
thinking. But in these cases, the ideologues may be committed to theoretical
as much as to political ideologies. Indeed, this is *more* likely among technocrats than among "ordinary citizens," for technocrats (regulators and their
scholarly advisers) are in particular need of a sorting mechanism to weed
out irrelevant information, lest their minds become filled with trivia about
the topic of their expertise—their thoughts merely echoing the "blooming,
buzzing confusion" produced by a surfeit of unorganized data. Social-
science paradigms, such as economism, can provide the needed cognitive
order, but at the cost of putting the technocrat in a conceptual straitjacket.

In the case of the financial crisis, the regulators' actions were based on what academic economists judged to be the best economic theories (Acemoglu 2011; Colander et al. 2011). In the particular case at hand, the most important theories were the theory of moral hazard associated with deposit insurance, which justified to the financial regulators capital-adequacy regulation of ever-greater complexity, discussed in Chapter 2; and the standard economic notion that securities markets require the "transparency" provided by marking assets to market, so that investors get the "perfect information" necessary to make self-interested decisions that actually achieve their objective (e.g., Stiglitz 2010b, 156). This was the version of economism that stood behind the accounting regulations discussed in Chapter 3.

Transparency would be blocked, of course, by "information asymmetry." Information asymmetry is exemplified by corporations hiding *known* information from shareholders; MTM is meant as a remedy. Standing behind the particular information asymmetry addressed by MTM is the incentive of corporate executives to hide losses from shareholders. But the tacit assumption of the regulators was that in the *absence* of such moral hazard (i.e., in a market regulated by MTM accounting rules), "market prices" *would* approximate perfect information; to achieve this end, therefore, market prices were written into the law.

Once again, the regulators were in no sense free-market fundamentalists: they did not trust unregulated markets, due to the risk of moral hazard. Once again, however, markets *could* be trusted if regulations removed the risk of moral hazard. Hence FAS 115 and FAS 157.

"Ideological" behavior among regulators is to be expected. But we are not saying that regulators can be expected to be dogmatic or "irrational." We mean simply that regulators can be expected to be human. Like anyone else, they will have little choice but to take actions that are consistent with their understanding of the way the society they are regulating works. This is not necessarily a bad thing: an ideology, or "belief system," may well be right, or mostly right. It depends on the accuracy of the beliefs. But if one does *not* share the economists' default assumption of perfect knowledge (in the absence of imperfections such as moral hazard), one has to acknowledge that errors can creep into any human being's ideas, including those contained in their theoretical as well as their political belief systems. For this reason, the history of ideas is by no means a story of the progressive triumph of the truth (not, at least, in the history of social science ideas).

And for the same reason, regulators can be expected to be as mistake-prone as those they regulate.

The Ubiquity of Ignorance

The more complex the world gets, the more serious we can expect the problem of human error to be. Thus, the regulators' trust in the "external rating agencies" was shared by a great many investors. Consider, for example, the rich, experienced investors, often institutions, that bought into the two Bear Stearns-sponsored subprime mortgage hedge funds. Mounting worries about the value of these two hedge funds' holdings led to their demise on June 22, 2007, when the parent company had to bail them out. Lingering concerns about Bear Stearns's own subprime holdings later prompted a classic mark-to-market panic (Cohan 2009, 307–8 and passim) that bankrupted the investment bank in March 2008.

Shares in the two Bear Stearns hedge funds had been marketed with a sales pitch that was compared to "a broken phonograph record . . . that basically says, 'The fund is 90 percent invested in AA and AAA structured finance assets'" (Cohan 2009, 311). Nobody who knew about the legally protected status of the rating agencies would have been impressed by that pitch, nor would they have been shocked if the agencies' ratings turned out to be unreliable. But to someone who was ignorant of the firms' legal protection, a double- or triple-A rating would seem to be extremely important information.

Thus, when Moody's suddenly downgraded some of its triple-A PLMBS ratings in the second half of 2007, executives at such gigantic investment firms as Vanguard, Pimco, and BlackRock flooded their counterparts at Moody's with outraged e-mails:

> "If you can't figure out the loss ahead of the fact, what's the use of your ratings?" asked an executive with Fortis Investments, a money management firm, in a July 2007 e-mail message to Moody's. "You have legitimized these things, leading people into dangerous risk." (Morgenson 2008, 32)

If such investors had known that Moody's, S&P, and Fitch could prosper no matter how inaccurate their ratings, they surely would not have been so stunned when the ratings turned out to be inaccurate. They were as surprised as were, we imagine, the BCBS and the U.S. financial regulators.

In hindsight, the three rating agencies' cardinal error seems to have been their use of mathematical approaches to risk assessment, such as the Gaussian copula (Coval et al. 2009; Jones 2009), to predict the default rates of MBS. These probabilistic bell curves—similar to the value-at-risk formulae used by investment banks in their assumptions about the predictability of "risk"—have famously been criticized by Nassim Taleb (2005 and 2007) for their naïve reliance on past patterns to predict the future. In open competition with the Big Three, another ratings firm might have exposed the foolishness of such models, or at least raised doubts about them. If one cannot imagine a rating firm run by the outspoken Taleb, there were plenty of disgruntled employees at the Big Three agencies who, as early as 2000, might have been able to start a competitor firm if the SEC's legal barrier to entry had not been in place. Frank Raiter, an S&P managing director, "and his counterpart at Moody's, Mark Adelson, say they waged a losing fight for credit reviews that focused on a borrower's ability to pay and the value of the underlying collateral" of the PLMBS—that is, the value of the mortgages themselves. "Adelson, 48, who quit Moody's in January 2001 after being reassigned out of the residential mortgage-backed securities business," told a reporter that in his view, "there is no substitute for fundamental credit analysis" (Smith 2008a).

One can only speculate about the other strategies that might have been used by competitors with the rating agencies, had there been any. By way of example, we can point to the very competitive market in equities-investment ratings, which includes not only firms such as Morningstar and publications such as *Investor's Business Daily* and *Forbes*, which rate stocks and mutual funds; but which encompasses many different approaches, ranging from "technical" analysis (which is akin to the historical-probability assessment used by the rating agencies) to "value" investing (which is akin to the fundamental credit analysis advocated by Adelson and Raiter).

Due to deregulatory pressure exerted on the SEC by Congress in 2006,[10] NRSRO status was extended to four new entrants, including Lace Financial in 2008. In 2010, Kroll, Inc., known as a successful "corporate sleuthing" company, bought Lace and its NRSRO status for $1.9 billion. Kroll plans to perform "due diligence" that goes beyond information provided by bond issuers (Lucchetti and Neumann 2010)—that is, to mix probability assessments with spot checks of fundamental credit quality. Meredith Whitney, the banking analyst who is credited with more prescience than most in detecting the weaknesses of the banks during the financial crisis, also announced in November 2010 that she was applying to the SEC for an NRSRO license (Varghese 2010). Unfortunately, the loosening of NRSRO regulations came too late to prevent the financial crisis.

Of course, competing bond raters need not necessarily have obtained NRSRO status: they could have offered their ratings to the investing public for a price. But the price was limited by the investing public's apparent ignorance of the fact that legal protections, not accuracy, were the basis of the Big Three's continued existence and profitability. The fact that the bond-rating agencies were shielded from competition is, even now, not widely known among scholars, let alone financial reporters—and such obscure matters are unlikely to be well known to bond investors if they are not reported.[11]

The investors who bought triple-A MBS, then, appear to have fallen victim to the same aspect of the human condition—ignorance—that bedeviled the "financial" regulators, the "securities" regulators, and the "retirement" regulators (Chapter 3). All of them were unaware of a key fact that might have undermined their confidence in the rating agencies.

Radical Ignorance

They had every *incentive* to know all the key facts, of course, but incentives are effective against ignorance only when one already knows what it is that it might be valuable to learn. If you are unaware of the legal protection of Moody's, S&P, and Fitch, all the incentives in the world cannot make you look into whether they are, indeed, legally protected—it wouldn't occur to you that they might be, since this is, to you, an "unknown unknown." Incentives are impotent in such cases, which are sometimes called cases of "radical ignorance" (Ikeda 2003). Radical ignorance is left out of all mainstream "economistic" models, including all models in "the economics of information" (Evans and Friedman 2011), perhaps because, being impervious to incentives, this type of ignorance *cannot* be corrected through an incentives-based policy fix.

Radical ignorance would afflict markets even in which all incentives for discovering and sharing information were perfectly aligned. This, we believe, is why Stiglitz resists acknowledging the importance of Keynes's "uncertainty," as opposed to "risk" (Chapter 1). We single out Stiglitz because his is the most prominent attempt to challenge the mainstream view of perfect markets, premised on perfect information (e.g., Stiglitz 2010a, 242–43). By omitting the concept of radical ignorance, however, this attempt fails. And it appears that the reason Stiglitz omits it is his economistic commitment to reducing all market failures to incentives problems.

If capitalism is inherently infected by radical ignorance because capitalists are human beings, and *if radical ignorance is important*, then the fact that "incentives matter" cannot be the basis—if there is any—for preferring capitalism to socialism, or for preferring capitalism to the type of close regulatory supervision toward which each version of the Basel rules takes another step, because radical ignorance has an equal chance of distorting the predictions of anyone, including regulators. But how do we know that radical ignorance is indeed important?

In truth, the reason that *we* believe that it is important is introspective: we are both quite aware of our *own* radical ignorance, because we are frequently *surprised*. One is usually surprised by an unexpected event or discovery—that is, the occurrence or the discovery of an unknown unknown. (The poverty of contemporary economic epistemology is illustrated by the fact that it can account for only deliberately arranged surprises, such as surprise parties, where the surprise to the honoree is a known known to the organizers of the event.) However, for those who are more prescient than we are, the financial crisis can serve as Exhibit A in the importance of radical ignorance.

The capitalist bankers seem to have been as ignorant of what was to come as other investors were, and as ignorant as the regulators. We have already seen (Chapter 2) that in the aggregate, bankers' preference was for safety before yield. This suggests that bankers were not ignoring risks that they knew about. Rather, they were ignorant of the fact that triple-A securities might be much riskier than advertised. Unfortunately, this evidence is indirect. As Tarullo (2008, 143) has written in a slightly different context, "the theoretical research has not been accompanied by what seems the logical adjunct of simply asking bank executives" why they did what they did. However, we are fortunate to have direct evidence about two key investment bankers—Ralph Cioffi and Matthew Tannin, who ran the two Bear Stearns subprime hedge funds.

It was Cioffi's pitch to investors that consisted of endlessly repeating the fact that the funds' assets had triple- or double-A ratings. Not only did his clients believe the pitch; so did he. Thus, he was willing to court a jail term by lying to his clients from December 2006 to February 2007, when news of subprime defaults was spreading and the CDS insurance price of subprime CDOs was rising (Cohan 2009, 311–12). To reassure his clients, Cioffi reported that he was selling subprime CDO bonds during this period when he was actually buying them. He must have been sure that by doubling down on highly rated subprime securities, he would produce excellent returns for his investors, such that no complaints would be filed and no investigation would reveal his fraudulent statements. He was mistaken: the hedge funds imploded, there was an investigation, and there was a trial. Surprise!

Cioffi's partner, Matthew Tannin, was also a believer in the ratings. Tannin followed Alan Greenspan (Zandi 2008, 72–73) and Ben Bernanke (2005) in denying that there was a nationwide housing bubble, as opposed to local bubbles in some cities (Cohan 2009, 305). E-mails to Cioffi uncovered by the FBI show that Tannin believed that buying subprimes was a good idea as late as February 28, 2007 (Cohan 2009, 322)—just four months before the Bear Stearns hedge funds collapsed. Both Tannin and Cioffi had millions of dollars invested in the two hedge funds they ran, and Cioffi moved $2 million of his $6 million investment out of these funds only on March 23, 2007 (Cohan 2009, 325), when he began managing a new fund to which he apparently needed to demonstrate his commitment. As of March 28, however, Tannin was still "ideologically" committed, one might say, to what he and Cioffi were selling: "'I simply do not believe anyone who shits all over the ratings agencies,' he wrote. 'I've seen it all before. Smart people being too smug'" (326).

It was not until April 22, 2007—two months before the funds' implosion—that Tannin began to have doubts. A new internal analysis of subprime CDOs suggested to him that "the subprime market looks pretty damn ugly. If we believe the [new CDO report] is ANYWHERE CLOSE to accurate, I think we should close the funds now" (quoted, Cohan 2009, 328). This was toward the end of a tortured e-mail in which Tannin reflected on how much he loved his work with Cioffi, and how he had no doubt "I've done the best possible job that I could have done. Mistakes, yep, I've made them," he admitted, but "all one can do is their [sic] best— and I have done this."

If Tannin and Cioffi were guilty of anything, it was the mistake of believing the ratings. A jury on November 9, 2009, acquitted them of *knowingly* making this mistake.

Cioffi and Tannin were just about the two best-placed bank executives in the world to have known that there was excessive risk in highly rated tranches of subprime securities. Bear Stearns securitized $61 billion of subprime loans annually in the peak period, 2005–6 (Luce 2009). Tannin had spent seven years intimately involved in the securitization process itself, and two more years studying the valuation of securitized assets, before he joined Cioffi in buying them for the Bear Stearns hedge funds (Cohan 2009, 283). By contrast, the *commercial* bank employees who bought these securities typically would not have been in a position to know much about them except that they were rated AAA. If Cioffi and Tannin were ignorant of the "true" risks, despite all the incentives to know, we have every reason to think that commercial bankers were just as ignorant of them.

This appears to be true as well of executives above Cioffi and Tannin in the banks' corporate hierarchies. When the market for the securities that Cioffi and Tannin were selling dried up and Bear Stearns had to absorb the losses, Paul Friedman (no relation), chief operating officer of the bank's fixed-income division, reports how bewildered everyone was: "At that point we still believed that an AAA rating meant an AAA rating, and we all believed that these things were reasonably well structured" (Cohan 2009a, 365). At around the same time in 2007, "members of the fixed-income department" of Merrill Lynch, another of the stand-alone investment banks that went under, "reported to [CEO E. Stanley] O'Neal that they were reducing the firm's subprime exposure, but no one in the department, or in the risk and finance departments, mentioned the CDOs accumulating on the balance sheet." A former Merrill executive told the *New Yorker:* " 'I can only believe that they saw the risk inherent in the CDOs in a different way. These securities were triple-A rated" (Cassidy 2008, 88).

This was the same mistake made by the money managers at Vanguard, Pimco, and BlackRock, and by investors around the world. It was also, of course, a mistake made, in effect, by the SEC and by the world's banking regulators, who rectified Basel I's crude risk buckets by using ratings to weight risk in the Recourse Rule and in Basel II. All of them were human, and all made the same error.

The ultimate cause of errors rooted in radical ignorance is the mismatch between our cognitive capacities and the complexity of the world we are trying to understand. In October 2010, the *New York Times* asked prominent economists why they couldn't agree on such policy issues as whether the Fed should engage in a second round of "quantitative easing," or

"QE2."Among economists, there could hardly be a higher incentive to discover a decisive way to resolve such disagreements: an economist who did so would immediately win a Nobel Prize. But what is as yet undiscovered is an object of radical ignorance, so we should not be surprised that disagreement persists (cf. Popper 1961).[12]

What, however, is the source of radical ignorance? In response to the *New York Times* query, Robert Solow suggested the analogy of economists' legitimate disagreements even about a policy that, unlike QE2, had already been implemented, and thus did not involve the inherently treacherous task of predicting the future: that is, their disagreements about the effects of the economic stimulus bill that had been enacted by the Obama administration early in 2009. "It has run its course over the past year and a half," Solow said, "but it is not an isolated event. One thousand other things were happening that had an effect on employment and real G.D.P.," and any of those things might have either counteracted the positive effect of the bill or hidden its negative effect.

Ignorance, Error, and Disagreement

Economist Dan Ariely added to this discussion an important observation. "If you have a simple problem," he said, "you can offer a simple solution. But the economy is a hugely complex problem. So we either simplify the problem and offer a solution, or embrace the complexity and do nothing" (Segal 2010).

We suspect that Ariely was advising that we simplify and take action: this is the ethos that follows necessarily from the policy mindset, which in turn is encouraged by the modern democratic culture of social and economic problem solving. Without the simplification brought about by the models we have criticized so harshly, economists could make no policy proposals, and neither could anyone else. But all simplifications carry the risk of *over*simplification, producing erroneous policy recommendations.

Resignation to the human condition—radically limited in our knowledge by our cultural contexts, life spans, and feeble powers of logic and imagination, relative to the task of understanding a complex world—is not, however, the conclusion one should necessarily draw. For there are ways of (fitfully) getting around these cognitive limitations.

Natural scientists use controlled experimentation to adjudicate among their competing, fallible theories. In this way they collectively compensate for the inevitable ignorance and fallibility of any given scientist. Unfortunately, controlled experimentation is usually available in the social sciences only when they are not really "social" at all. Laboratory experimentation in psychology *may* reveal underlying, genetically programmed constants, present in most individuals (although it is easy to mistake for psychological invariants what are actually traits peculiar to the undergraduates of a given historical era, who are the usual subjects of psychological experimentation). But when it comes to understanding how "the modern economy" works, we enter territory where each topic of investigation is historically unique—"path dependent," in the argot—and therefore unfit to be the basis of generalizations that have very much sweep. Time's arrow goes in only one direction, so conclusions about one historical episode cannot necessarily be extrapolated to another historical episode, let alone to the future. And if the modern economy is, as Solow and Ariely suggest, "complex"—that is, difficult for us to decipher, given our human limitations—then retrodiction may be nearly as difficult as prediction.

We certainly could not say, for example, that because the financial crisis that began in 2007 was (arguably) caused in large part by capital-adequacy regulations, this must have been true of the Asian financial crisis of 1997. There are too many known but historically peculiar variables, such as country-by-country exchange rates and capital flows, and too many unknown unknowns: who can say, in advance, what an investigation such as this one might reveal about the effect on the Asian crisis of obscure regulations in the various countries involved?

However, an imperfect institutional parallel to controlled natural science experimentation can be found in the very capitalist economies that regulators, backed by social science, are trying to perfect. That institution is, as in natural science, experimentation, as embodied in "competition." By competition we do not mean interpersonal rivalry. We mean the deployment by competing capitalist enterprises of various fallible hunches, heuristics, theories, even "ideologies" that address how, in a specific context, a company can make profits and avoid losses.

We are not suggesting that "perfect competition" is necessary or even desirable, or that "market discipline" will somehow incentivize capitalists to overcome their radical ignorance. We are not pointing to the *number* of firms or the doggedness of entrepreneurs, but the heterogeneity of the ideas that they collectively put into play.

Consider the impact of the Recourse Rule. While the aggregate data presented in Table 2.3 suggest that the regulation had the desired effect—

overall, bankers shifted into the allegedly safer bonds with lower risk weights—different banks did so to very different degrees. As they competed against each other, they took different approaches to the question of where to find profit—and how to avoid loss.

At the Swiss megabank UBS, chairman Peter Kurer admits that "people did not ask too many questions" about the triple-A ratings, so the bank invested heavily in AAA-rated subprime securities, particularly CDOs, and suffered huge losses. At Deutsche Bank, however, internal risk controls curtailed such investments (Tett 2009a, 136). Citigroup accumulated $10 billion of MBS on its balance sheet, but it barely maintained any usable capital cushion, so it hit the Tier 1 capital floor of 5 percent and then began holding CDO bonds in off-balance-sheet SIVs (see Appendix II), where $25 billion of them accumulated (Tett 2009a, 136). But JPMorgan Chase's CEO, Jamie Dimon, decided that imitating Citigroup was too risky (124–28), even though the cost of failing to do so was that JPMorgan Chase received much lower short-term profits (ibid., 117) due to its relatively low leverage.

JPMorgan Chase aimed for an 8–8.5 percent Tier-1 capital ratio, creating a 3–3.5 percent "real" capital cushion above the Tier 1 floor (see Chapter 2). With a higher Tier-1 capital level, Morgan was also able to increase its level of loan-loss reserves in Tier 2 (Rieker 2010), since Basel I capped Tier 2 in relation to Tier 1. Loan-loss reserves are reservoirs of capital that, unlike most capital, actually are "set aside" against defaults rather than being invested alongside borrowed funds. Dimon also raised the pay of Morgan's risk-monitoring personnel (ibid., 115). Years before Dimon's arrival, moreover, the Morgan employees who originally developed CDO tranching had had the opportunity to apply this technology to MBS. But they realized that even though "the last time house prices had fallen significantly" across the United States as a whole "was way back in the 1930s," a similar event might make all the losses within a mortgage-backed CDO "correlate" with each other, which "might be catastrophically dangerous." Therefore,

> to cope with the uncertainties the team stipulated that a bigger-than-normal funding cushion be raised, which made the deal less lucrative for J. P. Morgan. The bank also hedged its risk. That was the only prudent thing to do. . . . Mortgage risk was just too uncharted.
>
> The team at J. P. Morgan did only one more [such] deal with mortgage debt, a few months later, worth $10 billion. Then, as other

banks ramped up their mortgage-backed business, J. P. Morgan largely dropped out. (Tett 2009b)

As a result of its conservatism, JPMorgan Chase emerged from the crisis as far and away the strongest of the nationwide American commercial banks. But Morgan and Deutsche Bank were not the only banks to behave differently from the crowd. Goldman Sachs came to see the danger of its CDOs and used credit-default swaps to escape serious damage from them (Gjerstad and Smith 2010). So did Morgan, which single-handedly accounted for about 44 percent of the world's CDS exposure (Slater 2009). CapitalOne eschewed the mortgage business altogether. Wells Fargo avoided the dangers well enough that it literally had to be forced by the government to take Troubled Asset Relief Program money (Levy 2009).

There were also many smaller examples of what turned out to be prudent banking, ranging from regional giants BB&T, PNC, and U.S. Bancorp (Cox and Cass 2009) to tiny Beal Bank of Plano, Texas, which accumulated capital during the mid-2000s but avoided participating in what its president and chief stockholder, D. Andrew Beal, thought was credit-fueled craziness. In turn, his fellow bankers and the regulators thought *he* was crazy— literally (Condon and Vardi 2009; cf. Tett 2009a, 128). When the crisis began, Beal was ready to take advantage of the mistakes of other banks, buying about $5 billion of distressed assets by April 2009 and angling to become a major bank by buying another $23 billion in short order.

Disagreement in the Public and the Private Sectors

Basel I and Basel II encouraged banks to invest in mortgages; the Recourse Rule and Basel II encouraged banks to invest in highly rated ABS. The rules penalized bankers if they invested in securities the regulators deemed riskier by requiring that these securities be funded with greater amounts of useless *regulatory* capital, as opposed to useful (cushioning) capital (Chapter 2). For the most part, the bankers did what the regulators wanted them to do. But since the regulations did not *command* anyone to take advantage of the low capital charges on low-risk-weight assets, it was still possible for bankers who disagreed to resist the herd, if they could absorb the competitive costs of doing so while other banks were being subsidized with low capital charges. In other words, there was enough leeway in the regulations that a determined banker who disagreed with the regulators' view about which investments were prudent might be able to resist the tide for a period of time—if he or she happened to be sitting on a large enough pile of cash.

That is what Beal, Dimon, and the other "dissident" bankers did. We are fortunate, then, that the regulations were not so tight that they forbade all heterogeneity in market behavior. But that is undeniably the tendency of economic regulation, and all other regulation. By its very nature as a law, a regulation is imposed on every market participant in a jurisdiction. This means that even if, as with the Basel rules, the regulation takes the form of a "tax" on behavior the regulators wish to discourage rather than an outright prohibition, it has a homogenizing effect on market behavior overall.[13] The very point of regulation, after all, is to get market participants to behave differently than they otherwise would; this is why regulations have the force of law. Through the power of law, every regulation imposes one opinion— the regulators'—on all market participants, even if only, as in the case of capital-adequacy regulations, by imposing financial penalties on those who do not go along with that opinion.

It must surely be true that, just as among the bankers, there was disagreement among the regulators about the wisdom of using the rating agencies, or about the precise 20 percent risk weight that the regulations assigned to AAA ratings. But heterogeneous opinions among regulators do not matter, any more than do heterogeneous opinions among voters. Just as, after an election, only the opinion of the winning candidate or party prevails, only one regulation becomes the law in any jurisdiction (regarding any given activity)— regardless of whatever arguments occur among regulators before the decree is issued. This renders heterogeneous opinions among regulators or voters fundamentally different from heterogeneous opinions among capitalists, for when capitalists disagree, they can (in effect) test their discordant theories against each other by competing with each other.

Capitalist heterogeneity does not need to take the form of actual, verbal disagreement. Instead, it takes the more concrete form of different enterprises "structured" (from an analytical perspective—not necessarily from the deliberate perspective of the founders or managers of the enterprises) by different theories: theories about how best to compensate executives and other employees, theories about how to make a profit, and theories about how to avoid risk.

For example, JPMorgan Chase and the Morgan line of predecessor banks had, for half a century, cultivated an ethos that worked against any temptation to disregard known risks: "While at other banks, the emphasis had turned to finding star players, offering them huge bonuses, and encouraging them to compete for preeminence, at the Morgan Bank the emphasis was on teamwork, employee loyalty, and long-term commitment to the bank" (Tett 2009a, 15). By the same token, some banks were "integrated more closely [than others] in the firm-wide risk management process" because the risk-management chain of command ended with the company's treasurer; "firms that experienced more significant unexpected losses tolerated a more segregated approach to internal communications about risk management," which "may have contributed to the lack of awareness among managers of the risks they faced and the resulting losses" (Senior Supervisors Group 2008, 9). Each capitalist enterprise tacitly combines any number of such "institutions," ranging from incentives to traditions to norms to rules, with the enterprise as a whole embodying (from an analytical perspective) a metatheory about what the enterprise should do, and how to do it, in order to make profits and avoid losses. If an enterprise loses out in competition to others, then one or all of the theories contained in its metatheory have been falsified in that particular time and place.

The greatest advantage of this implicit competition among capitalists' theories is that it places relatively low cognitive demands on the "theorists." The "theories" in question need not have actually been thought up or written down by any of the participants for competition among them to take place. Nor does the success of the competition, as a competition, require that the competitors understand the reasons for their "wins" or "losses," any more than members of a species who carry a genetic mutation need to know why it is that—it will turn out, in the future—their progeny will, or won't, proliferate more than the progeny of other members of the same species.

By the same token, economic competition, like biological evolution, need not have some master note-taker standing above it and learning its lessons if the process is to do its work. This is crucial because such a synoptic perceiver, being human (hence ignorant and fallible), could not be relied upon to learn the right lessons from the process being observed. The process of competition "learns" these lessons as mechanically as evolution does—not by anyone thinking about them, let alone engaging in debate about them, but instead by weeding out—through bankruptcy in the limit case—the erroneous theories embodied in loss-making firms (Alchian 1950).[14] The participants in this system need not be well informed, prescient, or even particularly intelligent. They need only be heterogeneous.

By contrast, regulators *are* required to be synoptic perceivers, codifying in law their predictions about which practices will lead to market failure and should therefore be curbed. If they err in this analysis, the mistake is imposed homogeneously on the entire system. They need, therefore, to be able to grasp in detail the complexity of the system they are trying to regulate—which no *participant* in the system needs to do.

A system of regulation is therefore much more cognitively demanding than a system of competition. Consider how difficult it would be to reverse-engineer a complex biological organism, such as a human being, merely by observing and thinking about its behavior. Instead, the design of all complex biological organisms was produced by a completely unconscious process: natural selection among figuratively "competing" genes. The only requirement was heterogeneity, achieved through genetic variation. Certainly the results of natural selection are not perfectly adaptive reproductively, but just as certainly, they are more reproductively adaptive than could have been produced by "intelligent design"—unless the designer were, indeed, omniscient and thus infallible.

The regulators were neither omniscient nor infallible. Only their error in equating safety with high ratings from the NRSROs can explain why commercial banks proved, on the whole, to be three times more susceptible to the lure of private mortgage bonds than were other investors—who were equally impressed with high ratings, but who were not penalized by the Recourse Rule for failing to invest in highly rated asset-backed securities. The huge asymmetry between the proportion of commercial-bank portfolios that was devoted to triple-A mortgage bonds and the proportion of other investors' portfolios devoted to them (Table 2.3) cannot be explained by the bankers' quest for high yield in a low-interest-rate environment, nor by their performance bonuses, nor even by their prudence, since the same factors applied, *ceteris paribus,* to other investors. The chief difference between commercial bankers and everyone else was that specific capital-adequacy regulations covered the former. There is, therefore, no reason to think that ABS would have been issued in such volume, nor that they would have been so highly concentrated in the hands of U.S. commercial banks, in the absence of the Recourse Rule. Nor is there reason to think that, absent Basel I, banks across the entire world would have been so heavily invested in mortgage lending, and thus that they would have found such a profitable business in selling ABS whose collateral was mortgages. Nor is there reason to believe that market concern about the value of these securities would have caused a panic, let alone the Great Recession, if not for the accounting regulators' misguided theory about the "informational value" of market prices, which was enforced by MTM accounting.

The accounting regulators had persuasive reasoning behind them, and there is no doubt that they were well intended. But they were human, fallible, and quite possibly ignorant of the interaction of their action with capital-adequacy regulations. To be sure, fallibility does not entail error. All-too-human regulators may still get it right. Conversely, market competition does not entail good outcomes. Consumers may not know what they want, at least not at first—and, ultimately, consumer purchases are the systemic filter that screens out mistaken businesses' "theories." Likewise, the entrepreneurs with access to capital—or the bankers and investors who supply it—might tend homogeneously to make the same error. If everyone learns the same erroneous theory, such as the efficient-markets hypothesis, in business school, the system as a whole may be in trouble.

However, where there are competing powers, as in a capitalist economy, there is more chance of heterogeneity than when there is a single regulator with power over all the competitors. At worst, in the limit case of a market that, through "herd behavior" (caused, for instance, by homogeneous cultural exposure), universally converged on an erroneous idea or practice, unregulated capitalism would likely be no worse than regulated capitalism, since an idea or practice that is homogeneously accepted by all market participants in a given time and place is likely to be accepted by the regulators of that time and place, too. But at best, competing businesses will embody different theories, with the bad ones tending to be weeded out.

The systemic advantage that capitalism enjoys, in this respect, has as its flip side the comparative epistemological burden on regulators of capitalism. Disagreement, as we maintained in Chapter 3, occurs almost every time an asset is bought: the buyer thinks the asset will be worth more than the seller does. It would be hubristic to predict in advance which side in such a dispute is correct. But that is exactly what Treasury Secretary Geithner, the lead regulator during the crisis, had no choice but to do. At an early April 2009 "breakfast with a dozen or so corporate and banking executives in New York," he said that "many banks believe the investments and loans on their books are worth far more *than they really are*." In short, he disagreed with them. But this disagreement, according to Geithner, was "unacceptable. The banks, he said, will have to sell these assets at *prices investors are willing to pay*, and so must be prepared to take further write-downs" (Dash 2009, emphasis added).

There are at least two ways to interpret Geithner's statement. In the first interpretation, he was repeating the MTM doctrine that *market prices* are omniscient, and thus that the prices that investors were currently willing to pay were *equivalent to* what they were really worth—that is, in the case of asset-backed bonds, what the future payment stream from the triple-A tranches really would be. In the second interpretation, Geithner was making an independent judgment that in this particular case, the prices investors were willing to pay, as of April 2009, happened to be accurate forecasts of the amount of revenue that the triple-A tranches would yield in the future. The second interpretation is entirely plausible, given that the Treasury, and the Federal Reserve, had by then done a great deal of investigation of the matter. However, in this interpretation, Geithner was simply shifting the burden of omniscience from investors onto himself. As much as the epigraph shows that Geithner is aware of regulators' fallibility, his role as lead regulator compelled him, in this interpretation, to proceed as if he and his colleagues at Treasury and the Federal Reserve were, indeed, "clairvoyant."

In this case, however, it appears that neither Geithner nor "the market" was right, let alone clairvoyant. The fate of the AIG-insured mortgage bonds that ended up in the Fed's Maiden Lane III, as described in Chapter 3, suggests that by January 2010, the Fed, at least, had decided that these triple-A tranches were worth fighting over with Goldman Sachs and Société Générale, because they had already outperformed investors' previous predictions—just as had been predicted by the bankers with whom Geithner had disagreed, seven months earlier. The difference is that Goldman Sachs and Société Générale were two among many market participants, each of which had its own opinion about the future value of mortgage bonds and thus the reliability of the ratings, and none of which, as a private player, would have had its opinion stamped by law on society as a whole.

A Limited Case for Regulation—And a Limited Case
Against the Case for Regulation

The systemic advantage of capitalism is that it allows heterogeneous interpretations of what is going on to be "enacted" simultaneously by competing businesses. The disadvantage of modern democracy is that in attempting to solve social and economic problems, either the people or their agents—legislators and regulators—must adopt a single interpretation that, in legal form, homogenizes behavior throughout the entire system. If this single interpretation is erroneous, the entire system may be jeopardized. That, we believe, is the chief explanation of both the financial crisis and the Great Recession.

However, in drawing broader conclusions about capitalism, one has to factor in problems that are not caused by error. On the one hand, we can think of no plausible reason to believe that regulators will be smarter or better informed about a complex world than those they regulate. This fact tends to be invisible to economists, regulators—and citizens—when, in their preoccupation with incentives, they overlook the possibility of innocent cognitive mistake. If the polity blames capitalists' greed for whatever errors they make, then it is perfectly sensible for the polity to demand "adult supervision" of the greedy capitalists by regulators who—however greedy they might be—are not rewarded for it, unless they are corrupt.

Yet there are often cases where self-interest, not radical ignorance, really is the problem. For instance, in genuine cases of moral hazard, when the costs of a capitalist's actions are not borne by him or her but by others (e.g., pollution), a purely self-interested capitalist will have no incentive to refrain from imposing these costs on others. In such cases, there *is* a case for regulation. Since it is relatively easy to police self-interest among a handful of regulators who are, in addition, enjoined by cultural norms to be honest in seeking the public good, then it *is* logical to entrust them with the job of restraining the actions of potentially avaricious capitalists in such situations, traditionally known to economists as cases of "externalities" or "public goods."

The case *for* regulation, then, covers cases in which market participants' self-interest is served at the expense of others. This rationale for regulation is no different, in principle, than the case for regulation that we saw at work among the financial and accounting regulators and the mainstream economists whose assumptions we have criticized—except for one thing. Once we acknowledge that the regulators, too, may err, then we need to recognize as well that their errors, with the weight of the law behind them, may have even more disastrous consequences than the behavior they are regulating. This is true even when there seems to be a genuine case for regulation due to the need to curb externalities or produce public goods.

Such a case did seem to exist, for most economists and regulators, in the case of banking.

The disastrous consequences of the financial crisis are beyond dispute. The fact that these consequences were caused by regulatory error has, we hope, been established prima facie by Chapters 2 and 3. However, the errors that we attribute to the regulators were of two varieties, one more disturbing than the other.

It is bad enough that, arguably, the FASB failed to anticipate the future consequences of requiring banks' securities portfolios to be marked to market. The accounting regulators' error was a failure of prediction that may proximately have been caused by economistic ideology, but was ultimately rooted in the latent fact that ignorance of the future is endemic. This is an instance of the cognitive advantage of markets—to the extent that they are heterogeneous—over regulation; but as we have seen, there are cases in which regulation may nevertheless be desirable because of general, albeit not universal, differences in the motivations of private- and public-sphere decision makers.

The other errors, however—those of the financial regulators in introducing ratings into capital-adequacy regulations—are much more worrisome, because they involved one and possibly two mistakes in the *classification* of whether there *was* moral hazard. First, as we contend in Chapter 3, the regulators were apparently ignorant of the regulations that had created a legally protected ratings oligopoly, so they failed to predict the future consequences of having made the opinions of the firms benefiting from this protection into the basis of capital-adequacy regulations. Here, ignorance of the past led to ignorance of a possible future outcome. That is, the financial regulators failed to see that there was *at least* a moral-hazard problem with the ratings agencies,[15] and more widely a "cognitive hazard" problem with them, inasmuch as the regulations that had canonized their ratings had insulated these corporations from heterogeneous competition. We do not know whether, as a result, the agencies deliberately or accidentally misrated so many mortgage-backed bonds (or, as we have suggested in Chapter 3, whether they really *did* misrate them). But the strong possibility that either or both forms of "hazard" might afflict a legally protected oligopoly would have been apparent to regulators who were knowledgeable about the legal protections—and who were not blinded to the very possibility of cognitive hazard by their ideology. In this case, the regulators' ignorance and/or ideology led to an error of omission in their agenda of "hazards."

It will be useful to label this failure to recognize the dangers of relying on the ratings as a "Type II error" (a false negative). However, the financial regulators also committed a Type I error (a false positive) when they inaccurately assumed that deposit insurance was necessary to prevent bank runs, at least if we accept the declarations of economic historians presented at the beginning of this chapter. If so, then the entire edifice of capital-adequacy regulation—with the disastrous consequences that its most recent forms have produced—was unnecessary. Another possible Type I error is the assumption that deposit insurance, once enacted, created a moral hazard that, in turn, required capital-adequacy regulation to rectify it. Without fully exploring the issue here, two indirect forms of evidence against this line of reasoning were presented in Chapter 2.

For one thing, the maintenance of extra capital cushions by banks, usually treated by economists as a paradox (given their assumption that deposit insurance created a moral hazard), suggests that despite the fact that *depositors* would be bailed out if the banks were to become insolvent, bank managers—who would *not* be bailed out in that event, but instead would be fired and humiliated—were not actually in a situation of moral hazard that kept them from trying to maintain a capital cushion against insolvency on their own.[16] For another thing, even if deposit insurance did create a moral hazard, regulatory capital minima *cannot serve as effective capital cushions*, because legal penalties follow from drawing on the cushion. Thus, the relative stability of the banking system after the joint imposition of deposit insurance and capital-adequacy requirements may not be attributable to anything but the overall prudence of bankers (there have been many exceptions, of course). Yet if Chapter 2 is correct, capital-adequacy requirements—premised on a false positive that overlooked this evidence—were responsible for the worst economic calamity in eight decades.

Whatever one may think of these particular claims, we take it to be uncontroversial that Type I errors by regulators *can* occur, given the overabundance of data and their susceptibility to a wide variety of interpretations. In such cases, regulations may be imposed that have no point—but that may pose a severe systemic risk, given that the regulators' remedy for a nonexistent problem[17] is just as subject as any other human decision to producing unintended consequences. The consequences, however, are greatly magnified by the homogeneous imposition of regulations across entire societies.

CONCLUSION

Because our argument has covered a lot of ground, a summary is in order. We present it with its vulnerabilities (as we see them) exposed; after the summary, we briefly consider counterarguments directed at those vulnerabilities.

"Moral Hazard" and the Financial Crisis

We began in Chapter 1 with the fact that the mortgage-backed bonds on the balance sheets of U.S. commercial banks appear to have been either guaranteed by the GSEs or rated triple-A. This well-known fact poses serious problems for the two most prominent hypotheses about the cause of the crisis, both of which are "moral-hazard" stories.

According to one of the moral-hazard stories, bankers made bets on mortgage-backed bonds that they knew were risky because they also knew that they would be bailed out if disaster struck. According to the other story, they knowingly made bets on risky mortgage-backed bonds because they were paid to pursue short-term profit at the expense of long-term safety. In Chapter 1, we pointed out that there is literally no evidence that either of these hypotheses is true (see also Appendix I); and we noted that if either or both of them were true, it would be difficult to explain why banks bought low-yielding GSE-guaranteed and triple-A privately issued mortgage bonds, including triple-A CDOs, instead of much-higher-yielding double-A, single-A, triple-B, or double-B bonds or CDOs.[1]

Moreover, contrary to conventional wisdom, neither commercial banks in general nor the biggest of them were, on the whole, increasing their leverage *to the legal limit* in the years before the crisis (although some were indeed levering up, while others were deleveraging). For the moral-hazard stories to be true, bankers should have been taking risks that would pay off, and one way to increase the payoff on any bet is to use as much borrowed money as possible. In reality, bankers seem to have been trying to play it safe by betting on government-guaranteed or privately issued but low-yielding, tranched, overcollateralized mortgage bonds rated AAA, and by falling well short of using all the leverage they could to make these bets.

The Basel Thesis

The relatively low yields of the mortgage bonds and the relatively low leverage of the commercial banks form, respectively, the conceptual beginning and end of Chapter 2. First, we explained U.S. commercial banks' and savings and loans' $1.324 trillion in GSE-guaranteed and triple-A mortgage bond purchases (Table 1.1) as due to the 80 percent capital relief that these types of bonds received under the Basel I accords and the Recourse Rule, the latter of which applied only to U.S. banks. What is of particular interest is the $472 billion portion of this amount that was invested in AAA-rated "private-label" mortgage bonds (PLMBS). In 2001, the year in which the final version of the Recourse Rule was issued, PLMBS issuance increased by nearly 100 percent after having actually declined in 2000 (Figure 2.1). By the eve of the crisis, U.S. commercial banks had accumulated $383 billion of AAA-rated PLMBS and $90 billion of AAA-rated CDO bonds (Table 1.1). This amounted to 4.3 percent of the total assets of U.S. commercial banks and S&Ls, or three times the proportion of PLMBS and CDOs to be found in other U.S. investors' portfolios (Table 2.3).

The Mystery of Banks' Steady Leverage Levels

However, if banks were accumulating all of these relatively low-yielding PLMBS/CDOs primarily because of the capital relief they offered under Basel I and the Recourse Rule, why weren't they *using* the capital relief by increasing their leverage, which remained steady (in the aggregate) and low during the years before the crisis? What is the point of accumulating low-yielding bonds that, under the Recourse Rule, allowed banks to borrow more if they did not then borrow more?

Our answer, presented at the end of Chapter 2, turned on the distinction between usable and legally mandated capital cushions. A prudent unregulated bank would maintain a capital cushion because leverage can be dangerous: unpredictable defaults on its loans and losses on its other investments may prevent a bank from being able to pay back the funds (borrowed from depositors and other creditors) with which the bank has financed these loans and investments. For just this reason, legally required capital minima—leverage ceilings—are a key tool in the "prudential regulation" of banks. However, capital minima are enforced by threatening to fire the management, and seize the assets, of a bank that does not maintain the required cushion. Paradoxically, the severity of this enforcement mechanism prevents the required cushions from being prudentially useful.

While a prudent unregulated bank would need a capital cushion to stave off bankruptcy if disaster strikes, a regulated bank needs a capital cushion to stave off seizure if its capital level falls below the legal minimum. A *prudent but regulated* bank needs *both* of these "cushions": it needs to maintain the legal minimum if it is to be allowed to do business, and it needs an extra cushion above the legal minimum in order to avoid breaching the legal minimum should unforeseen problems with its loan and investment portfolio occur. Capital devoted to the extra cushion is necessary in the face of an unpredictable future, but capital devoted to the legal cushion is wasted.

This may resolve the mystery of why banks lobby against more onerous capital regulations even as they regularly maintain capital levels well in excess of the legal minimum. And it may explain why, in the years before the crisis, banks engaged in "capital arbitrage" even while maintaining an extra cushion—and even while *not* increasing their non-risk-weighted leverage (Figure 2.4). By using capital arbitrage to obtain capital relief, a bank reduces the size of the legally required—and useless—regulatory capital minimum. Thus, even while they kept their leverage levels steady, banks were (in the aggregate) acquiring huge quantities of assets that the regulators deemed to be safe, thereby reducing the amount of regulatory capital that banks had to maintain. This had the effect of expanding the banks' "extra," prudential capital cushion by lowering the legally mandated capital floor. The problem was that the combination of Basel I and the Recourse Rule offered banks seeking to engage in this strategy only three ways of doing so: issuing proportionately more mortgage loans, risk weighted at 50 percent, than business and consumer loans risk weighted at 100 percent; buying proportionately more agency bonds or double- or triple-A asset-backed securities, including PLMBS, risk weighted at 20 percent; or buying more government bonds, risk weighted at 0 percent.

Mark-to-Market Accounting

In the first half of Chapter 3 we turned from the financial crisis itself to the Great Recession that followed. Here we argued that Basel I and the Recourse Rule interacted with "fair-value" or MTM accounting to unnecessarily shrink the amount of banks' legally recognized capital, putting them in jeopardy of legal action once the banks' usable (nonregulatory) capital cushion had been run through—merely because the current market prices of mortgage- and other asset-backed bonds fell.

A bond's value consists of the actual revenue it ends up producing over its lifetime, not the price it commands at a given moment. That price is based on "the market's" collective prediction of the size of the bond's future revenue stream. When investors began to worry about the consequences of the burst housing bubble for subprime mortgage bonds, their prices plummeted; indeed, markets for them dried up, so there often were no actual prices for them. Low prices, and proxies for low prices, were treated as the "real" prices by MTM accounting regulations, and banks' paper losses on these bonds were therefore subtracted from their earnings, reducing their legally recognized capital levels dollar for dollar, and therefore reducing by a multiple of 10 (for well-capitalized banks) or 12.5 (for adequately capitalized banks) the lending capacity of the banks.

Using the more conservative 10 percent capital minimum for well-capitalized U.S. banks, the 2.2 percent write-downs against total bank assets taken by August 2008—even before the height of the market panic—could have translated into a 22 percent decline in commercial banks' lending capacity. Fortunately, banks were, with massive government assistance, able to raise capital to counteract some of this decline in lending capacity, but *business* lending still fell by 67 percent (Figure 1.2) even before it became crystal clear in September 2008 that a major recession was about to occur.

Why the Regulators Were Ignorant

In Chapter 3 we also began turning to the question of why the regulators promulgated such disastrous regulations. Our general answer is that they were human. People find it hard to predict the consequences of their actions even under the most favorable circumstances—but contemporary circumstances are particularly unfavorable for regulators. An extremely complex web of regulation has been enacted during the last century and a half, and it is humanly impossible for any given regulator to be anything but ignorant of the vast bulk of these regulations—let alone to understand their implications.

Thus, we argued that the accounting regulators either did not understand how capital-adequacy regulations could interact with MTM to devastate banks' lending capacity and thus the economy as a whole, or that they were blinded by their adherence to an ideology that equates market prices with true economic value. And we argued that similar things can be said about why the financial regulators (as opposed to the accounting regulators) made what we consider to be the master regulatory mistake that precipitated the crisis: using the bond ratings produced by Moody's, S&P, and Fitch as the determinant of the capital levels required of banks by law, even though these three firms had been effectively granted an oligopoly by the SEC.

As with the accounting regulators, we considered two possible explanations for the financial regulators' action: that they were ignorant of the legal oligopoly of the "ratings agencies," and that they were blinded by "economism," or the belief that markets are, in the default position, perfect, such that market participants are, in effect, omniscient. However, economists make a narrow exception to the rule of omniscience: they recognize that the omniscient default position (equilibrium) can be disturbed in cases where the information flow is blocked by incentives problems such as moral hazard.

The ignorance explanation and the ideology explanation are not mutually exclusive, and in Chapter 4 we present evidence in favor of both. This evidence consists of the financial regulators' continual refrain that the ratings agencies' judgments could be trusted because of the "market discipline" exerted upon them, even though the SEC, in particular, had long prevented such discipline from occurring. The financial regulators appear to have been ignorant of what the SEC had been doing, or else they were ignorant of the effect that the SEC's regulations might have had on the reliability of the ratings. But in the very words that suggest the financial regulators' ignorance of the securities regulators' actions, the financial regulators also displayed the underlying assumption of so many *economists*: not that markets do not need regulation, but that markets are, in effect, infallible when there are no misaligned incentives. Therefore the putatively market-disciplined rating agencies' predictions about the default rates of mortgage bonds could be trusted.

Price Fetishism, Market Fundamentalism, and Economism

The default assumption of market omniscience shared by the accounting and financial regulators may seem equivalent to "market worship" or "free-market fundamentalism," but in fact none of the regulators were by any means libertarians: they believed that without regulatory intervention, capitalist banks would leverage themselves to the hilt in pursuit of the profits that could flow from risky loans and investments, and that without regulatory intervention, corporations would deceive investors by hiding losses. In the case of the accounting regulators, the underlying assumption was not that capitalists' *behavior* should be left alone, but rather that market *prices* somehow have the ability to overcome human limitations and accurately predict the future. In Chapter 3 we called this assumption "price fetishism": a fetish is an object to which magical powers are attributed.

The distinction between market fetishism and free-market ideology is important, we think, because one may fetishize market prices (nearly all economists do) without being a free marketeer (most economists aren't).[2] The economistic coexistence of market fetishism with a fierce devotion to regulations that prevent moral hazard explains why the accounting regulators, who held market prices in such high esteem, held corporate executives in such low esteem. Because executives are paid to run a profitable firm, they had an incentive to hide losses from the investing public, creating a condition of moral hazard. By the same token, deposit insurance had, in the view of the financial regulators, created a moral hazard for bankers, who now had an incentive to overleverage and to make risky but profitable loans and investments. One readily sees parallels to the most influential theories of the cause of the crisis: that bankers experienced additional moral hazards due to their performance bonuses and/or their alleged assurance that their banks were too big to fail.

Our case against economism is not that capitalists would never behave in the self-interested manner in which economists assume that they always behave. In fact, our theory about the financial crisis is itself an "incentives" story: capital-adequacy regulations created incentives to load up on assets that the regulators considered safe, such as PLMBS rated AAA.

Nor do we object (here)[3] to the related but separate assumption, common among economists, that all human behavior is, as Weber ([1968]

1978, 24–25) put it, "instrumentally rational" (that is, that all human behavior is calculated to be instrumental to some further end), even though this assumption overlooks Weber's categories of traditionalistic behavior and "value-rational" or duty-bound behavior, where certain actions are taken because they are considered ends in themselves. The economists' reduction of all motives to instrumental calculations also leaves out Weber's "affectual" behavior, in which actions are not calculated or "considered" at all.

We set aside the partiality of economists on this score because we agree with Weber's larger point: that increasingly, modern behavior *is* instrumentally rational (Weber [1920–21] 1958). We have seen no evidence that the crisis was caused by any upsurge in "irrationality," in the sense of emotionality; and our theory of the crisis imputes instrumental rationality to the bankers who bought MBS in pursuit of capital relief, as well as to the regulators who enacted rules that they hoped would encourage prudent banking and honest accounting.

Therefore, in Chapter 1 we devoted considerable space to rebutting the "irrational exuberance"/"animal spirits" hypothesis advanced by George Akerlof and Robert Shiller. They share our dissatisfaction with the partial view of human nature entertained by mainstream economists. But we believe that Akerlof and Shiller's critique of economism is founded on an error in logic: a conflation of *irrationality* with *error*. One can be perfectly rational and as unemotional as *Star Trek*'s Mr. Spock, yet make a *mistake* in thinking that a given action will, indeed, be instrumental to one's desired end.

Psychologism is thus only a slight improvement (because of its acknowledgement of the possibility of emotional decision making) over *economism*. The glaring problem with both "isms" is that they leave out genuine human errors, which may *not* be caused by emotional excitation; and which may well produce results that are contrary to the objectives, selfish or otherwise, to which one intended an action to be instrumental. This is especially the case when people do not understand that something they do not know would, if known, upend their current belief about some aspect of the truth. Such unknown unknowns, or cases of "radical ignorance," will frustrate the plans of even most unemotional, logical, and well-informed human being. Indeed, we believe that they frustrated the good intentions of the accounting and financial regulators.

Ignorance and Ideology in Action

The meta-mistake that economists make in ignoring ignorance (or in reducing it to "rational" or *deliberate* ignorance or to "asymmetrical information," where one party *does* know the truth)[4] is suggestive, we think, of the problems that modern democracy faces: If economists are our most important advisers, but their worldviews have no place for genuine human error, we are in deep trouble. But our argument is not *merely* suggestive. The economistic assumption that only incentives really matter had real-world consequences in the form of the regulations that, we contend, were central causes of the crisis. For that assumption accounts for the *particular* forms of ignorance that seem to have afflicted the regulators.

Thus, the accounting regulators apparently were ignorant of at least two things: First, that capital-adequacy regulations were such that if asset values were marked down to the market price due to a panic, it might severely constrain banks' lending capacity and thus cause or aggravate an economic downturn. Second, that market prices, as aggregations of fallible, ignorance-prone human opinions, might be mistaken—like any consensus of human opinions. The first mistake might be accounted for by the thicket of regulations that can potentially interact with one other, and that no human being can master, in practical terms; the second mistake, however, requires the active interposition of an ideology, since we find it impossible to believe that anyone's natural or default view would be that market prices are "wise."

Neither markets nor prices existed in the environment of evolutionary adaptation that, for all but the last 13,000 years, shaped the evolution of human cognition. Thus, no opinion of any kind about market prices, in and of themselves, could have a source other than culture. The peculiar content of the regulators' opinion suggests that the cultural source here is the doctrine taught to most economists by other economists. This is exactly how we should expect an ideology to operate: Its tenets, drawn from a selective reading of the world around us—the only kind of reading that is possible for human beings who are not omniscient—convince the ideologue that some aspect of the world that has been targeted by the ideology is representative, not merely of opinions one has learned from fallible teachers, but of the larger, objective reality with which the ideas are concerned.

The financial regulators appear to have been ignorant of at least *three* things. The first, of course, was the fact that their capital-adequacy regulations could encourage banks to make mortgage loans, and to invest in MBS, even while heading into a huge housing bubble—a bubble to which these very regulations may have contributed. The second was the fact that the bond-rating corporations constituted a legally protected oligopoly. The third, however, was that even if the bond raters were not legally protected, they, like the financial markets whose judgments the regulators attributed to them, could be mistaken.

Did Capitalism Cause the Crisis?

To be sure, many capitalists, including the crucial ones in this case— bankers—must have been ignorant of some of the same things that the financial regulators were ignorant of, or they would not have bought privately issued mortgage-backed bonds, regardless of their ratings and regardless of the capital relief conferred by the financial regulators for doing so. However, even though radical ignorance often renders probabilistic predictions of future outcomes dubious, at best, it is not unreasonable to think about the future by using rough estimates of likelihood; that is the best we can do. These estimates will vary from banker to banker, for example, based on what a given banker "knows" to be true (including things that he or she may think are true but are false) about the past and the present; and based on her interpretation, or theory, of the implications of these "facts" for the future. Against a given banker's rough estimate of the low "probability" of future events that could upset her predicted scenario, she must weigh her estimates of the costs of taking precautions against such risks (or, rather, uncertainties).

After following a similar process, at least vaguely, most U.S. investors' overall estimates of the costs and benefits of buying triple-A PLMBS and CDOs was such that they devoted only 1.4 percent of their portfolios to them (Table 2.3). In retrospect—at least in the retrospective judgment of, say, October 1, 2008—this was a mistake that must have been due to radical ignorance: if these investors had known on, say, October 1, 2006, what they "knew" two years later, the proportion of PLMBS/CDOs in their portfolios would have been zero. If we take 1.4 percent as a baseline for what the bankers' default behavior would have been in the light of *their* ignorance, then the 4.3 percent of U.S. commercial banks' portfolios devoted to these bonds suggests that *the financial regulators'* ignorance aggravated the ignorance of the bankers by giving them three times the benefit, overall, to plug into their estimates of the benefit versus the cost.

Ours is, as we said, an "incentives story," but it is not a moral-hazard story, because as we showed in Chapter 1, there is no reason to think that the bankers, in any significant number, *knew* that they were making a mistake by buying these securities, and there is every reason to think otherwise—given that theirs was such a low-paying mistake, compared to the higher yields that were available for buying low-rated mortgage-backed bonds (and other securities) *not* privileged by the Recourse Rule.

Why, finally, is *this* important? Why should anyone—except policy makers "going forward"—care about what caused the financial crisis, and about our answer to the question?

It is not because regulators should be "blamed" for the crisis: nobody should be blamed for honest mistakes or even for ideological thinking, both of which, we maintain, are inherent to the human condition and are, moreover, involuntary. Rather, it is important because once one recognizes that "deregulated" capitalist finance did not cause the crisis, but rather that regulatory ignorance and ideology, apparently transmitted to the regulators by modern democracy's most trusted academic experts, may have caused it, one has to wonder whether modern democracy has a potentially fatal flaw: the mistakes that may flow from the cognitive limitations of modern democracy's all-too-human decision makers.

The cognitive limitations of capitalist decision makers are, of course, just as likely to lead to mistakes. But capitalists may simultaneously put into practice heterogeneous, competing interpretations of the world—all of them fallible, all of them ignorant of most aspects of the world, all of them, in one sense or another, "ideological." At least some of these interpretations, if not all of them, are very likely to be mistaken, but some may be less mistaken than others.

Society might therefore be well advised to diversify its asset portfolio by allowing capitalist competition to proceed unhindered, rather than by predicting that a single interpretation is best in advance and then imposing it on all capitalists' behavior at once.

Some Objections to Our Argument

Here we would like to present what we view as the weakest parts of our argument, as well as obvious objections that we believe can be answered.

1. Despite the critique of ideology, does the argument not culminate in a new ideology, and one that is, in fact, a form of "market fundamentalism," if not "market fetishism"?

We accept as inevitable that we, like everyone, are ideological, in the sense that we have no choice but to see the world selectively—there is far too much world for us to see it unselectively. And yes, our contrast between the heterogeneity of capitalist competition and the homogeneity of regulation does suggest that capitalism has an advantage, in principle, in reducing the possibility of system-wide errors.

However, that advantage is by no means absolute. For one thing, as we pointed out in Chapter 4, capitalist behavior is not always heterogeneous; "herd behavior" is common, and we suspect that it will grow more common as education and culture are increasingly homogenized on a global scale. Thus, the putative advantage of capitalism is not universal and it may shrink.

Moreover, nothing in our argument would sustain a critique of "big government" in general, or of all government "intervention." Our argument applies only to regulation, not redistribution. One can infer, however, that our argument also applies to government "ownership" of, say, entire industries, or the educational system, or the health-care system, since that, too, would have homogenizing effects.

2. How does the contrast between homogeneous regulation and heterogeneous competition avoid appealing to the very doctrine of "market discipline" that the financial regulators thought would police the rating agencies (Chapter 3)?

Market discipline connotes market participants who deliberately avoid mistakes because of the incentives to do so when faced with competitors. Our objection is twofold. First, the rating agencies were not, in fact, faced with competitors; the SEC had placed a legal barrier to entry in their way. Second, only errors of carelessness, not errors caused by radical ignorance, can be affected by incentives. Most error is involuntary, and no amount of discipline can beat it out of fallible human beings. A heterogeneous competitive market does not so much discipline error as it affords consumers the opportunity to "exit" from doing business with the firms that make the mistakes (Hirschman 1970). The erring firms may be "disciplined" after the fact by losses or bankruptcy, but this effect cannot magically confer inerrancy on competitors, or else no competitor would ever experience losses or bankruptcy.

3. *Why the special emphasis on* legal *barriers to entry? Capitalism itself is founded on a system of property law and contract law; property law grants monopoly privileges to property "owners," who can (literally) bar entry to, and can prohibit competitors from experimenting with, "their" property.*

We agree. There is no possible form of capitalism (or any other social system) that lacks law, or internalized equivalents to law (Foucault 1979); and property law is inherently monopolistic in regard to any parcel of property. So these are matters of degree. Contract law coupled with certain forms of property law allows relatively great scope for competing enterprises. The monopolies enforced by capitalist property law are small in scope compared to society-wide (or, rather, polity-wide) monopolies, or in this case, oligopolies, granted by law. By the same token we are not arguing against "government intervention." We are arguing against *homogenizing* intervention. There may well be new laws that could increase heterogeneity and therefore diminish systemic risk.

4. *Chapter 2 almost solely concerns the Recourse Rule's "amendment" of Basel I, which applied only in the United States. What about the international dimensions of the crisis?*

We consider this the biggest weakness of our argument. We were unable to find data that might reveal the possible effect of Basel II on non-U.S. bank holdings of highly rated mortgage-backed bonds. One of us (Kraus) intends to pursue further research on that. However, as we noted in Chapter 2, Basel I risk weighted *un*securitized mortgages at 50 percent, and Basel II reduced this risk weight to 35 percent. These risk weights may have played a role in encouraging housing bubbles across the world, not just in the United States. Bank losses were not confined to securitized mortgages (although losses on unsecuritized mortgages were not marked to market).

5. *The Basel Thesis is monocausal. What about other factors that may have contributed to the crisis?*

We agree that this is almost certainly a problem for our argument, even though, in Chapter 1, we indicated that low interest rates and federal housing policies—not just Basel I/Recourse Rule incentives to originate and securitize mortgages—may have contributed to the bubble. But we have not gone beyond previous discussions of those factors or provided any new evidence. And there certainly may be other factors that we are leaving out—especially, as we said, international factors or factors specific to other countries. Similarly, our argument about MTM accounting surely provides too simplistic an account of the initial cause of the recession, even setting aside the many factors that came into play after the panic of September 2008.

Thus, we are virtually certain that critics will point out many key factors that we have omitted—as well as aspects of the law and of regulators' and bankers' behavior that we have misinterpreted, and flaws in our reasoning. We have done our best, but we, too, are human.

Scholarship About the

Corporate-Compensation Hypothesis

We point out in the text the thinness of the scholarship on the claim that banks' incentive compensation systems helped to cause the crisis. We know of only two studies of the matter, in fact; they warrant a close look.

The first of the studies, by Rüdiger Fahlenbrach and René Stulz (2009), finds that the higher the proportion of stock held by the top executives of a bank, the worse the bank did in the crisis. Thus, for example, Bear Stearns CEO James Cayne and Lehman Brothers CEO Richard Fuld lost nearly $1 billion each during the financial crisis, and Citigroup Chairman Sanford Weill lost half that amount (Cohen 2009). In this context, Fahlenbrach and Stulz's findings undermine the compensation hypothesis and suggest, instead, the ignorance hypothesis: the executives did not realize that their banks were taking excessive risks, or else they would have either put a stop to the risk taking or sold their stock. As Ira Kay (2010) has pointed out, it is illogical to build up billions of dollars in downside risk knowingly, in the form of unsold stock, in exchange for the tens of millions of dollars of potential upside gain that might be produced by an increase in the price of that stock in any given year due to risky decisions—*if* one knows that one's decisions have put one's firm in harm's way.

The second study, by Lucian Bebchuk, Alma Cohen, and Holger Spamann (2009), is couched as a rebuttal to the Fahlenbrach and Stulz study and, more generally, to "commentators"[1] who have "dismissed the possibility that incentives generated by pay arrangements played a significant role in the risk-taking decisions financial firms made in the years preceding the financial crisis" (Bebchuk et al. 2009, 1). These commentators have noted

that financial firms' executives suffered significant losses when the
stock prices of their firms fell sharply. In these commentators' view,
these losses imply that, to the extent executives took excessive risks,
such risk-taking resulted fully from mistakes—excessive optimism,
failure to perceive risks, or even hubris—rather than from incentives. (1)

This characterization of the commentators' view is something of a straw
man, since no good social scientist would assert that any single hypothesis,
including the ignorance hypothesis, could explain the actions of thousands
of people "fully." It is true that a question raised by the commentators to
whom Bebchuk et al. are responding is whether there is any evidence *in
favor* of the alternative, moral-hazard explanation of the crisis, which is
defended by Bebchuk et al.; simply put, there is not (as of this writing). But
surely it is possible, even likely, that some among the thousands of executives and traders might have recognized the risks they were taking and gone
ahead because of their performance incentives. The more important question, then, is whether the behavior of the banks' executives, who lost billions of dollars by not selling their stock, constitutes evidence *against* the
moral-hazard hypothesis. The authors never confront this evidence, and
they inadvertently strengthen it.

The main point made by Bebchuk and his colleagues is that executives
of Bear Stearns and Lehman Brothers sold large quantities of stock in the
seven years *preceding* the crisis. For instance, Cayne sold $289 million of
stock in those years, while Fuld sold $470 million. However, these gains
were dwarfed by the losses the two CEOs sustained due to the crisis: after
subtracting the nearly $1 billion each that Cayne and Fuld lost, they netted
a negative $642 million and $461 million respectively.

These data come from Bebchuk et al. (2009, 8).[2] In what sense, then,
do the authors believe that they have they provided evidence *in favor* of the
executive compensation hypothesis, rather than evidence against it? They
offer three answers.

First, they point out that taken together, all of the executives at the two
firms sold more *shares* of stock during the pre-crisis period than they
owned at the end of it (Bebchuk et al. 2009, 16). We cannot understand
why this makes any difference; what matters is the amount of money the
executives left on the table, which is of course the number of shares multiplied by the price. The share prices of these stocks went up during the

pre-crisis period, accounting for the huge financial losses the executives sustained on a (relatively) small number of shares during the crisis. The small number of shares is irrelevant; surely they were aware of the share price and could have sold the relatively small number of shares to reap huge rewards if they had any notion that their actions, or actions that they had allowed, had put their banks in jeopardy.

Second, the authors point out that the value of the shares the executives sold in the pre-crisis years was higher than the value of their holdings at the *beginning* of the period (Bebchuk et al. 2009, 21–24). Again, we do not see the relevance of this fact, since the evidence against the moral-hazard hypothesis is the amount of money the executives lost at the *end* of the period by failing to sell their stock, not the amount they had lost (or gained) beforehand.[3]

The authors' main argument, however, is simply the fact that the executives sold any stock at all during the pre-crisis period. This, the authors believe, is proof that "executives *had incentives* to place some weight on short-term stock prices throughout the period," which in turn might have led them deliberately to take risks that would drive up prices in the short term (Bebchuk et al. 2009, 9, emphasis added). However, the fact that the executives objectively "had incentives" to engage in ex post risky behavior (if they thought it would have been profitable) was never in question; the question is whether these incentives actually did subjectively motivate *reckless* behavior that was *deliberately* designed to boost the value of the executives' compensation. The evidence against this hypothesis begins with the recognition that perverse incentives would have had to motivate the executives' behavior through *conscious choices* to take excessive risks, based on at least a rough calculation of the personal gains to which these choices might lead. If, as in that scenario, the executives *knowingly* initiated or tolerated excessive risk taking, then they would have known as well that they were jeopardizing their banks—as well as the billions of dollars of stock holdings that they did not sell. This key fact, to which their paper is supposed to be a response, is never squarely confronted by Bebchuk et al.

One might still wonder why the executives cashed in some of their stock during the years before the crisis. However, payment in equities has long constituted the vast majority of executive compensation at the top twenty-four American commercial and investment banks, including Lehman Brothers and Bear Stearns (Core and Guay 2010, Fig. 10). One would not expect people who spend their lives trying to get rich to fail to cash in some of the riches so they can be spent. Thus, the fact that the executives sold some of their stock over the years has no necessary bearing on their perceptions of the risks their banks were taking. In contrast, the fact that they did *not* cash in the *bulk* of their stock (in terms of its cash value, not in terms of the number of shares) suggests that they were largely or entirely ignorant of the existence of these risks.

The ignorance hypothesis is supported as well by book-length accounts of the fall of Bear Stearns and Lehman Brothers (Cohan 2009; McDonald 2009), which indicate that Cayne and Fuld were unaware of any of the details of their firms' mortgage-backed investments, and that Cayne was obsessed with building a new headquarters building for Bear Stearns that would testify to the *permanence* of its leap in stature under his stewardship. Having once been a "Jewish investment bank" that had been looked down upon by the WASP establishment, Bear Stearns had, under Cayne, risen into the upper echelon of investment banking, and he was determined to memorialize this achievement. It is implausible to think that he would have deliberately risked the destruction of this achievement just to make a few more millions of dollars.

We do not (as of this writing) have insider accounts of the commercial banks that did the worst in the crisis, such as Citigroup and Bank of America. However, the Bebchuk et al. study, even though it was confined to two investment banks, requires the attention we have paid to it because it presents the most widely cited argument in favor of the corporate compensation thesis—though its documentation of the net *losses* of the CEOs at Bear Stearns and Lehman Brothers points to the very opposite of what its authors argue.

In the end, surprisingly, this fact is acknowledged by the authors, who concede that their "analysis does not show these incentives in fact had an effect" (Bebchuk et al. 2009, 26). However, they go on to claim that their analysis "does show that concerns that this might have happened should not be dismissed, but rather taken seriously." We agree, but the best way to take a hypothesis seriously is to test it against evidence. Bebchuk et al. neither rebut the evidence against the corporate-compensation theory that they themselves present, nor do they provide evidence in favor of the theory. Yet they conclude that even if their theory explains nothing about the actual financial crisis of 2008—such that in reality, just as the "commentators" had claimed, "misperceptions and excessive optimism" did indeed drive "risk-taking"—there is nonetheless "a good reason to get rid of incentives for excessive risk-taking going forward, lest they produce excessive risk-taking in the future." This "good reason" is the fact that "one of the powerful lessons of economics is that incentives matter."

That, however, is precisely what is at issue in the case of Bear Stearns, Lehman Brothers, and the other banks that failed: *Did* (performance-compensation) incentives matter, and if so, how significantly did they matter? If our concern is to find out what happened, rather than to make policy proposals, we cannot conflate the economists' a priori conviction that incentives always and everywhere matter (and that they matter more than anything else) with an actual demonstration of whether a particular set of incentives matter *significantly*—at least not in the explanation of a real-world event.

It turns out, however, that the main concern of Bebchuk and his colleagues *is* to make policy proposals, which they proceed to make (Bebchuk et al. 2009, 259–80), on the entirely reasonable grounds that "getting rid of" a perverse incentive might do some good in the future. However, the financial crisis happened in the past, and the behavior of executives at Bear Stearns and Lehman Brothers in the years 2002–8 is germane to the wisdom of any proposal for future reform only if, as a matter of fact, that behavior was caused by the factor that the policy proposal is designed to address.[4]

Neither of these two studies addresses the question of whether lower-level employees, such as traders, were responsible for the ex post excessive risks that were taken by banks. This possibility has been suggested, inter alia, by Viral V. Acharya and Matthew Richardson (2011, 196–7). It is a more persuasive theory than the *executive*-compensation theory for two reasons: first, since bonuses to lower-level employees tended to be paid in cash rather than stock, the "incentives" line up better to produce perverse short-term behavior. Second, there is (arguably) some evidence in favor of thinking that these incentives actually had the posited behavioral effects, at least in the case of the Swiss banking conglomerate UBS.[5] Third, the previously cited book-length accounts of executive decision making at investment banks suggest that the executives essentially had no idea what the employees who were actually purchasing assets were doing.

We present further evidence of the ignorance of the executives in Chapter 4, but regrettably our evidence is also drawn only from Bear Stearns and UBS. We note in passing that the large commercial banks (UBS, Citigroup,

Bank of America, and so on) were even bigger and more complicated organizations than were the stand-alone investment banks such as Bear Stearns and Lehman Brothers, making it likelier, ceteris paribus, that executive ignorance was at work in the commercial banks; thus, the problem is likelier to have been deliberately excessive risk taking by lower-level employees whose compensation packages encouraged recklessness. But this does not mean that there is evidence that the problem was significant; as yet, there is not.

The Basel Rules off the Balance Sheet

Chapter 1's account of the process by which mortgage bonds were produced is an oversimplification (of course), in large part because of its omission of the role of off-balance-sheet entities (OBSEs), legal vehicles into which banks could place assets.

Again oversimplifying, there are two basic types of such vehicles, for our purposes: Those that were instrumental to the *creation* of "structured" (tranched, overcollateralized) as well as unstructured asset-backed bonds (pools of assets that were rated but were not tranched or overcollateralized); and those that were the final resting places of these bonds. Often bonds sold against unstructured collateral pools—asset-backed commercial paper, or ABCP—would be used to fund the creation of structured bonds, such as PLMBS. This process was countenanced and, indeed, encouraged by the Basel rules.

Why would a bank hold assets off its balance sheet, how would this be done, and why would regulators countenance it?

The easiest question to answer is "how." A bank would establish a special-purpose vehicle (SPV) or special-purpose entity (SPE), whose assets were sometimes accounted for on, but usually off, of a bank's balance sheet. An SPV/SPE is a legal entity that purchases certain assets—"receivables"— from the sponsoring bank.

As for "why," Al L. Hartgraves and George J. Benston (2002, 246) explain:

> Also called special purpose vehicles, SPEs typically are defined as entities created for a limited purpose, with a limited life and limited activities, and designed to benefit a single company. They may take the legal form of a partnership, corporation, trust, or joint venture.

SPEs began appearing in the portfolio of financing vehicles that investment banks and financial institutions offered their business customers in the late 1970s to early 1980s, primarily to help banks and other companies monetize, through off-balance-sheet securitizations, the substantial amounts of consumer receivables on their balance sheets. A newly created SPE would acquire capital by issuing equity and debt securities, and use the proceeds to purchase receivables from the sponsoring company, which often guaranteed the debt issued by the SPE. Because the receivables have limited and reliably measured risk of nonrepayment, a relatively small amount of equity usually was sufficient to absorb all expected losses, thus making it unlikely that the sponsoring company would have to fulfill its guarantee. In this way the sponsoring company could convert receivables into cash while paying a lower rate of interest than the alternative of debt or factoring, as the debt holder could be repaid from the collection of the receivables by the sponsor. SPEs also allow the sponsors to remove receivables from their balance sheets, and avoid recognizing debt incurred in the securitization.

In the case of structured PLMBS, the "receivables" are the payments expected from the mortgagors. Investors bought PLMBS partly on the strength of various types of commitments that the sponsors offered to back up the bonds issued against these receivables. For instance, a bank that retained the equity tranche of a PLMBS thereby offered a *credit enhancement* to investors in bonds issued from the rated tranches. For unstructured asset-backed bonds, such as asset-backed commercial paper (ABCP), a commercial bank that sponsored the SPE into which it sold its mortgages offered *liquidity enhancements* to the bond purchasers.

Asset-Backed Commercial Paper

The ultimate appeal of each type of bond to investors (whether the investors held the bonds on or off their balance sheets) varied considerably. Chapter 1 explains how overcollateralization and tranching, or "subordination," made PLMBS, CDOs, and other structured pools of assets appear ultrasafe to investors in the senior (AAA) tranches, even when the collateral in the pool, such as subprime mortgages, seemed unsafe individually. The appeal of the mezzanine tranches, by contrast, was that investors in these tranches received much higher coupons, in exchange for bearing the brunt of the risk of default.

The appeal of ABCP, which paid even lower coupons than did the senior tranches of PLMBS and CDOs, was primarily its safety. As Hartgraves and Bentston put it, the receivables backing ABCP "have limited and reliably measured risk of nonrepayment." We would be the first to point out that *historically* reliable risks do not necessarily translate into future probabilities. But as we argue in the Conclusion, this does not necessarily make investors, or regulators, unwise in supposing that there is enough general continuity between the past and the most "likely" future scenarios that they can safely suppose—usually—that the past can be used as a guide to the future.

In the case of ABCP, an additional safety factor is the extremely short term of the bonds—usually 1–4 days—which allows an investor to stop investing in such bonds, by refusing to "roll them over," at a moment's notice. However, this would be akin to a Ponzi scheme unless somebody— the sponsoring bank—guaranteed to the holders of ABCP that if other ABCP investors suddenly stopped rolling over the "paper," the bank would step in and pay off the remaining ABCP holders itself. Such liquidity enhancements are among the strongest commitments made by sponsors to their SPEs, as Acharya, Schnabl, and Suarez (2010) have pointed out.

At the other end of the spectrum, special investment vehicles (SIVs), were typically funded with only 27 percent ABCP, and the liquidity support offered by the sponsoring bank covered only 10–15 percent of the senior (AAA) debt issued by the typical SIV (IMF 2008a, 71). These were the weakest SPE commitments to investors by their sponsoring bank. Apart from the liquidity support for about a quarter of their funding (that is, the portion funded by ABCP), SIV sponsors' commitments were informal. The reputation of, say, Citigroup, the biggest SIV sponsor in the United States, or Deutsche Bank, the largest sponsor abroad, would help to gain the confidence of investors in the SIVs' assets—usually meaning the purchasers of ABS or CDO bonds. According to the IMF (71), SIVs held $412 billion in assets, of which approximately 46 percent was PLMBS or CDO bonds (which tranched the tranches of many different PLMBS and other ABS).[1] In these cases, reputational ties were supplemented by credit enhancements such as subordination and overcollateralization.[2]

There is plenty of confusion about the nomenclature of SPEs; the IMF calls them OBSEs. We prefer this ungainly usage because it allows us to distinguish terminologically among different subcategories. We also follow the IMF (2008a, 71), then, in calling a *conduit* an SPE funded entirely by liquidity-enhanced commercial paper, such as ABCP, in contradistinction to SIVs. ABCP-funded conduits were used, among other things, for the following relevant purposes.

1. To hold pools of mortgages through their maturity. Here, the mortgage pools serve as the collateral for ABCP (Poszar et al. 2010, 16). This was possible once the mortgages in the pools were rated with the short-term equivalent (A-1, A-2, etc.) of the more familiar AAA, AA, and other letter ratings that are used for long-term bonds.[3] Acharya and Schnabl (2010, 13) estimate that "credit arbitrage conduits" such as these held about $55 billion of securitized, unstructured residential mortgages. However, 92 percent of the assets in conduits were not mortgages. They were other receivables such as unpaid bills, car loans, corporate loans, and other miscellaneous assets (IMF 2008a, Box 2.5).

2. To warehouse pools of mortgages and other receivables awaiting structuring (tranching and re-rating) into ABS, including PLMBS, with the pools again serving as securitized, rated collateral against which ABCP would be issued. Instead of being held to maturity, however, the mortgages in this case would eventually be used as collateral against which PLMBS or CDO bonds were issued (Poszar et al. 2010, Exhibit 27).[4] Acharya and Schnabl (2010, 13) estimate that $173 billion in assets were held in such warehousing conduits, mostly consisting of residential mortgages.

In short, unstructured ABCP asset pools could be the final destination of unstructured pools of assets, or they could be instrumental to the creation of structured pools of assets.

The Regulation of ABCP by Basel I

In contrast to assets held in OBSEs to which banks had not made any legal commitments—such as SIVs (apart from the commitments made to their ABCP holders)—certain types of legal commitment to OBSEs triggered a 100 percent "credit conversion factor" (CCF) under Basel I, such that the sponsoring bank would have to hold capital amounting to 8 percent of the value of the assets in the OBSE (or, for well-capitalized U.S. banks, 10 percent). However, if the assets were, say, mortgages, the requisite capital would be determined by multiplying 8 (or 10) percent by the conversion factor of 100 percent and then by the risk weight of 50 percent, yielding a 4 (or 5) percent capital requirement.

Other types of legal commitment to OBSEs triggered a 50 percent CCF, still others a 20 percent CCF, and others a 0 percent CCF (BCBS 1988, Annex 3). Unlike the 100, 50, 20, and 0 percent risk buckets created by Basel I for on-balance-sheet assets, these off-balance-sheet conversion factors were determined not by the type of asset but by the duration and other features of the commitments to them offered by a bank.

The governing principle was to set higher conversion factors in accordance with "the likelihood that the [commitment] would become an asset" on the balance sheet, and thus would "create [default] exposure for the bank" (Tarullo 2008, 59). However, despite the fact that liquidity support for a conduit was one of the strongest commitments a bank could make to SPE, Basel I placed liquidity "commitments with an original maturity of up to one year, or which can be unconditionally cancelled at any time" (BCBS 1988, 24), in the 0 percent CCF bucket. The effect was to allow a bank to completely avoid capital requirements for off-balance-sheet commitments of fewer than 365 days, including conduits with ABCP liquidity support. The BCBS explained in a 1998 annex to Basel I that the 0 percent CCF was justified because "shorter-term commitments or commitments which can be unconditionally cancelled at any time, it is agreed, generally carry only low risk and a nil risk weight for these is considered to be justified on de minimus grounds" (1998, 12).

FIN 46, FIN 46-R, and the New Rule

Just as the Recourse Rule was about to take effect in late 2001, it was revealed that Enron, an American energy corporation, had hidden much of its debt off of its balance sheet to make its investors think it was less leveraged than it really was—exactly the type of moral hazard against which mark-to-market accounting was to be a corrective (Chapter 3).

In response to the Enron scandal, the FASB, an arm of the SEC, announced that it was contemplating the introduction of FIN 46 (FASB Interpretation 46), which was enacted in January 2003. The effect of the

regulation would be to require banks to "consolidate" many of their conduits, i.e., bring the assets onto their balance sheets. In October 2003, FASB
proposed clarifications of the consolidation standards imposed by FIN 46,
and it enacted these clarifications in a revision of FIN 46 issued in December 2003, FIN 46-R (see Gilliam 2005).

However, in October 2003, the same U.S. financial regulators that had
issued the Recourse Rule in 2001—the FDIC, the Fed, the OCC, and the
OTS—intervened with a temporary rule, effective until June 30, 2004, that
exempted banks' ABCP liquidity-supported assets from consolidation
under FIN 46-R. The banking regulators reasoned (as had the BCBS) that
"sponsoring banking organizations generally face limited risk exposure to
ABCP programs."[5] On July 28, 2004, the financial regulators issued the so-
called New Rule,[6] which made the temporary reversal of FIN 46-R (for
banks) permanent.

However, the New Rule also recognized that an ABCP program supported by a bank through liquidity enhancement ran the risk of requiring
the bank to pay off the conduit's ABCP creditors in a crisis. A 1999 BCBS
proposal for Basel II had also recognized this risk, and had proposed replac-
ing Basel I's 0 percent CCF for short-term commitments with a 20 percent
conversion factor (BCBS 1999, para. 26). Thus, a well-capitalized U.S. bank
that provided liquidity support to an OBS conduit would have to hold
capital amounting to 2 percent (.10 x .20) of the value of the ABCP that
funded the assets in the conduit if the assets were risk weighted at 100
percent. This was the formula eventually contained in Basel II (except, of
course, using the non-U.S. capital adequacy standard of 8 percent, not 10
percent) (BCBS 2006, para. 579), and it had also been proposed by the
U.S. financial regulators in October 2003, when, concurrently with their
provisional exemption of banks' conduit assets from consolidation under
FIN 46-R, they had announced their intention to make the exemption permanent and had requested public comment.

In issuing the New Rule, however, the banking regulators reported that
"seven commenters stated that the proposed 20 percent credit conversion
factor for short-term liquidity facilities was too high given the low historical
losses and the overall strength of the credit risk profiles of such liquidity
facilities," and "one commenter noted that the proposed capital charge
would put U.S. banks at a disadvantage relative to foreign banks," which
were still subject to the 0 percent CCF for ABCP under Basel I. In addition,
the regulators noted that banks tended to maintain capital equivalent to a

10 percent CCF on their own, despite the Basel I allowance for zero capital, so the New Rule permanently established a 10 percent CCF for U.S. commercial banks.[7]

The net effect of countermanding FIN 46 by means of the New Rule was, therefore, to increase the amount of capital that U.S. commercial banks were required to hold against their conduits from "nil" under Basel I to 10 percent of the basic capital charge, producing a 1 percent capital charge for well-capitalized U.S. banks that provided liquidity support to conduit assets in the 100 percent risk bucket (.10 x .10 x 1.00), and a .5 percent capital charge for mortgages (in the 50 percent risk bucket).

The Role of Regulation in Encouraging ABCP Issuance

The period of regulatory uncertainty in 2002–4, when the SEC issued FIN 46 and FIN 46-R and then the financial regulators temporarily overrode the securities regulators, saw a flattening of the trend line in U.S. ABCP issuance, which previously had spiked at the end of 2001. In the years prior to 2002, Basel I had conferred no capital charge on OBSE assets funded with ABCP; the capital charge went up to 2 percent under the temporary rule that prevailed from October 2003 to July 2004, and then it went down to 1 percent under the New Rule, beginning in July 2004. Figure II.1 suggests the importance of capital relief as a motive in issuing ABCP, since it reveals not only the "flatlining" of ABCP issuance during the two years of uncertainty, but also the fact that, as Acharya, Schnabl, and Suarez (2010) have pointed out, ABCP issuance resumed its sharp upward climb once the New Rule took effect.[8]

All this suggests that the low capital charges on ABCP liquidity were the driving force behind the volume of ABCP issuance; but however suggestive, the evidence is not conclusive.

Consider the fact that Basel II assessed a capital charge of 20 percent for liquidity enhancements, twice the level imposed in the United States by the New Rule in 2004 (which remained in effect through the financial crisis). As Chapter 2 explains, it is at this point difficult to say anything very precise about the timing of Basel II's implementation across the world, but we do know that the final version of Basel II was issued in 2005. Yet Figure 2.4 shows that in 2005 and 2006, when we might expect to see European ABCP issuance *fall* because of the higher risk weights imposed by Basel II (in

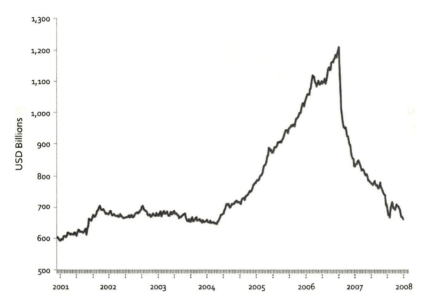

Figure II.1. The rise and fall of U.S. asset-backed commercial paper. Acharya and Richardson 2011, Fig. 7.1.

comparison to the New Rule in the United States), ABCP issuance instead rose sharply in most European countries, and in others continued its previous trend unhindered—as in Britain, the country that Blundell-Wignall and Atkinson (2008) single out as the earliest to start the implementation of Basel II. There, ABCP issuance rose unrelentingly until the crisis began in 2007.

This may be reason to doubt Blundell-Wignall and Atkinson's claim that Basel II took effect soon enough to have been an important contributory factor to the financial crisis. However, another possibility is that (depending on the country) European ABCP issuance spiked in 2005 and 2006, or that it continued rising, precisely in anticipation of the implementation of Basel II, with its doubling of the capital charge for ABCP assets. To the extent that European ABCP issuance was instrumental to the production of longer-term ABS, European banks may have been ramping up their ABCP issuance so that they could finish creating as many PLMBS as possible before Basel II took effect. This interpretation suggests that indeed, capital relief was the driving force behind ABCP issuance—but it would also suggest that we should not neglect the capital relief that Basel II promised for assets held *on* banks' balance sheets: the same 20 percent risk weight for AA- or AAA-rated ABS, including PLMBS, that had been initiated by the Recourse Rule years earlier in the United States. The low-to-nonexistent capital charges that had been established for ABCP by Basel I (no capital charge) and, in the United States, by the New Rule (0.5 percent capital charge for ABCP issued against mortgage pools) may have provided additional capital relief for banks that were engaged in creating tranched, over-collateralized ABS by pooling individual receivables into unstructured ABS and then structuring them to be rated.

The low capital charges imposed by Basel I and the New Rule might thus have been important enough to have been necessary preconditions for this process to make sense for the banks involved. However, this would also mean that while the root cause of the rise of ABCP—the end to which it was a means—was in some large measure capital relief, it was the capital relief offered by the Recourse Rule and possibly (depending on the timing of its implementation) Basel II for highly rated, structured ABS on banks' balance sheets. That is, even if the off-balance-sheet capital relief for ABCP was a necessary precondition for the production of structured ABS that were economical enough to be sold at a profit—something that we do not pretend to know—the sufficient condition in precipitating the financial crisis, and perhaps in calling forth a large proportion of ABCP issuance, was the on-balance-sheet capital relief that structured and highly rated ABS would achieve.

The Overrated Role of SIVs

That brings us to the much-discussed topic of SIVs.

To the extent (roughly three quarters) that SIV assets were *not* funded by ABCP, they offered *complete* capital relief under Basel I, since the sponsoring banks made no legal commitments to SIV investors other than the liquidity enhancements that they offered to ABCP purchasers. As we have seen, however, the banks' reputations, although not legally binding, still stood behind SIVs. By the end of 2007, after the financial crisis had begun and ABCP was not being rolled over, Citigroup felt compelled to bring all $87 billion of its SIV assets onto its balance sheet despite the lack of a legal commitment to do so (Jablecki and Machaj 2011, 223–24). Citigroup's and other banks' SIV consolidations brought approximately $412 billion (IMF 2008a, 71) onto banks' balance sheets in short order, helping to create the impression that lax regulation helped cause the financial crisis, since SIVs were—except for their ABCP component—unregulated by Basel I or the Recourse Rule.

However, as with ABCP, we need to distinguish cause and effect. Neither SIVs nor their consolidation caused the panic about asset-backed paper of all kinds, including both ABCP and ABS. The panic was caused by worries about the implications of subprime mortgage defaults for the soundness of all highly rated asset-backed bonds (although undoubtedly the consolidation of SIVs must have helped to stoke these worries). If triple-A subprime PLMBS could have been misrated, what other highly rated bonds might have been misrated? (Most ABCP was rated A-1 or A-2, the short-term equivalent of AAA or AA.) For that matter, who knew how many subprime mortgage bonds were funded by ABCP—or were held in SIVs? These fears, which led ABCP investors to refuse to roll over their bonds, also led, directly and indirectly, to the consolidation of the SIVs. For example, in the case of Citigroup, the consolidation was intended to head off a feared ratings downgrade (Harrington and Hester 2007).

In reality, however, according to the IMF (2008a, 70), while 29 percent of SIV assets worldwide were PLMBS of one type or another, only 8 percent of SIV assets were *subprime* PLMBS. An additional 15 percent were CDO bonds, 8 percent were commercial mortgage-backed real estate bonds, 12 percent were nonmortgage ABS, and 6 percent were collateralized loan obligations; the rest of the SIVs' assets were not ABS of any kind. Fewer than 1 percent of the Citigroup SIV assets were subprime bonds, apparently CDOs (Harrington and Hester 2007). While Greenlaw et al. (2008, Exhibit 3.8) estimate that the subprime portion of U.S. banks' PLMBS holdings came to $250 billion, or 65 percent of the total on-balance-sheet PLMBS figure of $383 billion, SIVs' subprime PLMBS constituted only 29 percent of SIVs' PLMBS holdings worldwide, with a value of a mere $33.2 billion (IMF 2008a, 70).

SIVs might have helped cause the crisis and the recession in the same way that, we argue in Chapter 3, the Recourse Rule did, when combined with MTM accounting: by offering capital relief to banks that acquired what later came to be *feared* (by "the market") as highly risky assets, even if in fact they turned out not to be. However, the small proportion of banks' assets that were held in SIVs suggests that most banks felt constrained by reputational concerns not to use SIVs for capital-relief purposes (or any other purposes)—even though a well-capitalized U.S. bank holding structured, triple-A rated ABS on its balance sheet received a 2 percent capital charge (.20 risk weight x .10 capital charge), compared to no capital charge at all if it were held off the balance sheet. The sum total of $412 billion in worldwide SIV assets constituted far less than 1 percent of the $62.3 trillion in North American and European banks' on-balance-sheet assets as of the end of 2007 (IMF 2009a, 177).

Even in the effect that their consolidation may have had on commercial banks' regulatory capital levels, and thus their lending capacities, it is not clear that SIVs were very important. Eight percent of SIV assets—the capital charge, before risk weighting, for non-U.S. banks under both Basel I and Basel II—would have amounted to $33 billion, producing a $412.5 billion decline in lending capacity; if we calculate the decline in lending capacity using the 10 percent capital charge for well-capitalized U.S. commercial banks, it would come to $330 billion. However, in contrast to the unstructured asset pools backing ABCP, which would have taken the full capital charge on the underlying receivables once they were consolidated, 70 percent of SIV assets were structured ABS (IMF 2008a, 70), 68 percent of SIV assets were rated AAA, and 20 percent were rated AA—which, under both the Recourse Rule in the United States and Basel II elsewhere, would have gone into the 20 percent risk bucket, drawing a capital charge of 2 percent in the United States or 1.6 percent outside the United States. All but 0.2 percent of the remaining SIV assets worldwide, or 11 percent, were rated A, which would have qualified for the 50 percent risk bucket under both the Recourse Rule and Basel II (Table 2.1), and thus for a 5 percent or 4 percent capital charge, respectively. We lack data on the international breakdown of SIV assets, so using the higher charge for (well-capitalized) U.S. banks in the interest of simplicity, the total capital charges on the consolidated ABS might have amounted to $5 billion for the AAA and AA assets, $317 million for the A assets, and $183 million for the BBB assets, summing to $5.5 billion—leading to a $55 billion decline in lending capacity if all of the SIVs were (contrary to fact) in the United States; or to a $66 billion decline in lending capacity if they were all (contrary to fact) outside the United States, and were all subject to Basel II's 8 percent capital minimum, that is, its leverage ratio of 12.5:1.

To be sure, the true figures are not so easy to arrive at. For one thing, after having been consolidated, SIV assets would be subject to MTM write-downs that, as we saw in Chapter 3, would have magnified the reduction in lending capacity by subtracting from banks' earnings amounts equal to the difference between the face value of ABS and their temporary market price. Based on the experience of triple-A PLMBS tranches, this might have meant the loss of up to 60 percent of the face value of the consolidated assets, or an additional $33–40 billion in lending capacity (depending on whether we use the 8 percent or 10 percent capital minimum). Moreover, even with the simplifications already described, we have left out of these calculations the 30 percent of SIV assets that were not ABS. In the United States, these assets would have drawn the full 10 percent capital charge (100 percent risk weight) regardless of their short-term ratings, or $12 billion, although under Basel II they would have been risk weighted in the 20 and 50 percent buckets, just like ABS, reducing the capital charge dramatically. Even in the worst-case scenario, however, the total lending-capacity reductions due to SIV asset consolidations would have amounted only to $118 billion worldwide, which is relatively inconsequential compared to the $2.5 trillion lending-capacity reduction in the United States alone that write-downs on the triple-A tranches of on-balance-sheet PLMBS might have caused, and the $131 billion reduction due to ABCP consolidations in the United States alone (Chapter 3). To refer once more to the Citigroup case, the effect of the SIVs' asset consolidation on Citi's Tier 1 capital ratio was merely to reduce it from 7.32 to 7.16 percent (Harrington and Hester 2007). Tier 1 constituted only half the regulatory capital required under the Basel rules, so the effect on Citi's overall regulatory capital was minuscule.

Because of the relatively small quantity of SIV assets worldwide, and because of the instrumental—even if perhaps necessary—role of the capital relief that Basel I and the New Rule conferred on ABCP, we conclude that the main arena in which capital arbitrage played a role in fomenting the financial crisis and the Great Recession was on the banks' balance sheets, not off them.

NOTES

Introduction

1. Even "rational ignorance" and "asymmetric information," the two main theo-retical concessions economists make to ignorance, posit ignorance as a deliberate deci-sion, made by an agent who is either weighing the cost of learning something against its benefit, or an agent whose self-interest is served by hiding information from other agents (Evans and Friedman 2011). Given the lack of conceptual space in contempo-rary economics for genuine, inadvertent ignorance, economists have little choice but to turn to "irrationality" theories to account for *errors*. We criticize both sides of this dilemma in Chapter 1.

Chapter 1. Bonuses, Irrationality, and Too-Bigness: The Conventional Wisdom About the Financial Crisis and Its Theoretical Implications

1. Fannie Mae was created by the Federal Housing Authority in 1938. In 1968, in an effort to remove Fannie Mae's costs from the federal budget, Congress passed the Charter Act, reconstituting Fannie Mae as a "government-sponsored private corpora-tion" regulated by the Department of Housing and Urban Development. In other words, Fannie was "privatized" so that its debt would no longer be on the federal books. The private status of Fannie Mae allowed its profits to accrue to shareholders rather than the U.S. government, but the implicit government guarantee for its debt remained, since this was essential to its purpose ever since it had been created during the Great Depression: to artificially stimulate the private origination of mortgages. The 1968 Act also authorized Fannie Mae to issue mortgage-backed securities, and it cre-ated the Government National Mortgage Association, or Ginnie Mae, to guarantee federally originated mortgages to veterans and government employees (this had for-merly been one of Fannie Mae's functions.) In 1970, Congress created the other GSE, Freddie Mac, to compete with Fannie Mae.

2. Specifically, we use the lower curve displayed in Ivashina and Scharfstein (2010, Fig. 2). The authors kindly provided us with the data.

3. Another part of the explanation for the size of the housing bubble, we believe, is the favorable treatment given to both mortgages and mortgage-backed securities by

the Basel rules, which we discuss in Chapter 2. However, the size of the housing bubble is relevant only to its negative effect on banks' lending when the bubble popped, as we explain later on.

4. There were in fact often more than thirteen tranches, even more finely differentiated.

5. Usually the funding advantages enjoyed by the GSEs enabled them to monopolize the market for securitizing prime mortgages, but an exception was the securitization of "jumbo" prime mortgages, which are offered to borrowers with high credit scores who want to buy houses that are too expensive to "conform" to GSE guidelines.

6. For instance, in the second quarter of 2007, nationally chartered banks originated $73 billion worth of home mortgages, while state-chartered banks originated $28 billion worth. (This information was kindly provided by Katherine G. Wyatt of the FDIC.)

7. The figure for U.S. banks given here is one-third lower than in Table 1.1, row 1, column 2, partly because the figure here is based on numbers provided to Greenlaw et al. 2008 by Goldman Sachs a year before the report on which Table 1.1 is based (Lehman Brothers 2008), but mostly because some of the collateral of PLMBS consisted of mortgages that were prime but "jumbo"—too large for the GSEs to securitize. We rely primarily on the figures in Table 1.1 because they are more recent and because the prices of mortgage bonds, for mark-to-market purposes, were based primarily on their rating and vintage, not their collateral composition; this was especially true when active markets dried up and ABX indices of "representative" CDS tranches were used instead of actual prices (see Chapter 3).

8. Senator Phil Gramm, the driving force behind Gramm-Leach-Bliley, was a former economics professor, as was Representative Dick Armey, who at the time GLBA was enacted was the House majority leader. Virtually all decision-making personnel at the Federal Reserve, the FDIC, and so on are also university-trained economists.

9. Similar to that of Frank Knight (1921).

10. Because AIG had a triple-A rating, the company was released by many of its counterparties from posting the collateral that was customary with most credit-default swaps. As James Keller (2009) put it, "In the world of derivatives trading, Lehman, not AIG, was the norm. What this means is that in general, banks have adequate collateral against counterparty claims. Those who traded derivatives with Lehman seem to have had sufficient collateral to cover the unwinding of their trades following Lehman's bankruptcy filing. . . . [But] AIG would often not have to post collateral . . . provided it maintained its AAA rating." On September 16, 2008, AIG's credit rating was downgraded, forcing it to come up with collateral it did not have.

11. Fannie Mae and Freddie Mac, however, were tied in an obvious way to mortgages. Fears about their solvency might therefore have contributed to the decline in bank lending that began in mid-2007, although as we have seen, they do not actually seem to have done so. In the case of AIG, however, it was not widely recognized until September 2008 that a small unit of the huge insurance company had issued large

enough numbers of mortgage-bond CDS to put AIG itself in financial jeopardy. The spread of AIG bonds over Treasuries remained completely unchanged until September 16, 2008, when AIG lost its AAA credit rating and therefore had to provide collateral to its CDS counterparties (RiskMetrics 2008). So it is even less likely that fears about AIG's abilities to pay off those contracts contributed to the decline in bank lending, which had begun in mid-2007.

12. It is preliminary in that these figures combine the exposures of U.S. investment banks and commercial banks (a distinction that does not exist in other countries); and in that they include an indeterminate quantity of agency bonds, as opposed to PLMBS, held by non-U.S. banks. More precise measures of the overconcentration of PLMBS in U.S. commercial banks' portfolios, based on Table 1.1, will be presented in Chapter 2, but we have found no such measures for non-U.S. banks.

13. The relevant statutes are sections 23a and 23b of the Federal Reserve Act, U.S. Code 12 § 371c, c-1.

14. Judge Posner was a founder of the law-and-economics movement, which imports incentives analyses into legal studies.

15. We leave aside theoretical papers such as Bolton, Mehran, and Shapiro 2010; normative papers, such as Core and Guay 2010; theoretical/normative papers, such as Bebchuk and Spamann 2009; and empirical papers on performance incentives that do not cover the period of the financial crisis, such as Mehran and Rosenberg 2009.

16. We refer, however, to more than just the assumption that "rational representative agents" know the correct macroeconomic theory—the efficient-markets assumption on which Colander and his colleagues focus their criticism; we take this assumption to be merely a glaring example of a more widespread defect embedded in economists' *microeconomic* reasoning; for a critique, see Kirzner 1997. We also omit mention in the text of the "information asymmetry" literature spawned by Akerlof 1970, because this literature preserves the omniscience assumption in the form of the agents who know what they need to know in order to take advantage of the ignorance of other agents: used-car salesmen know what they need to know, for example, if they are to take advantage of their customers. This is indisputably true in some cases, but our objection is to the a priori assumption that all or most cases of ignorance are asymmetrical and thus are brought about by the deliberate deceptions of a knowledgeable party. (For a critique of the epistemology of "the economics of information," on which Akerlof relies, see Evans and Friedman 2011.) This assumption not only deadens the impulse to actually do research to find out if, for example, investment bankers knew they were selling overrated securities, or whether commercial-bank executives knew they were taking reckless risks, or whether bank executives or creditors acted on the basis of the belief that certain banks were too big to fail. It also substitutes, for the Chicago-school image of a utopia created by effectively omniscient self-interested agents, a dystopia in which greedy capitalists are omniscient enough always to dupe their counterparties, and never to make unforced errors. Both of these assumption-driven pictures of the world amount to ideology, not scholarship.

17. We mean by a fully *rational* agent the same thing that economists mean by this term. A rational agent is one who treats his or her actions as a means to given ends ("preferences"). Weber ([1968] 1978, 24) called such an agent *zweckrational*, or "instrumentally rational." However, economists often forget that an instrumentally rational agent is perfectly capable of acting in ways that fail to achieve her objectives if she is uninformed, underinformed, or misinformed about key facts, such as what the future holds (Simon 1985). Errors based on ignorance are therefore not instances of "irrationality," as economists so often assume (e.g., Akerlof and Shiller 2009; Caplan 2007; Shiller 2005 and 2008). See the final section of this Chapter.

18. We emphasize that this is an extreme possibility because it is one that would actually be susceptible to formal modeling, since random behavior could be expected to cancel out over large numbers of agents. In the real world, however, ignorance does not manifest itself in random behavior, because nobody is *completely* ignorant. Instead, people have access to different bundles of incomplete or partly misleading information, and they assess its completeness and adequacy according to theories and cognitive heuristics that they have built up over time through cultural (or biological) conditioning. The behavior of a given agent will thus be nonrandom but nonetheless unpredictable, unless one has perfect insight into his or her own cognitive genome and his or her entire history of perceptions and interpretations.

19. Well-capitalized banks are charged roughly twice the FDIC deposit insurance fees as adequately capitalized banks, and only well-capitalized banks can receive brokered deposits.

20. These figures do not include off-balance-sheet commitments, formal or informal, as discussed in Appendix II.

21. This evidence also undermines Stiglitz's (2009) assertion that because of GLBA, the risk-taking ethos of investment banks seeped into commercial banks that were owned by the same holding companies. Deliberate risk takers never would have bought or held senior PLMBS tranches or agency bonds, and they would have leveraged up to the maximum level allowed by law. In reality, commercial banks and investment banks had very different risk profiles, as indicated by rows 1 and 3 of Table 1.1: 61 percent of investment banks' private mortgage bonds were CDOs or were drawn from mezzanine tranches, while commercial banks and thrifts held no known mezzanine mortgage bonds and only 19 percent CDOs. These figures include the huge commercial banks that were parts of holding companies that included investment-bank arms.

22. The latter three figures are derived from data kindly provided by Stefano Giglio. One might ask why, as we noted in discussing Fannie and Freddie, the spreads of the big banks skyrocketed after Lehman Brothers was allowed to fail. Clearly this suggests that before Lehman failed, the big banks were enjoying lower funding costs because it was, indeed, widely believed that they were too big to fail. However, this would have made perfect sense after March 2008—when Bear Stearns was bailed out (by being absorbed into JPMorgan Chase at the arrangement, and with the financial

assistance, of the Fed). Bear Stearns was by far the smallest of the big banks. Its bailout must have established that the bigger banks were very likely to be bailed out, too. But this does not mean that in the years before 2008, when big banks were investing in MBS, they enjoyed lower funding costs because creditors were convinced that they were too big to fail.

23. A home-equity loan is cash lent to the mortgagor at interest. The loan amount and interest are added to the mortgage. A HELOC is like a credit card where the purchases and interest are added to the mortgage. Cash-out refinancings took place "when a homeowner took out a larger mortgage, paid off the previous one, and pocketed the difference. With mortgage rates low and falling, homeowners could increase the size of a loan without increasing the monthly payment" (Zandi 2008, 59).

24. "Fannie Mae's Raines Sees No Housing Bubble, Low Interest Rates," *Bloom berg.com*, June 6, 2003.

25. In *Animal Spirits* (2009), Shiller and Akerlof make occasional use of real cognitive psychology in the form of the heuristics/biases literature, as we have done in invoking hindsight bias. However, one would not properly call an arithmetical or interpretive error of the type catalogued by this literature "irrational"; in making such errors, one *is* engaging in rational processes, but is doing so incompetently. (Thus, we do not accuse Shiller of being irrational merely because he engages in hindsight bias; he is simply misremembering what he said in 2005, and misinterpreting what Alan Greenspan wrote in 2007.) Incompetence is not the same as "irrationality," at least not in the sense that Shiller evokes when he uses the term. See Simon 1985.

Real (scientific) cognitive psychology (e.g., Nisbett and Ross 1980; Kahneman, Slovic, and Tversky 1982) does not lend itself to diagnoses of irrationality, although neither does actual affect psychology; the goal of all scientific psychology is to *explain* behavior, including errors, not to explain it away. The explaining-it-away vocabulary deployed by Shiller and Akerlof is not based on scientific psychology, even when it is describing findings of cognitive psychology. It is mere psychologistic rhetoric that miscasts the interesting cultural-epistemological "story" that Shiller and Akerlof tell, about how people come to make economic mistakes, as if it were a tale of emotions run wild. The backdrop "psychology" here has not even advanced from Plato (who pitted emotions against reason) to Aristotle, let alone to modern empirically based psychology (e.g., Gigerenzer 2008). Moreover, the cognitive psychology of heuristics and biases is largely endogenous to the individual mind (presumably by means of biological processes), rather than being "social" in origin, as Shiller and Akerlof maintain. But our main objection is that Shiller and Akerlof provide little evidence that primitive Platonic psychological forces are at work in causing asset bubbles in general or the financial crisis in particular; for instance, Shiller (2005, 20) ascribes the illusion that housing has always been a good investment to the fact that when people sell their houses, so much time has usually passed that they misinterpret inflation-induced price increases as real investment payoffs. There is nothing irrational about such misinterpretations; yet the vocabulary of irrationality lends itself to vulgar (non-)explanations.

Chapter 2. Capital Adequacy Regulations and the Financial Crisis:
Bankers' and Regulators' Errors

1. This is not true of normal stock market transactions, which take place in "secondary" equities markets where investors buy shares of stock from other investors. Ultimately all of this stock was initially obtained by buying it from the issuing corporation, but most stock trading is between subsequent investors in that stock, not between the bank or other corporation and its investors.

2. See Tarullo 2008, 42–43.

3. Charles Rochet (2010, 30), however, contends that "the favorable treatment of mortgage risk was a response to demands made by American politicians."

4. Well-capitalized banks must maintain not only a minimum of 10 percent risk-adjusted capital (Tier 1 plus Tier 2), but a minimum level of Tier 1 risk-adjusted capital of 6 percent, and a Tier 1 leverage ceiling of 5 percent, i.e., a minimum level of non-risk-adjusted capital of 5 percent (FDIC Rules and Regulations, § 325.103). These complications are ignored in the subsequent examples for the sake of simplicity.

5. These scenarios are for illustrative purposes only. In reality, a U.S. commercial bank cannot legally be leveraged at 50:1; see previous note.

6. As well as the U.S. financial regulators, who released a proposal for using credit ratings to judge the risk and therefore the appropriate level of capital for senior (AAA-rated) asset-backed securities in 1994; see Chapter 3.

7. The Recourse Rule was officially called the 2001 Final Rule on Risk-Based Capital Guidelines; Capital Adequacy Guidelines; Capital Maintenance: Capital Treatment of Recourse, Direct Credit Substitutes and Residual Interests in Asset Securitizations. 66 Fed. Reg. 59614 (November 29, 2001).

8. 59 Fed. Reg. 27116 (May 25, 1994).

9. 62 Fed. Reg. 59943 (November 5, 1997); 65 Fed. Reg. 57993 (September 27, 2000).

10. See Mabel 2001 and Smith 2002 for definitions and explanations of the various types of credit enhancement covered by the Rule.

11. Cf. 66 Fed. Reg. 59616.

12. Brief treatments of the effects of Recourse Rule can be found in Friedman 2009; Kling 2009, 2010; Acharya and Richardson 2009a, ch. 2, and 2009b; Jablecki and Machaj 2009; Taylor 2009; and Wallison 2009a.

13. We wish we could display data on the change over time in the proportion of ABS and PLMBS that were rated AA or AAA, but we have not been able to find such data.

14. Blundell-Wignall and Atkinson also argue that the behavior of Citigroup anticipated Basel II's eventual adoption in the United States, but we find this implausible, because much of the ratings arbitrage that they document at Citigroup occurred *before* Basel II was announced in 2004 or finalized in 2005, and the differences between Basel II and the Recourse Rule were in most cases negligible.

15. Obviously this is an oversimplification: bankers presumably cared about all these factors, among which there were tradeoffs. (Moreover, two of the three factors—yield and capital relief—are eventually supposed to translate into profit, when weighed against risk.) Thus, if the yield on AA PLMBS had been even higher, they probably would have found some purchasers among commercial banks.

16. That is, unless they had raised capital or sold assets during those three months sufficient to bring them back above the 8 percent legal capital minimum, in which case, however, one again wonders at the purpose of the legal minimum. If the idea is to give bankers time to "work things out," a special provision of bankruptcy law might work just as well, but without requiring bankers in the meantime to change the composition of their asset portfolio and engage in elaborate off-balance-sheet activities so as not to waste capital on a pointless regulatory "cushion." We are not suggesting this as a policy proposal, but are trying to emphasize that the net effect of legal capital minima—promoting regulatory capital arbitrage so that banks do not fall below the "well" or "adequately" capitalized levels—probably is not mitigated very much by the uncertainty of a three-month window in which regulators decide whether a bank's management is adequately doing what needs to be done if the bank is to escape seizure, and if not, should be dismissed. See GAO 2007, 13–14.

Chapter 3. The Interaction of Regulations and the Great Recession: Fetishizing Market Prices

1. *Accounting for Certain Investments in Debt and Equity Securities*, Statement of Financial Accounting Standards 115 (FASB 1993).

2. No two *products* are identical, even if we are dealing with physically identical objects, because consumers' response to a physical object will vary according to contingent (broadly speaking, historical as well as idiosyncratic) circumstances. An iPad purchased in 2010 may strike a given consumer as a wonderful innovation, while the same consumer would not think so two years later, and a different consumer in 2010 might consider a physically identical iPad a waste of money or an affront to the pleasures of the bound paper book. If Apple were to forecast 2011 sales (let alone 2012 sales) as a straight-line extrapolation of 2010 sales, it would not stay in business for long. In other words, the same physical object will be categorized differently by different people at the same time, or by the same person at different times; the producer's "job," to use Stiglitz's language, is not to ferret out "the relevant information," but to *interpret* which information is relevant, based on theories about how consumers are categorizing a certain product now and how they might do so differently in the future.

3. *Fair Value Measurements*, Statement of Financial Accounting Standards 157 (FASB 2006), §40.

4. We are bracketing asset sales caused by the seller's liquidity needs, or other differences between buyer and seller over the utility of the asset to them personally—as with consumption goods—rather than asset sales caused by different views of the income potential or eventual resale value of the asset.

5. *Accounting for Certain Investments in Debt and Equity Securities*, §16.

6. *Disclosures About Fair Values of Financial Instruments*, Statement of Financial Accounting Standards 107 (FASB 1991).

7. *Accounting by Creditors for Impairment of a Loan—an Amendment of FASB Statements No. 5 and 15*, Statement of Financial Accounting Standards 114 (FASB 1993).

8. One might think that this provision gives the banks, through their accountants, the power to circumvent MTM simply by failing to declare an asset other-than-temporarily impaired (OTTI). But here FAS 115 interacts with a statute, the Sarbanes-Oxley Act, that was enacted just after the Recourse Rule went into effect: "After the passage of the Sarbanes-Oxley Act in 2002, the role of public company auditors shifted from service provider to regulator. Auditors began to exercise much more authority over the financial statements of their clients, and the Financial Accounting Standards Board (FASB) was crowned by the SEC as the rule maker for the auditing industry. The auditors could not defy FASB, and as a practical matter, public companies could not defy their auditors in this new regime" (Burton 2009, 130).

9. *Fair Value Measurements*, Statement of Financial Accounting Standards 157 (FASB 2006).

10. Ibid., §5.

11. A third method, relying on either "consensus pricing services" or "unobservable inputs" that reflect a firm's own estimates of valuation, was used for 7 percent of the banks' assets. This method may sound like a loophole that would allow a bank to undo the effects of MTM, by estimating an asset based on cash-flow projections rather than market sentiment, but accountants, not banks themselves, make the actual determinations, and these would not be made to begin with had the accountants not already decided that an asset was OTTI, and hence must be marked down.

12. These figures, drawn from Lehman Brothers 2008, Fig. 4, include SIV assets, which had been consolidated onto banks' balance sheets by the end of the fourth quarter of 2007. See, e.g., IMF 2008a, Fig. 2.2; and Gorton 2008.

13. In principle, the three agencies might at least have competed with each other, although in reality they seem to have found it more profitable to allow clients to "ratings shop" so as to find the most lenient rater of a particular security; if there was any competition, it was competition to lower standards. The lowering of standards may have been encouraged by the Recourse Rule and other regulations' requirements of two NRSRO ratings (Jones 2008), which would have left a dissident agency bereft of any business if it did not play along with the other two (which could then have monopolized the two-ratings business between them). Given the two-ratings regulations, three happened to be the ideal number to keep the agencies' methods fairly homogeneous and to keep any doubts about each other's methods quiet. And it may explain why their standards began an apparent decline after Fitch, long a minor agency (albeit one of the three NRSROs), became a serious player in the 1990s.

14. In 2003 the SEC granted NRSRO status to a Canadian bond rater, and in 2005 to an insurance-company rater (White 2011, 393), but it does not appear that either company tried to compete with the Big Three in rating asset-backed securities.

15. From the report of the BIS (2005, 27, emphasis added): "Although high entry costs—*possibly aided by regulation*—have limited the number of agencies active in structured finance markets, competition among the agencies and from sophisticated arrangers appears to have promoted continual improvements in structured finance rating methodologies." However, the report notes that "CDO rating methodologies used by the three major rating agencies Fitch, Moody's and Standard and Poor's are broadly similar" (19), and it does *not* note that the NRSRO designation was an insurmountable barrier to entry, not just a high one. It seems that the regulators were dimly aware of regulations surrounding the rating agencies but were not interested in finding out exactly what they were. What interested them instead was the moral hazard posed by the "issuer pays business model" used by the rating agencies.

16. 66 Fed. Reg. 59614 (November 29, 2001), 59626.

17. 59 Fed. Reg. 27116 (May 25, 1994).

18. 62 Fed. Reg. 59943 (November 5, 1997), 59951.

19. 65 Fed. Reg. 12320 (March 8, 2000), 12323–24.

20. "The Silence of Mammon," *Economist*, December 17, 2009.

21. But see DeCanio 2000 and 2006, which emphasize the autonomy that regulators and other state officials enjoy due to the public's ignorance of their actions.

22. Nouriel Roubini did predict the main features of the financial crisis and the Great Recession in 2006 (see Roubini and Mihm 2010, 1–3). However, he was right for the wrong reason: He foresaw a financial crisis and a worldwide recession caused by high leverage, after having in earlier years foreseen crises caused by a run on U.S. Treasury debt, protectionism, derivatives, easy money, and hedge funds (Hoffman 2009). In fact, however, the causal agents in the Great Recession—commercial banks, as opposed to investment banks—maintained flat leverage ratios throughout the 2000s, as can be seen in Figure 2.3; and, if anything, they effectively *deleveraged* by shifting into low-risk-weighted assets, as explained in Chapter 2.

Chapter 4. Capitalism and the Crisis: Ignorance, Heterogeneity, and Systemic Risk

1. For a brief explanation of the clearinghouse mechanism, see Gorton 2008, 64.

2. We have seen in Chapter 1 that Stiglitz (2010b) is dismissive of the very concept of "uncertainty," such that he might dismiss, too, the possibility that the regulators could have been *wrong* in their predictions about the "riskiness" of various asset classes.

3. This may sound reminiscent of the logic of the TBTF theory that we disputed in Chapter 1. But we did not argue there that the cost of debt—whether a bank's debt, a mortgagor's debt, or a national government's debt—has no effect on the behavior of

the debtor. We merely disputed whether the reason for the low cost of debt for large banks was investors' conviction that these banks would be bailed out.

4. 66 Fed. Reg. 59614 (November 29, 2001), 59626.

5. 65 Fed. Reg. 12320 (March 8, 2000), 12323–24.

6. 59 Fed. Reg. 27116 (May 1994), 27127.

7. Ibid.

8. Competition would not make these human beings any less fallible, but it would allow rating companies that used methods that consistently led to errors to be displaced by companies that used better methods.

9. Including ourselves, of course. Ideology, or at least the use of less comprehensive cognitive schemas, is *inevitable.* However, some schemas may more accurately model the data that they screen than others do.

10. 15 U.S.C.A. § 78o-7

11. No news about this crucial aspect of the rating agencies can be found even in the best journalistic reports before and during the crisis, such as Dizard 2009, Jones 2008 and 2009, and Plender 2009 in the *Financial Times*; Norris 2009 in the *New York Times* business section (or Morgenson 2008 on the front page of the *New York Times*); Smith 2008b in Bloomberg.com. The sole exception we found is Lowenstein 2008, which buried the information about the 1975 SEC decision, without comment, deep inside an excellent article in the *New York Times Magazine*.

12. Given our critique of the economic mainstream, we hope it is clear that we are not implying that when economists agree, they must be right. Just as any given economist who disagrees with his or her peers may be mistaken, so may an economist who agrees with the consensus. See Bennett and Friedman 2008, 201–6 and passim.

13. A law that imposes fines, jail sentences, or the death penalty for an action does not actually force anyone to obey it. People still have the choice of disobedience if they consider the penalty less important than whatever they view as being at stake if they obey the law. Even pointing a gun at someone and threatening him or her does not, strictly speaking, force her to cooperate; only grabbing someone and physically restraining her limbs does that. On the other hand, in common usage all of these actions are seen as "coercive." By that standard, threatening a bank with higher capital charges if it invests in assets the regulators deem to be relatively unsafe is equivalent to threatening a taxpayer with a fine if he or she does not comply with the Internal Revenue Code.

14. The evolutionary filter that "runs" this process is the ultimate need to sell products that consumers like at prices consumers will pay. Fallible consumer like/ dislike decisions constitute the final selection mechanism that leads to the extinction of maladapted *businesses*—not individuals (Friedman 2006, 477–81). For this reason, Alchian's comparison of economics with evolution has nothing to do with Social Darwinism, as a careless journalist has recently suggested (Fox 2009, 93; cf. Stiglitz 2010a, 273). Individuals enter the evolution analogy, as consumers, only in the form of the "environment" that determines the competing businesses' adaptive fitness. Nor does

Alchian attach normative weight to adaptivity per se, as Social Darwinists did. Only if one inserts the normative premise that consumers' felt needs should be attended to can the competitive economic process described by Alchian qualify (arguably) as "good." One would insert this premise only if one believed that consumers, as human beings, were entitled to something like happiness, satisfaction, or relief from discomfort. But such a premise is inherently egalitarian (see Sen 1979), contradicting the Social Darwinist notion that "unfit" human beings should be left to perish.

15. The BIS researchers worried about moral hazard caused by the "issuer-pays" business model, but since they did not seem to be aware that the small number of rating corporations was due to their legal protection, they concluded that "market discipline" would handle the problem; see Chapter 3.

16. If we relax the usual assumptions about economic agents' motivations and include public humiliation as something that people are eager to avoid, however, the case for the moral-hazard theory of deposit insurance is strengthened, because the depositors would be less likely to make failed bank managers the object of their fury if the depositors were bailed out.

17. Winston 2006 shows that in every area except environmental regulation, regulatory policy has produced more costs than benefits, often in response to Type I errors.

Conclusion

1. Throughout, we have based this assertion on Table 1.1, from which Tables 2.2 and 2.3 are also derived. Table 1.1 consolidates data from the widely cited Figure 4 (e.g., Acharya and Richardson 2011, Table 1.1, and Krishnamurthy 2008, Table 1) of a Lehman Brothers report dated April 11, 2008 and written by Akhil Mago, Rahul Sabarwal, and Madhuri Iyer. This is the only comprehensive data source on the distribution of mortgage bonds, including their ratings, that we could find. The report explains that the data come from "Federal Reserve, FDIC, [and] websites of various financial institutions." We surmise that the first two sources provided the data on the PLMBS holdings of investment banks, commercial banks, and thrifts, and these data are very closely corroborated by other sources, such as the IMF's October 2009 Global Financial Stability Report (Table 1.2) for total mortgages and securitized mortgages held by U.S. banks, and a report by a different team of Lehman analysts half a year earlier (Lehman Brothers 2007) on the 100-percent dominance of AAA-rated PLMBS and CDOs among U.S. banks (on the balance sheet). The Lehman 2008 data are also consistent with an analysis by Greenlaw, Hatzius, Kashyap, and Shin (2008), based on privately provided data from Goldman Sachs. However, the websites of various financial institutions cannot be expected to be a precise source of information about the investment portfolios of thousands of insurance companies, REITs, and hedge funds. This consideration suggests that the 2008 Lehman analysts may have underestimated the amount held by these investors. On the other hand, the total amount that the Lehman analysts attributed in April 2008 to all investments in PLMBS, $2.233 trillion,

closely tracks the Federal Reserve's July 2008 Statistical Supplement, Table 1.54, line 71, which gives the total of securitized U.S. mortgages outstanding at the end of 2007 as $2.132 trillion (http://www.federalreserve.gov/pubs/supplement/2008/07/table1_54.htm). It appears, then, that Lehman extrapolated from its website discoveries to account for approximately all PLMBS purchased by the various types of private investor that they listed. We remain skeptical about the specific amounts attributed to different subclasses of nonbank investor, though, and remedy the problem in Tables 2.2 and 2.3.

2. See Caplan 2007, 183–85.

3. In Friedman 1996, one of us does criticize the application of this assumption to the political sphere.

4. For a critique, see Evans and Friedman 2011.

Appendix I: Scholarship About the Corporate-Compensation Hypothesis

1. Bebchuk et al. (2009, nn6–8) list as the commentators to whom they are responding Fahlenbrach and Stulz, Kevin Murphy, Joseph Grundfest, and Jeffrey Friedman.

2. Unfortunately, while Bebchuk and his colleagues provide data on all the revenue the top five executives at the two banks *took in* over the 2002–8 period, they provide figures for how much they *lost* by not selling stock before the crisis only in the cases of the two CEOs, Cayne and Fuld, for whom these data had already been reported by the commentators to whom Bebchuk et al. are responding. The gigantic amount that the executives left on the table, however, is the only relevant issue, since it suggests that they had little idea that their actions, or the actions they had allowed, had endangered their firms. The Bebchuk paper's failure to come to grips with this issue is manifest in its failure to investigate the total losses of *all* the executives at the two firms during the crisis.

3. Bebchuk et al. may be trying to prove that the executives *profited* from the actions that led to the crisis, even though they made net *paper* losses: despite the losses, after all, they emerged from the crisis much richer than they were at the beginning of the pre-crisis period. But nobody questions that. The question is whether the actions they took in the pre-crisis years were *deliberately* reckless responses to the incentives created by their compensation packages, not whether they got rich because of their actions (or factors out of their control). For instance, Cayne and Fuld could have gotten three times as rich if they had sold their stock before the crisis, suggesting that they did not know that their firms were at risk.

4. Bebchuk et al. consistently conflate normative and historical issues, or "policy implications" "going forward" with the causes of what happened in the past. Naturally we see policy tunnel vision at work (see Chapter 1).

5. Specifically, a UBS report to the Swiss government shows that UBS employees had performance incentives to buy CDOs that, despite their triple-A rating, had been

built from mezzanine tranches of MBS, and which therefore brought in higher revenue streams. However, there is no evidence that the employees knew the risks involved and suppressed the information so as to increase their compensation. Rather, the responsibility for evaluating risk was assigned to a different group of employees, and they "relied on the AAA rating of certain Subprime positions, although the CDOs were built from lower rated tranches of RMBS. This appears to have been common across the industry" (UBS 2008, 39).

Appendix II: The Basel Rules off the Balance Sheet

1. CDOs, in turn, tranched PLMBS and other ABS that were first warehoused in conduits.

2. However, residual interests, such as retained equity tranches, that were provided directly by a sponsoring bank, might constitute a form of credit enhancement that would count as "recourse" to the sponsor, triggering capital charges, because if a sponsor holds residual interests, it suggests that there was no "true sale" of the assets from the sponsor into the SPE. "Consequently, the residual interest is held by another SPV, not the sponsor. The 'true sale' occurs with respect to this second vehicle" (Gorton and Souleles 2005, 11).

3. Moody's and Fitch use different symbols to designate what S&P calls AAA, AA, and other levels of bond safety, and they likewise use different short-term symbols, but we follow the convention of using S&P symbols, which are the most widely known.

4. In the interest of simplicity, we have massively understated the various uses to which ABCP conduits were put, as readers of Poszar et al. 2010 will discover.

5. 69 Fed. Reg. 44,909.

6. 69 Fed. Reg. 44,908–25 (July 28, 2009).

7. 69 Fed. Reg. 44,909–10.

8. From 2002 to 2004, European banks also slowed the pace of ABCP issuance, as can be seen in Figure 2.3. This appears to have been due to European banks waiting "until the dust settles" to see the competitive lay of the land once the U.S. regulatory situation was clear (BancOne Capital Markets 2004, 5). We thank Philipp Schnabl for pointing us to this source.

REFERENCES

Acemoglu, Daron. 2011. "The Crisis of 2008: Lessons for and from Economics." In Friedman 2011.

Acharya, Viral V., and Matthew Richardson, eds. 2009a. *Restoring Financial Stability: How to Repair a Failed System.* New York University Stern School of Business/ John Wiley.

————. 2009b. "Causes of the Financial Crisis." *Critical Review* 21 (2–3): 195–210.

————. 2011. "How Securitization Concentrated Risk in the Financial Sector." In Friedman 2011.

Acharya, Viral V., and Philipp Schnabl. 2010. "Do Global Banks Spread Global Imbalances? Asset-Backed Commercial Paper During the Financial Crisis of 2007–09." *IMF Economic Review* 58: 37–73.

Acharya, Viral V., Philipp Schnabl, and Gustavo Suarez. 2010. "Securitization Without Risk Transfer." Working Paper 15730, National Bureau of Economic Research. February.

Akerlof, George A. 1970. "The Market for 'Lemons:' Qualitative Uncertainty and the Market Mechanism." *Quarterly Journal of Economics* 89: 488–500.

Akerlof, George A., and Robert J. Shiller. 2009. *Animal Spirits: How Human Psychology Drives the Economy, and Why It Matters for Global Capitalism.* Princeton, N.J.: Princeton University Press.

Alcaly, Roger. 2010. "How They Killed the Economy." *New York Review of Books,* March 25.

Alchian, Armen A. 1950. "Uncertainty, Evolution, and Economic Theory." *Journal of Political Economy* 58 (3): 211–21.

Ashcraft, Adam B., and Til Schuermann. 2008. "Understanding the Securitization of Subprime Mortgage Credit." Federal Reserve Bank of New York, Staff Report 318, March.

Bair, Sheila C. 2010. "Statement of Sheila C. Bair, Chairman, Federal Deposit Insurance Corporation, on the Causes and Current State of the Financial Crisis, Before the Financial Crisis Inquiry Commission." January 14.

Baker, Dean, and Travis McArthur. 2009. "The Value of the 'Too Big to Fail' Big Bank Subsidy." Washington, D.C.: Center for Economic and Policy Research, September.

Balachandran, Sudhakar, Bruce Kogut, and Hitesh Harnal. 2010. "The Probability of Default, Excessive Risk, and Executive Compensation: A Study of Financial Services Firms from 1995 to 2008." Paper presented at conference on Governance, Executive Compensation and Excessive Risk in the Financial Services Industry, Sanford C. Bernstein & Co. Center for Leadership and Ethics, Columbia Business School, May 27–28.

BancOne Capital Markets. 2004. "Asset Backed Commercial Paper: 2003 Review and 2004 Outlook."

Bank for International Settlements (BIS). 2005. "The Role of Ratings in Structured Finance: Issues and Implications." Report submitted by a Working Group Established by the Committee on the Global Financial System, BIS. January.

Barnett-Hart, Anna Katherine. 2009. "The Story of the CDO Market Meltdown: An Empirical Analysis." Honors thesis, Department of Economics, Harvard College.

Barth, James R. 2010. *The Rise and Fall of the U.S. Mortgage and Credit Markets.* New York: Wiley.

Barth, James R., Tong Li, and Triphon Phumiwasana. 2008. "The U.S. Financial Crisis: Credit Crunch and Yield Spreads." Manuscript, Auburn University.

Basel Committee on Banking Supervision (BCBS). 1988. "International Convergence of Capital Measurement and Capital Standards" (Basel I). Basel: Bank for International Settlements, July.

———. 1998. "International Convergence of Capital Measurement and Capital Standards" (Basel I, updated to reflect several textual changes made since Basel accords of July 1988). Basel: Bank for International Settlements, April.

———. 1999. "A New Capital Adequacy Framework." Consultative paper issued by the Basel Committee on Banking Supervision, June.

———. 2006. "International Convergence of Capital Measurement and Capital Standards: A Revised Framework, Comprehensive Version" (Basel II plus elements of Basel I left in place by it). Basel: Bank for International Settlements, June.

———. 2009. "Report on Special Purpose Entities." Basel: Joint Forum, Bank for International Settlements.

Bass, Kyle. 2007. "Testimony before the Subcommittee on Capital Markets, Insurance, and Government Sponsored Enterprises." September 27.

Bebchuk, Lucien A., Alma Cohen, and Holger Spamann. 2009. "The Wages of Failure: Executive Compensation at Bear Stearns and Lehman [sic] 2002–2008." Working paper, Harvard Law School, November 22.

Bebchuk, Lucien A., and Holger Spamann. 2009. "Regulating Bankers' Pay." Discussion paper, John M. Olin Center, Harvard Law School. Revised version, October.

Bennett, Stephen Earl, and Jeffrey Friedman. 2008. "The Irrelevance of Economic Theory to Understanding Economic Ignorance." *Critical Review* 20 (3): 195–258.

Bernanke, Ben S. 2005. "Testimony Before the Joint Economic Committee." October 20.

———. 2010. "Monetary Policy and the Housing Bubble." Address at annual meetings of the American Economic Association, Atlanta, January 3. http://www.feder alreserve.gov/newsevents/speech/bernanke20100103a.htm.

Bhattacharya, Sudipto, Arnoud W. A. Boot, and Anjan V. Thakor. 1998. "The Economics of Bank Regulation." *Journal of Money, Credit and Banking* 30: 745–70.

Bhidé, Amar. 2009. "An Accident Waiting to Happen." *Critical Review* 21 (2–3): 211–48.

———. 2010. *A Call for Judgment: Sensible Finance for a Dynamic Economy.* New York: Oxford University Press.

Blinder, Alan S. 2009. "Crazy Compensation and the Crisis." *Wall Street Journal*, May 28.

Blundell-Wignall, Adrian, and Paul Atkinson. 2008. "The Sub-prime Crisis: Causal Distortions and Regulatory Reform." Discussion paper, Organization for Economic Cooperation and Development.

Boettke, Peter J. 1997. "Where Did Economics Go Wrong? Modern Economics as a Flight from Reality." *Critical Review* 11 (1): 11–64.

Bolton, Patrick, Hamid Mehran, and Joel Shapiro. 2010. "Executive Compensation and Risk Taking." (Preliminary and incomplete draft.) Paper presented at conference on Governance, Executive Compensation and Excessive Risk in the Financial Services Industry, Sanford C. Bernstein & Co. Center for Leadership and Ethics, Columbia Business School, May 27–28.

Bordo, Michael. 1985. "Financial Crises, Banking Crises, Stock Market Crashes and the Money Supply: Some International Evidence, 1870–1933." *Revista di Storia Economica* 2: 41–78.

Brereton, Natasha. 2010. "Data Show Big Exposure for Banks in Euro Zone." *Wall Street Journal*, June 14.

Burton, Edwin T. 2009. "The Mark-to-Market Controversy and the Valuation of Financial Institutions." In *Insights into the Global Financial Crisis*, ed. Laurence B. Siegel. Charlottesville, Va.: Research Foundation of the CFA Institute.

Caballero, Ricardo J. 2010. "Macroeconomics After the Crisis: Time to Deal with the Pretense-of-Knowledge Syndrome." *Journal of Economic Perspectives* 24: 85–102.

Calomiris, Charles W. 2010. "The Political Lessons of Depression-Era Banking Reform." *Oxford Review of Economic Policy* 26: 540–60.

Caplan, Bryan. 2007. *The Myth of the Rational Voter.* Princeton, N.J.: Princeton University Press.

Carlson, Mark, and Kris James Mitchener. 2006. "Branch Banking, Bank Competition, and Financial Stability." *Journal of Money, Credit, and Banking* 38 (5): 1293–328.

Cassidy, John. 2008. "Subprime Suspect." *New Yorker*, March 31.

———. 2009. *How Markets Fail: The Logic of Economic Calamities.* New York: Farrar, Straus and Giroux.

Cheng, Ing-Haw, Harrison Hong, and Jose Scheinkman. 2009. "Yesterday's Heroes: Compensation and Creative Risk-Taking." Manuscript, SSRI, October.

Cohan, William D. 2009. *House of Cards: A Tale of Hubris and Wretched Excess on Wall Street*. New York: Doubleday.

Cohen, Richard. 2009. "How Is Cramer to Know What Insiders Don't?" *Investor's Business Daily*, March 17.

Colander, David, et al. 2011. "The Financial Crisis and the Systemic Failure of the Economics Profession." In Friedman 2011.

Condon, Bernard, and Nathan Vardi. 2009. "The Banker Who Said No." *Forbes.com*, April 3.

Converse, Philip E. [1964] 2006. "The Nature of Belief Systems in Mass Publics." *Critical Review* 18 (1–3): 1–74.

Core, John E., and Wayne R. Guay. 2010. "Is There a Case for Regulating Executive Pay in the Financial Services Industry?" Manuscript, Wharton School, January 25.

Cotter, Richard V. 1966. "Capital Ratios and Capital Adequacy." *National Banking Review* 3: 34–46.

Coval, Joshua, Jakub Jurek, and Erik Stafford. 2009. "The Economics of Structured Finance." *Journal of Economic Perspectives* 23: 3–25.

Cox, Rob, and Dwight Cass. 2009. "Tests May Spur Bank Mergers." *New York Times*, May 8.

Crews, Clyde Wayne, Jr. 2010. "Ten Thousand Commandments: An Annual Snapshot of the Federal Regulatory State." Washington, D.C.: Competitive Enterprise Institute.

Dash, Eric. 2009. "Banks Holding Up in Tests, but May Still Need Aid." New York Times, April 9.

DeCanio, Samuel. 2000. "Bringing the State Back In . . . Again." *Critical Review* 14 (2–3): 139–46.

———. 2006. "Mass Opinion and American Political Development." *Critical Review* 18 (1–3): 143–56.

Dewatripont, Mathias, Jean-Charles Rochet, and Jean Tirole. 2010. *Balancing the Banks: Global Lessons from the Financial Crisis*. Princeton, N.J.: Princeton University Press.

Dimon, James. 2009. "Letter to Shareholders." JPMorgan Chase Annual Report 2008.

Dizard, John. 2009. "The Inside Story on Reforms Is that There Is No Story." *Financial Times*, February 17: 10.

Dowd, Kevin, ed. 1992a. *The Experience of Free Banking*. London: Routledge.

———. 1992b. "U.S. Banking in the 'Free Banking' Period." In Dowd 1992a.

Evans, Anthony, and Jeffrey Friedman. 2011. "Search vs. Browse: A Theory of Error Grounded in Radical (Not Rational) Ignorance." *Critical Review* 23 (1–2).

Fahlenbrach, Rüdiger, and René M. Stulz. 2009. "Bank CEO Incentives and the Credit Crisis." Manuscript, Fisher College of Business, Ohio State University.

FDIC (Federal Deposit Insurance Corporation). 1984. *The First Fifty Years: A History of the FDIC, 1933–1983*. Washington, D.C.: FDIC.

Federal Reserve Board. 2007. "Flow of Funds Account of the United States." Z1. March 8.

Federal Reserve Board. 2008. *Profits and Balance Sheet Developments at U.S. Commercial Banks in 2007.* Washington, D.C.: Federal Reserve System.

Fischhoff, Baruch. 1982. "For Those Condemned to Study the Past: Heuristics and Biases in Hindsight." In Kahneman et al. 1982.

Foucault, Michel. 1979. *Discipline and Punish: The Birth of the Prison.* New York: Vintage.

Fox, Justin. 2009. *The Myth of the Rational Market.* New York: HarperCollins.

Freeman, Gaylord A., Jr. 1952. "The Problems of Adequate Bank Capital." Analysis Prepared for the Illinois Bankers Association.

Friedman, Benjamin M. 2009. "The Failure of the Economy and of the Economists." *New York Review of Books*, May 28.

Friedman, Jeffrey. 1996. "Introduction: Economic Models of Politics." In *The Rational-Choice Controversy: Economic Models of Politics Reconsidered*, ed. Jeffrey Friedman. New Haven, Conn.: Yale University Press.

———. 2006. "Taking Ignorance Seriously: Rejoinder to Critics." *Critical Review* 18 (4): 467–532.

———. 2009. "A Crisis of Politics, Not Economics: Complexity, Ignorance, and Policy Failure." *Critical Review* 21 (2–3): 127–84.

———, ed. 2011. *What Caused the Financial Crisis.* Philadelphia: University of Pennsylvania Press.

Friedman, Milton, and Anna Jacobson Schwartz. 1963. *A Monetary History of the United States.* Princeton, N.J.: Princeton University Press.

Frydman, Roman, and Michael D. Goldberg. 2009. "Financial Markets and the State: Price Swings, Risk, and the Scope of Regulation" Working Paper 29, Center on Capitalism and Society at Columbia University, February.

GAO (Government Accountability Office). 2007. "Deposit Insurance: Assessment of Regulators' Use of Prompt Corrective Action Provisions and FDIC's New Deposit Insurance System." Report to Congressional Committees, February.

———. 2009. "Fannie Mae and Freddie Mac: Analysis of Options for Revising the Housing Enterprises' Long-Term Structures." Report to Congressional Committees, September.

Geanakoplos, John. 2010. "Solving the Present Crisis and Managing the Leverage Cycle." Paper presented to the Financial Crisis Inquiry Commission, Washington, D.C., February 27–28.

Gigerenzer, Gerd. 2008. *Rationality for Mortals: How People Cope with Uncertainty.* New York: Oxford University Press.

Gilliam, Lee. 2005. "Accounting Consolidation versus Capital Calculation: The Conflict Over Asset-Backed Commercial Paper." *North Carolina Banking Institute Journal* 9: 291–315.

Gjerstad, Steven, and Vernon L. Smith. 2011. "Monetary Policy, Credit Extension, and Housing Bubbles: 2008 and 1929." In Friedman 2011.

Gorton, Gary. 2008. "The Panic of 2007." Prepared for Federal Reserve Bank of Kansas City Jackson Hole Conference, August.

———. 2009. "Slapped in the Face by the Invisible Hand: Banking and the Panic of 2007." Prepared for Federal Reserve Bank of Atlanta 2009 Financial Markets Conference, "Financial Innovation and Crisis," May 11–13.

Gorton, Gary, and Nicholas S. Souleles. 2005. "Special Purpose Vehicles and Securitization." Manuscript, National Bureau of Economic Research.

Graham, Jed. 2009. "Geithner Calls for Systemic Regulator and More Capital." *Investor's Business Daily*, March 27.

Greenspan, Alan. 2007. *The Age of Turbulence: Adventures in a New World.* New York: Penguin.

———. 2009. "The Fed Didn't Cause the Housing Bubble." *Wall Street Journal*, March 11, A15.

———. 2010. "The Crisis," 2nd draft. Manuscript.

Greenlaw, David, Jan Hatzius, Anil K. Kashyap, and Hyun Song Shin. 2008. "Leveraged Losses: Lessons from the Mortgage Market Meltdown." U.S. Monetary Policy Forum Report 2.

Grossman, Sanford J., and Joseph E. Stiglitz. 1980. "On the Impossibility of Informationally Efficient Markets." *American Economic Review* 70: 393–408.

Hanson, Samuel, Anil K. Kashyap, and Jeremy C. Stein. 2010. "A Macroprudential Approach to Financial Regulation." Manuscript, Harvard University and National Bureau of Economic Statistics. First draft: July.

Harrington, Shannon D., and Elizbeth Hester. 2007. "Citigroup to Consolidate Seven SIVs on Balance Sheet" (Update 3). Bloomberg, December 13.

Hart, Oliver, and Luigi Zingales. 2010. "Curbing Risk on Wall Street." *National Affairs* 3 (Spring): 20–34.

Hartgraves, Al L., and George J. Benston. 2002. "The Evolving Accounting Standards for Special Purpose Entities and Consolidations." *Accounting Horizons* 16 (3): 245–58.

He, Zhiguo, In Gu Khand, and Arvind Krishnamurthy. 2009. "Balance Sheet Adjustment." Presentation at Jacques Polak Research Conference, Washington, D.C., November 5–6.

Hellwig, Martin. 2010. "Capital Regulation After the Crisis: Business as Usual?" Preprints, Max Planck Institute for Research on Collective Goods, Bonn.

Hetzel, Robert L. 2009. "Should Increased Regulation of Bank Risk-Taking Come from the Regulators or from the Market?" *Economic Quarterly* 95 (2): 161–200.

Hirschman, Albert O. 1970. *Exit, Voice, and Loyalty: Responses to Decline in Firms, Organizations, and States.* Cambridge, Mass.: Harvard University Press.

Hoffman, Damien. 2009. "Is Nouriel Roubini a False Prophet?" *Wall St. Cheat Sheet*, August 19.

Ikeda, Sanford. 2003. "How Compatible Are Public Choice and Austrian Political Economy?" *Review of Austrian Economics* 16 (4): 63–75.

IMF (International Monetary Fund). 2008a. "Global Financial Stability Report: Containing Systemic Risks and Restoring Financial Soundness." April. Washington, D.C.: IMF.

———. 2008b. "Global Financial Stability Report: Financial Stress and Deleveraging." October. Washington, D.C.: IMF.

———. 2009a. "Global Financial Stability Report: Responding to the Financial Crisis and Measuring Systemic Risk." April. Washington, D.C.: IMF.

———. 2009b. "Global Financial Stability Report: Navigating the Challenges Ahead." October. Washington, D.C.: IMF.

Isaac, William M. 2009. "Testimony Before the Subcommittee on Capital Markets, Insurance, and Government Sponsored Enterprises of the Committee on Financial Services of the United States House of Representatives." March 12.

Ivashina, Victoria, and David Scharfstein. 2010. "Bank Lending During the Financial Crisis of 2008." *Journal of Financial Economics* 97(3) (September): 319–38.

Jablecki, Juliusz, and Mateusz Machaj. 2009. "The Regulated Meltdown of 2008." *Critical Review* 21 (2–3): 301–28.

———. 2011. "A Regulated Meltdown: The Basel Rule and Banks' Leverage." In Friedman 2011.

Jarsulic, Marc. 2010. *Anatomy of a Financial Crisis*. New York: Palgrave.

Johnson, Simon, and James Kwak. 2010. *13 Bankers: The Wall Street Takeover and the Next Financial Meltdown*. New York: Pantheon.

Jones, David. 2000. "Emerging Problems with the Basel Capital Accord: Regulatory Capital Arbitrage and Related Issues." *Journal of Banking and Finance* 24: 35–58.

Jones, Sam. 2008. "How Moody's Faltered." FT.com, October 17.

———. 2009. "Of Couples and Copulas." *Financial Times*, April 25–26.

Kacperczyk, Marcin, and Philipp Schnabl. 2009. "When Safe Proved Risky: Commercial Paper During the Financial Crisis of 2007–2009." Manuscript, NYU Stern School of Business. November.

Kahneman, Daniel, Paul Slovic, and Amos Tversky. 1982. *Judgment Under Uncertainty: Heuristics and Biases*. Cambridge: Cambridge University Press.

Kashyap, Anil K., Raghuram G. Rajan, and Jeremy C. Stein. 2008. "Rethinking Capital Regulation." Paper presented at Federal Reserve Bank of Kansas City symposium, "Maintaining Stability in a Changing Financial System," Jackson Hole, Wyoming, August 21–23.

Kay, Ira T. 2010. "Risk Taking or Mistake Making." Comments delivered at National Bureau of Economic Research Conference on Risk, June 17.

Keller, James. 2009. "The Myth of Systemic Collapse." RealClearMarkets.com, March 4.

Kirzner, Israel M. 1997. "Entrepreneurial Discovery and the Competitive Market Process." *Journal of Economic Literature* 35: 60–85.

Kling, Arnold. 2009. "The Unintended Consequences of International Bank Capital Standards." *Mercatus on Policy* 44 (April).

———. 2010. "The Financial Crisis: Moral Failure or Cognitive Failure?" *Harvard Journal of Law and Public Policy* 33: 507–18.

————. 2011. "Macroeconometrics: The Science of Hubris." *Critical Review* 23 (1–2).

Knight, Frank. 1921. *Risk, Uncertainty, and Profit.* Boston: Houghton Mifflin.

Kraus, Wladimir. 2011. "The Financial Crisis and the Future of Law and Economics." *Critical Review* 23 (1–2).

Krishnamurthy, Arvind. 2008. "The Financial Meltdown: Data and Diagnoses." Paper prepared for NBER Corporate Finance Credit Crisis meeting, Boston, November 20.

Kuritzkes, Andrew, and Hal Scott. 2009. "Markets Are the Best Judge of Bank Capital." *Financial Times*, September 23.

Labaton, Stephen. 1999. "Agreement Reached on Overhaul of U.S. Financial System." *New York Times*, October 23.

————. 2009. "S.E.C. Nominee Offers Plan for Tighter Regulation." *New York Times*, January 16: B3.

Lachman, Desmond. 2008. "Is U.S. Monetary Policy Really Too Loose? *The American*, September 3.

Landler, Mark, and Sheryl Gay Stolberg. 2008. "As Fingers Point in the Financial Crisis, Many of Them Are Aimed at Bush." *New York Times*, September 20.

Lane, Charles. 2010. "Contending with Paul Krugman, Part II." *Washington Post Online*, 10 June.

Lavoie, Don C. 1985. *Rivalry and Central Planning: The Socialist Calculation Debate Reconsidered.* Cambridge: Cambridge University Press.

Lehman Brothers. 2007. "Who Owns Residential Credit Risk?" U.S. Securitized Products Fixed Income Research, September 7.

————. 2008. "Residential Credit Losses—Going into Extra Innings?" U.S. Securitized Products Fixed Income Research, April 14.

Leonhardt, David. 2008. "Washington's Invisible Hand." *New York Times Magazine*, September 28.

————. 2010. "Heading Off the Next Financial Crisis." *New York Times Magazine*, March 22.

Lewis, Michael. 2010. *The Big Short: Inside the Doomsday Machine.* New York: Norton.

Levy, Ari. 2009. "Wells Fargo Assails TARP, Calls Stress Test 'Asinine.'" Bloomberg.-com, March 16.

Lewis, Michael. 2010. *The Big Short: Inside the Doomsday Machine.* New York: Norton.

Lowenstein, Roger. 2008. "Triple-A Failure." *New York Times Magazine*, April 27.

Lucchetti, Aaron, and Jeannette Neumann. 2010. "Kroll Gets a License to Shoot (Bonds)." *Wall Street Journal*, August 31.

Luce, Edward. 2009. "Subprime Explosion: Who Isn't Guilty?" Graphic: "Top Underwriters in Peak Years 2005–06." Financial Times, May 6.

Mabel, Cynthia C. 2001. "Bank Capital Requirements for Retained Interests in Securitizations." *North Carolina Banking Institute Journal* 5: 233–63.

Madrick, Jeff. 2009a. "Can They Stop the Great Recession?" *New York Review of Books*, April 8.

———. 2009b. "How We Were Ruined and What We Can Do."*New York Review of Books*, February 12.

———. 2009c. "They Didn't Regulate Enough and Still Don't." *New York Review of Books*, November 5.

McDonald, Lawrence G., with Patrick Robinson. 2009. *A Colossal Failure of Common Sense: The Inside Story of the Collapse of Lehman Brothers.* New York: Crown Business.

Mehran, Hamid, and Joshua Rosenberg. 2010. "The Effect of CEO Stock Options on Bank Investment Choice, Borrowing, and Capital." Manuscript, Federal Reserve Bank of New York Research and Statistics Group.

Mill, John Stuart. [1836] 1967. "On the Definition of Political Economy and the Method of Investigation Proper to It." In *Collected Works of John Stuart Mill*, vol. 4. Toronto: University of Toronto Press.

Morgenson, Gretchen. 2008. "Debt Watchdogs, Caught Napping." *New York Times*, December 7.

Narayanan, V. G., Fabrizio Ferri, and Lisa Brem. 2010. "Executive Pay and the Credit Crisis of 2008 (A)." Harvard Business School case study 9–109–036, rev. June 24.

Nisbett, Richard, and Lee Ross. 1980. *Human Inference: Strategies and Shortcomings of Social Judgment.* Englewood Cliffs, N.J.: Prentice-Hall.

Norris, Floyd. 2008. "Another Crisis, Another Guarantee." *New York Times*, November 25.

———. 2009. "It May Be Outrageous, But Wall Street Pay Didn't Cause the Crisis." *New York Times*, July 31.

———. 2010. "Seeking a Safer Way to Securitization." *New York Times*, February 6.

Norton, Joseph J. 1995. "Devising International Bank Supervisory Standards." *International Banking and Finance Law* 3: 46–49.

New York State Bankers Association. 1952. "A Report of the Committee on Risk Asset Ratio Study."

Office of the Comptroller of the Currency (OCC). 2009. "Testimony of Kevin J. Bailey, Deputy Comptroller, Office of the Comptroller of the Currency, before the Subcommittee on Capital Markets, Insurance, and Government Sponsored Enterprises of the Committee on Financial Services of the United States House of Representatives." March 21.

Pittman, Mark. 2007. "Betting on a Crash: The Gamble of J. Kyle Bass." *Bloomberg News*, December 19. www.nzherald.co.nz/business/news/article.cfm?c_id = 3&objected = 10484879

Pittman, Mark, Alan Katz, and David Mildenberg. 2008. "Citigroup, Wells Fargo May Loan Less After Downgrades (Update 3)." *Bloomberg.com*, April 8.

Plender, John. 2009. "Error-Laden Machine." *Financial Times*, March 3: 8.

Popper, Karl R. 1961. *The Poverty of Historicism.* New York: Harper & Row.

Posner, Richard A. 2009. *A Failure of Capitalism: The Crisis of '08 and the Descent into Depression.* Cambridge, Mass.: Harvard University Press.

Poszar, Zoltan, Tobias Adrian, Adam Ashcraft, and Hayley Boesky. 2010. "Shadow Banking." Federal Reserve Bank of New York Staff Report 458, July.

Rajan, Raghuram. 2006. "Has Financial Development Made the World Riskier?" *European Financial Management* 12: 313–64.

———. 2008. "Bankers' Pay Is Deeply Flawed." *Financial Times*, January 8.

———. 2010. *Fault Lines: How Hidden Fractures Still Threaten the World Economy.* Princeton, N.J.: Princeton University Press.

Rieker, Matthias. 2010. "At J. P. Morgan, Eye on Consumer Banking." *Wall Street Journal*, January 15.

RiskMetrics. 2008. "On the White Board." December. http://www.riskmetrics.com/on_the_whiteboard/20081215.

Rochet, Jean-Charles. 2010. "The Future of Banking Regulation." In Dewatripont et al. 2010.

Rodriguez, Robert L. 2007. "Absence of Fear." Speech, CFA Society of Chicago, June 28.

Roubini, Nouriel, and Stephen Mihm. 2010. *Crisis Economics: A Crash Course in the Future of Finance.* New York: Penguin.

Ryon, Sandra L. 1969. "History of Bank Capital Adequacy Analysis." FDIC Working Paper 69–4. Washington, D.C.: FDIC Division of Economic Research.

Salmon, Felix. 2007. "The Weakness of Marking Subprime Bonds to Market." *Seeking Alpha* (blog), December 5.

Samuelson, Paul. 1973. *Economics.* 9th ed. New York: McGraw-Hill.

Schuler, Kurt. 1992. "The World History of Free Banking: An Overview." In Dowd 1992a.

SEC (Securities and Exchange Commission). 2008. "Report and Recommendations Pursuant to Section 133 of the Emergency Economic Stabilization Act of 2008: Study on Mark-to- Market Accounting." Washington, D.C.: Office of the Chief Accountant, Division of Corporate Finance, December.

Segal, David. 2010. "The X Factor of Economics." *New York Times*, October 17.

Selgin, George A. 1988. *The Theory of Free Banking.* Totowa, N.J.: Rowman and Littlefield.

———. 1994. "Are Banking Crises Free-Market Phenomena?" *Critical Review* 8 (4): 591–608.

Sen, Amartya K. 1979. "Equality of What?" In *The Tanner Lectures on Human Values*, vol. 1, ed. Steling McMurrin. Salt Lake City: University of Utah Press.

Sender, Henry. 2010. "Fed Makes 'a Killing' on AIG Contracts." *Financial Times*, January 20.

Senior Supervisors Group. 2008. "Observations on Risk Management Practices During the Recent Market Turbulence." Basel, March 6.

Shiller, Robert J. 2000. *Irrational Exuberance.* Princeton, N.J.: Princeton University Press.

———. 2005. *Irrational Exuberance.* 2nd ed. New York: Broadway.

———. 2008. *The Subprime Solution: How Today's Global Financial Crisis Happened, and What to Do About It.* Princeton, N.J.: Princeton University Press.

Simon, Herbert A. 1985. "Human Nature in Politics: The Dialogue of Psychology with Political Science." *American Political Science Review* 79:293–304.

Slater, John. 2009. "How Much Risk Is the Treasury Really Assuming from Financial Institutions?" *Seeking Alpha,* April 8. http://mergers.com/toughtimes/2009/how-much-risk-is-the-treasury-really-assuming-from-the-financial-institutions/

Smick, David M. 2010. "A Never-Ending Economic Crisis?" *Commentary,* January.

Smith, Joseph A., Jr. 2002. "The Federal Banking Agencies' Guidance on Subprime Lending: Regulation with a Divided Mind." *North Carolina Banking Institute* 6: 73–263.

Smith, Elliot Blair. 2008a. "Bringing Down Wall Street as Ratings Let Loose Subprime Scourge." Bloomberg.com, 24 September.

———. 2008b. "'Race to Bottom' at Moody's, S&P Secured Subprime's Boom, Bust." Bloomberg.com, 25 September.

Stanton, Richard, and Nancy E. Wallace. 2008. "ABX.HE Indexed Credit Default Swaps and the Valuation of Subprime MBS." University of California, Berkeley, Fisher Center for Real Estate and Urban Economics, working paper 312stanton-wallace. 15 February.

Stiglitz, Joseph E. 2009. "The Anatomy of a Murder: Who Killed America's Economy?" *Critical Review* 21 (2–3): 329–40.

———. 2010a. *Freefall: America, Free Markets, and the Sinking of the World Economy.* New York: Norton.

———. 2010b. "The Non-Existent Hand." *London Review of Books,* April 22: 17–18.

———. 2011. "The Anatomy of a Murder: Who Killed the American Economy?" In Friedman 2011.

Stiglitz, Joseph E., and Andrew Weiss. 1981. "Credit Rationing in Markets with Imperfect Information." *American Economic Review* 71: 393–410.

Story, Louise, and Gretchen Morgenson. 2010. "A Rift at the Fed over the Bailout of AIG." *New York Times,* January 23.

Taleb, Nassim N. 2005. *Fooled by Randomness: The Hidden Role of Chance in Life and in the Markets.* New York: Random House

———. 2007. *The Black Swan: The Impact of the Highly Improbable.* New York: Random House.

Tarullo, Daniel K. 2008. *Banking on Basel: The Future of International Financial Regulation.* Washington, D.C.: Peterson Institute for International Economics.

Taylor, John B. 2009. "Economic Policy and the Financial Crisis." *Critical Review* 21 (2–3): 341–64.

Taylor, John B. 2011. "Monetary Policy, Economic Policy, and the Financial Crisis: An Empirical Analysis of What Went Wrong." In Friedman 2011.

Tetlock, Philip E. 2005. *Expert Political Judgment: How Good Is It? How Can We Know?* Princeton, N.J.: Princeton University Press.

Tett, Gillian. 2009a. *Fool's Gold: How the Bold Dream of a Small Tribe at J.P. Morgan Was Corrupted by Wall Street Greed and Unleashed a Catastrophe.* New York: Free Press.

————. 2009b. "Genesis of the Debt Disaster." *Financial Times*, May 1.

Thanassoulis, John. 2009. "This Is the Right Time to Regulate Bankers' Pay." *Economists' Voice*, April.

Timiraos, Nick. 2010. "Mortgage Delinquencies Decline." *Wall Street Journal*, November 19.

UBS. 2008. "Shareholder Report on UBS's Write-Downs." April 18.

Varghese, Romy. 2010. "Analyst Whitney Plans to Start Credit-Rating Firm." *Wall Street Journal*, November 19.

Volcker, Paul. 2010. "'The Time We Have Is Growing Short.'" *New York Review of Books*, June 24.

Wallison, Peter J. 2009a. "Cause and Effect: Government Policies and the Financial Crisis." *Critical Review* 21 (2–3): 365–76.

————. 2009b. "Deregulation and the Financial Crisis: Another Urban Myth." Financial Services Outlook. Washington, D.C.: American Enterprise Institute for Public Policy.

————. 2011a. "Housing Initiatives and Other Policy Factors." In Friedman 2011.

————. 2011b. "Credit-Default Swaps and the Crisis." In Friedman 2011.

Weber, Max. [1918] 1946. "Science as a Vocation." In *From Max Weber: Essays in Sociology*, ed. H. H. Gerth and C. Wright Mills. New York: Oxford University Press.

————. [1968] 1978. *Economy and Society*, vol. 1. Ed. Guenther Roth and Claus Wittich. Berkeley: University of California Press.

————. [1920–21] 1958. *The Protestant Ethic and the Spirit of Capitalism*. New York: Charles Scribner's Sons.

Wesbury, Brian S. 2010. *It's Not as Bad as You Think*. Hoboken, N.J.: John Wiley.

WRCM (Western Reserve Capital Management). 2009. "Negative Feedback Loop." February 9.

White, Lawrence J. 2011. "The Credit-Rating Agencies and the Subprime Debacle." In Friedman 2011.

Winston, Clifford. 2006. *Government Failure vs. Market Failure*. Washington, D.C.: AEI- Brookings Joint Center for Regulatory Studies.

Zandi, Mark. 2008. *Financial Shock: A 360-Degree Look at the Subprime Mortgage Implosion, and How to Avoid the Next Financial Crisis*. Upper Saddle River, N.J.: FT Press.

INDEX

ACKNOWLEDGMENTS

This volume would not have been possible without the help of many scholars and researchers. At the top of the list are Viral V. Acharya and Philipp Schnabl of the NYU Stern School of Business, who never failed to share their pioneering research on asset-backed commercial paper, without which we could not have begun to navigate the very difficult landscape of off-balance-sheet banking activities. Moreover, Acharya's paper with Matthew Richardson on capital arbitrage, which appeared in *Critical Review*'s 2009 special issue on the causes of the financial crisis, served as our first introduction to the Basel rules, and their importance was reinforced by Juliusz Jablecki and Mateusz Machaj's paper in the same issue on the implications of the Basel rules off of banks' balance sheets. We thank all these scholars not only for opening our eyes to the path of research we would end up taking, but for their unstinting generosity in helping us to understand the many twists and turns we encountered.

In addition, we gained illumination, and often data, from John Allison of Wake Forest University; James H. Barth and "Cindy" Tong Li of the Milken Institute; Juan Carlos Climent, Meg Donovan, Michael Gordy, and Andreas Lehnert of the Federal Reserve Board; Darrell Duffie of Stanford University; Donna Fisher of the American Bankers Association; Karen Frenza and Jan Hatzius of Goldman Sachs; Stefano Giglio, Victoria Ivashina, and David Scharfstein of Harvard University; Steven Gjerstad of Chapman University; William M. Isaac, former director of the FDIC; Anil K. Kashyap of the University of Chicago; Ira Kay of Pay Governance LLC; Jodi Scarlata of the IMF; Aaron Steelman of the Federal Reserve Bank of Richmond; and Katherine G. Wyatt and Richard A. Brown of the FDIC. Rich Brown, in particular, was immensely helpful in guiding us to many of those listed here, and in never betraying annoyance in answering one "final" question, after another, after yet another, as we grew increasingly to understand that we needed to know even more. Viral Acharya, Howard

Baetjer, Amar Bhidé, David Bernstein, Peter J. Boettke, Tyler Cowen, Steven Gjerstad, Juliusz Jablecki, Garett Jones, Jeffrey Rogers Hummel, Ashwin Parameswaran, Philipp Schnabl, and Hal Scott read chapters of this book or versions of Friedman's introduction to *What Caused the Financial Crisis*, in which many of the ideas developed in this book were originally bruited. The usual caveat applies, with great emphasis in some cases!

Finally, we thank Erin Graham of the University of Pennsylvania Press for her faith in this project; Jeremy S. Davis of Houston, Texas. for a much-needed research grant to one of us (Kraus) at a crucial moment; and our wives, Shterna Friedman and Oksana Budnyk, for their long-suffering patience. Shterna also formatted the manuscript for publication and prepared the index, and engaged in much helpful parsing of the mysteries of leverage ratios and the hermeneutics of the Recourse Rule.

We are more grateful to all of you than we can say.